To Andy

~Best Regards

~Bill

A Wander Doon Memory Lane...

A pictorial history of Glasgow Road, Blantyre...

Glasgow Road, North & South

Compiled and edited by Bill Sim

A Pictorial History of Glasgow Road, Blantyre...

DEDICATION

James McGuigan Cornfield 1928 - 2012

I couldn't dedicate this work without starting with my friend and Mentor, Jim Cornfield, who was a sprightly 84-year-old ex-miner, firefighter and noted expert on all matters relating to Blantyre.

Jim was at one time the Chairman of The Blantyre Heritage Group and would often give talks and slide shows relating to Blantyre's rich history.

We participated together, along with Andy Paterson, on the History Project at the Blantyre Resource Centre.

Jim and I were about to produce a Wander Doon Memory Lane as a joint effort, but sadly Jim passed after just one meeting in 2012.

Jim's passing on 13th March 2012 is a sad loss to Blantyre and to me personally.

Secondly, I would like to dedicate this work to Thomas Dunsmuir Hartman, a life-long friend of Jim Cornfield also from Logan Street, now living in Chicago. Thomas's description and experiences of old Blantyre and along

Glasgow Road, in particular, was invaluable in putting together this history of Glasgow Road.
In addition, I would like to dedicate this compilation to all the Blantyreonians who shared their memories of growing up and living in Blantyre from the 50s, whose oral history played a big part in compiling the history within these pages.

Also in the memory of Peggy McGuigan an elderly cousin of James Cornfield, who gave us her detailed version of the Cornfield's flitting from Dixon's Raw's to Logan Street in her mother tongue. (See Page 101)

And, it would be amiss by me, if I were not to mention my friend from Blantyre, now living in Canada, for many years, for her support and motivation, she has shown me over the last fourteen years, Betty McGaulley.

Moreover, to those who remember, Glasgow Road as it was prior to the Clyde Shopping Centre being built.

Contents

Part One - Glasgow Road, North - Starting at Park Burn and travelling west along Glasgow Road, taking in all the side Streets and finishing at Rotten Calder meets River Clyde, Haughead.

Contents

Part Two - Glasgow Road, South - Starting at Springwell and travelling west along Glasgow Road, taking in all the side streets and finishing at The Hoolet's in Barnhill.

Acknowledgements

So many people and organizations need to be acknowledged for their input and source of information and photographs used in compiling this pictorial history of Glasgow Road, Blantyre. In no particular order, I would like to thank those individuals: Thomas Dunsmuir Hartman, Jim Cornfield (Dec), Neil Gordon (Dec), Andy Paterson, Lon McIlwrath, Jim Whelan, William Ross, Anthony Smith, Jim Brown, John Dunsmore, James McGuire, Ellen Clarkin, Ailean McLeman and organizations: Rhona Wilson and Richard Stenlake Publishers, Hamilton Advertiser, britishnewspaperarchive, TalkingScot and BritainfromAbove © RCAHMS. Those of you whose memories were used are listed here in alphabetical order by first name: ~

Agnes Flannigan	Andrew MacFarlane
Agnes Hynds	Andrew Mccluskie
Agnes McAllister	Andy Callaghan
Ailean McLeman (Roberts)	Andy Lynch
Aileen Farrell	Andy Macphee
Alan Baird	Angela Carty
Alan Burnett	Angela Mary McGlynn
Alan Smith	Angela Tallis
Alan Young	Angela Taylor
Alex Graham	Angela Timoney
Alex Mcdermott	Angela Vallely
Alex Young	Ann Crossar
Alice Murray	Ann Ferguson
Alison Walker-Hill	Ann Ford
Allan Love	Ann Higgins Crossar
Amanda O'Neill Gwynne	Ann McArdle
Amanda Palmer	Ann Millar
Amanda Price Campbell	Anna Carroll
Amelia Kane	Anna Konno – Cavanagh
Andrew Charles	Anne Bain

Anne Bell
Anne Callaghan
Anne Gilmour Callaghan
Anne Mccreadie
Annemarie Aitken
Anne-Marie Clarkin
Anne-marie Hart
Annie Miller Scoular
Annie M-Anderson Black
Anthony Smith
April Mcmahon
Archie Peat
Arlene Campbell
Audrey Marshall
Audrey Morrison
Barrie Pentney
Berty Booster
Bette Conner Houghton
Betty Hepburn
Betty McGaulley
Betty McLean
Betty Mcneill
Bill Graham
Bill Hunter
Bill McIntyre
Billy Mckinlay
Billy Purse
Bim Mcskimming
Bobby Dunsmuir
Boski Bell
Bruce Baldwin
Campbell Wylie
Carmen McGuire
Carol Crombie
Carol Jordan
Carol Lush
Carol Summers
Carolann Bate Graham
Carole Jamieson
Carole Mackie Rickard

Carole Marie Deplacido
Carole Miller
Caroline Baird
Caroline Lee
Carolyn Patterson
Catherine Burnett
Catherine McConnell
Catherine McCunnie
Catherine Sneddon
Catherine Stewart
Catherine Travers Leslie
Catriona Paterson
Chris Good
Christina Frame
Christine Allan Brown
Christine Brown
Christine Robertson
Claudia Wood
Colin Balfour
Colleen Mitchell
Dallas Carter
Daniel Anderson
Danielle McClymont
Danielle Scully
Danny Canavan
David Aitken
David Andrew Hilston
David Brown
David Hay
David Owens
David Scott
David Thomson
Davie McKinnon
Debbie Cochran-Reid
Deborah Buhagiar
Dee Mcewan
Diane Cunningham
Don Barkey
Donna Baird
Donna Timmins

A Wander Doon Memory Lane...

Drew Semple
Duncan Slater
Eain Gray
Eddie Mcguire
Edith Bulloch
Eileen Clark
Eileen Duffy Eger
Elaine Currie
Elaine Russell
Eleanor Duncan Nailon
Eleanor Ferguson Kelly
Eleanor Stenhouse
Elizabeth Ann Ward
Elizabeth Baillie Alemanno
Elizabeth Clelland
Elizabeth Dobson Grieve
Elizabeth Gallagher
Elizabeth O'Brien
Elizabeth Wallace
Elizabeth Weaver
Ellen Nimmo Pickering
Ellen Swift
Elspeth Shirkie
Emma Trevethan
Ethel Watson
Etta Morrison
Evelyn Graham Shaw
Fiona Allen
Fiona Broadley Semple
Fiona Glen
Fran Mcdermott Walters
Frances Clelland
Frances McDonald
Frank Glancy
Gary Doonin
Gary Mitchell
George Gibson
George Mackenzie
Georgina Durnan Mackie
Gerry Gillies

Gerry Mcnamee
Gerry Walker
Gord Fotheringham
Gordon McInnes Finbow
Grace Watson
Graeme Smith
Hannah Mcaleenan
Hari Docherty
Hazel Krawczyk
Helen Dyer
Helen Gilchrist Young Baird
Helen Grieve
Helen Henderson Mclaughlin
Helen Howe
Helen Lawson Taylor
Helen Stewart
Helen Whyte Dyer
Henerson Janette
Hugh Lennon Tonner
Hugh McDade
Iain Douglas
Ian Anderson
Ian Dino McDougall
Ian Mccaul
Ina Sanders
Irene Berry Milligan
Irene Steiner
Isabel Park
Isabell McGinty Cain
Ishbel McKinlay-Wilkie:
Isobel Bolger
Ivy Robertson
Jack Owens
Jackie Croft
Jacqui Lafferty Draper
Jacqui Williamson
Jade Sloey
James Cornfield
James Donnelly

James Faulds
James Gribben
James Hunter
James Mcguire
James Mclean
James Minto
James O'Donnelly
Jamie Boyle
Jan Ritchie
Jan Walsh
Jane Barkey
Jane Davies
Jane Dunleavy
Jane Maxwell
Jane Paterson
Janet Saunders
Janette Brown
Janette R Minto
Janice Cja Clark
Janice Clarkin
Janice Frank
Janice Fullerton:
Jannette McAllister
Jean Andrew
Jean Boyd
Jean Brown
Jean Gibson
Jean MacKie
Jean McIntosh
Jean McSorley
Jean Orr
Jeanette Allardyce Ward
Jeanette Bryan
Jeanette Henshaw
Jeanette Izzett
Jeanette Lee
Jessie Mclachlan
Jim Brankin
Jim Brown
Jim Caullay

Jim Hunter
Jim Macfie
Jim McDougall
Jim Tallan
Jim Walsh
Jimi O'neill
Jimmy Hislop
Joan Adams
Joan Anderson
Joan Baird
Joe Beetham
Joe Jones
Joe Kane
Joe Sneddon
Joey Campbell
John Allan
John Cornfield
John Crothers
John Dunsmore
John Fallon Jnr
John Hand
John Latta
John Maguire
John Mcadams
John McCourt
John McDermott
John Mcgaulley
John Murray
John Paterson
John Pollock
John Ryan-Park
John See
Joyce Traynor
Julie Anne Lindsay
Julie Anne Screen
Karen Baird
Karen Feelie
Karen McLachlan
Karen Rouse
Kate McInulty

Kathleen Anne Obrien
Kathleen Duffy
Kathleen McDermott
Kathleen McDermott Parks
Keith MacLean
Keith Mccormack
Laura Hamilton
Laurie Allan Crothers
Leigh Hynds
Len Northfield
Lesley Hartley
Letitia Mitchell
Liam Brown
Linda Halpin
Linda McEwan Ashton
Linda Mcgowan
Linda Warner
Liz Ali Ali
Liz Allan
Liz Anderson
Liz Boxall
Liz Campbell
Liz Cutts
Liz Daley
Liz Doonin
Liz Hughes
Liz Jack
Liz Mcginty
Liz Miller
Liz Nelson
Lon McIlwrath
Lorraine Barker
Lorraine Mcguire
Lyn Lappin
Lynn Dougela
Lynn Kelly
Lynn Telfer
Lynne Dunsmuir
Mae Donnelly
Maggie O'Brien

Maggie Tallis
Maggie Tonner McVeigh
Maisie Whittaker
Marc McAuley
Marc Moran
Margaret Barnes
Margaret Bell
Margaret Brown
Margaret Cunning
Margaret Duncan
Margaret Gallagher
Margaret Lappin
Margaret Mcculloch
Margaret McGuigan
Margaret Nimmo Lehmann
Margaret Quinn
Margaret Slaven McSorley
Margaret Steven McAuliffe
Margaret Stewart
Margaret Wilson
Margo Haughen
Maria L Azul
Marian Maguire
Marianna Caserta
Marianne Aitken
Marianne Stark Aitken
Marianne Timmions
Marie Cathcart
Marie Kelly
Marie Mc Millan
Marie McDermott
Marie McMillan
Marion Murdoch
Marion Robertson
Marion Smith
Marion Young
Mark Rock
Martin Cummiskey
Martin Smith
Nadine Gallagher

Mary Borland
Mary Boyle
Mary Crowe
Mary Davies
Mary McGuigan
Mary Mcguire
Mary Meekat
Mary Odonnell
Mary Queen
Mary Sambou
Mary Summers
Mary Wood
Maryon Allan
Mattie Taggart
Maureen Brown
Maureen Kelly Elliott
Maureen McGilligan Downie
Maureen Wood
May Hamilton
May Young Breen
Mazie Brown
Melanie Baird
Mhairi McGaulley
Michael Connor
Michael Docherty
Michael Mogan
Michelle Brankin
Michelle Devine
Modlifecrisis
Moira Lees
Moira Macfarlane
Moira McMenemy
Moira Mulvaney Pacheco
Monica McFall Holmes
Monica Whelan
Morag Campaigne
Morag Pickering
Moyra Lindsay
Mary (Scott) Sitters
Sheona Thomson Brennan

Nancy McFadden
Natalie Ward
Neil Forrest
Norma Foley
Olive Rawlings
Orlando Ancilotti
Pamela Bushell
Pamela Holland
Pat Cunningham
Patrick Gaughan
Patrick Mcdonagh
Patrick Sanaghan
Paul Anderson
Paul Gilligan-Black
Paul Hudson McGowan
Paul McGivern
Peter Murray
Rab Mccarrol
Ray Couston
Raye Kelly Robertson
Richard Rankin
Ricky Forrest
Robert Cairney
Robert Crothers
Robert Henderson
Robert McLeod-Wolohan
Rosemary Law
Ruth Haughen
Ruth Stannage
Sadie Dolan
Sally Fisher
Sandra Goodall
Sandra Mckeown
Sandy Wilkie
Sarah Sked
Saxonrose Law
Sharon Burt
Sharon Kerrigan
Sharon Mcmillan
Terry Hughes

A Wander Doon Memory Lane...

Sheryl McPhee
Shona Mccabe
Shug McNeill
Shuggie Whyte
Steph Burns
Stephen Allan
Stephen Hasson
Stephen Mcgowan
Stephen Morrison
Steven Johnstone
Stevie Brown
Stevie Fletcher
Stewart Campbell
Stewart Willis
Stuart Christie
Stuart Oneil
Susan Flannigan Mayes
Susan Walker Graham
Suzanne Wall-Duffy
Sylvia Wilson
Sharon Miller
Sheena Thomson

Thea Borland
Thomas Barrett
Thomas Dunsmuir Hartman
Thomas Hamilton-Hailes
Thomas Izzett
Tom McGuigan
Tracey Ann Campbell
Tracey McDougall
Tracy Feelie
Tracy Stirling
Una Mason Hynds
Unkle Cyril
Walter Campbell
Wendy Dalgleish
Wendy Monaghan
Wendy Wilson
William Ross
Willie Rouse
Wilma Hannah-Boyle
Wilma Murdoch MacPhail
Winifred Murphy
Wullie Mourning

Introduction

This, 'A Wander Doon Memory Lane', Part One, is a journey along Glasgow Road, Blantyre from Springwell to Haughead. Taking in all the side streets, including, Whistleberry Road, Forrest Street, John Street, Alpine Street, Station Road and Blantyreferme Road, with photos and comments on all major buildings as they were in the 50s, 60s and 70s.

It is your memories of the buildings, shops and characters that brings this pictorial history alive.

Part Two will be from Springwell to Barnhill, taking in Glasgow Road, Rosendale Place, Auchinraith Road, Herbertson Street, Jackson Street, Church Street, Elm Street, Logan Street, Craig Street, Victoria Street, Calder Street, Stonefield Road and Bardykes Road ending at the Hoolet's in Barnhill.

Together, Part One and Two represent a history of times gone by when Glasgow Road was a welcoming friendly place to shop and be entertained. Not a history by one historian but of the memories of over five hundred local people who lived it, experienced it and remembers it.

So, please enjoy your Wander Doon Memory Lane and save it for the next generation.

Don't forget that all proceeds from the sale of this book will go to local charities and good causes.

Bill Sim
http://blantyre.biz

About Blantyre

Blantyre Parish Map 1832

Before we start our wander doon memory lane of Glasgow Road, here is some information about Blantyre, a village eight miles South East of Glasgow.

Some refer to Blantyre as a "Town," but I have yet to find any evidence of when it became a Town and ceased, therefore, to be a village. If it were a Town, there would have been some sort of announcement or even celebration, or at least a Town Hall and Town Mayor! With our own administration.

No place becomes a town because of its population or facilities. It can only do so by governmental order in order to build new amenities or living accommodation which requires the 'village' boundaries to be extended. This is of course UK specific.

The natural boundaries of Blantyre are the rivers that surround it, and this is probably the most likely reason that Blantyre is still a village to this day, simply because the boundaries have never been enlarged to accommodate new facilities.

In size, Blantyre is not a large village, the parish being approximately 10 kms in length with an average width of about 1.5 km.

Those are 6 miles 2 Furlongs by 3 furlongs to 2.5 Miles, 6.5 square miles in all.

Did you know that you cannot enter Blantyre without crossing water?

River Clyde to the North

Park Burn to the East

Rottenburn to the South

Rotten Calder to the West

It is bounded by the River Clyde to the north, the Park Burn to the east, hence the name, Burnbank, the Rotten Burn to the south and the Rotten Calder to the west, running North until it meets the river Clyde.

River's Meet

Rotten Calder meets River Clyde - Haughead Pit in the background

~~~

Meaning of the name Blantyre...

It is assumed that Blantyre was an ancient British settlement and was built around the Old Blantyre Kirk Yard, which may have been a druid devout circle. The Kirk Yard is a large man made eight-foot-high mound of earth and if it was a druid circle, it would have been the centre of the settlement's religious activities. The old sixteenth century communion cups belonging to the Old Parish Church have no letter E in the spelling of BLANTYRE.

It would suggest that the old spelling Blantyr is a Gaelic corruption of LLANTYR. Llantyr contains two Welsh words, LLAN meaning 'consecrated' and TYR meaning 'ground/land'. The consecrated/church ground being the Old Kirk Yard at High Blantyre Cross.

In the 1791, Old Statistical Account of Scotland, the Rev. Henry Stevenson believed it had its origins in the Gaelic "Bla'an tir" meaning 'a warm retreat." Later in the New Statistical Account of Scotland of 1835 the Rev James Anderson agreed with him. However, the Rev. Stewart Wright explained in "The Annals of Blantyre" that it had its origins in two Gaelic words meaning "the field of the holy men."

Finally, an alternative explanation might be found in the 1952 Third Statistical Account of Scotland, wherein the Rev. A. Mackenzie put forward the idea that since Blantyre had its birth as a religious settlement, it would be probable that it had taken its name from an early Christian missionary to the area, St Blane. The Rev. Mckenzie believed it more likely that Blantyre had originated from "Blan-tyr" meaning "land of (St.) Blane".

The earliest written record of the name Blantyre was in 1275 where the Priory was included in a list of Scottish ecclesiastical establishments, which were taxed by Pope Clement IV to raise money to finance yet another crusade against the Saracens.

This document was known as Bagimond's Roll, named after the Pope's emissary, Baiamund De Vicci, who was sent to collect the hated tax.

Priory Ruins c1878

The Priory was most likely certainly mentioned in previous list issued by Pope Innocent IV in 1254 to finance an earlier crusade.

Most of the early priors are recorded as having attended the Scottish parliaments and being involved in many important incidents in Scottish history.

Blantyre Priory stood on Blantyr Craig, the high cliff directly opposite Bothwell Castle, and was founded between1238 and 1249.

The Priory was a cell of the Augustinian Canon of Jedburgh Abbey, who also used it over the years as a retreat from the wars between England and Scotland. The last Roman Catholic Prior was William Chirnside, who conformed to the new religion and became the first Protestant minister in Blantyre.

Part One ~ Glasgow Road, North

McCaffrie's Building

McCaffrie's Building, also known as McCafferty's, who owned the Public House, McCaffrie's Bar on the facing corner. The McCaffrie's lived in Thornhill Avenue, down the Dandy, next door to James Kelly of Kelly's Corner, Blantyre Engineering and Glasgow Celtic fame.

The building included Dougie Fraser's shop, Kane's Butchers and Parisimo Valerio's Confectionery. McCaffrie's Bar later became Enzio Caserta's Ice Cream Parlour.

Dougie Fraser's

Dougie Fraser's shop which he ran with his wife Ann, was very popular with the Springwell residents, not only because of the 'tick' that they offered but also their friendly attitude and welcoming smiles. The Fraser's owned their shop and the flat above where they lived. The shop was closed in 1971 after Dougie died and his wife, Ann sold the shop and land to Duncan's the scrap dealers who had the scrap yard behind the building. Ann then managed the Barbour's shop, formerly Nicholson's, in Station Road until she retired in 1977.

Your Memories:

Jim McDougall: I worked in Charles Ireland's in early 60s. We would have our rolls on spam and cheese in Dougie Fraser's, and Valerio's was famous for their pie and peas, what brilliant times and memories of those days. You have done it again Bill, you do a great job thanks mate.

Mary Davies: I remember Dougie Fraser. We had to go there for butter, and he patted it with the paddles. Ah the good old days.

Tom McGuigan: When I was a paperboy for Wullie Pate, I used to go to Dougie's for a bottle of milk and a piece of gingerbread. Then, when I worked in Robertson's, I would go to the Cafe for my rolls of Cheese and Tomato.

Elizabeth Wallace: HI Bill, My Grandpa Dougie was born in the back of the shop which was owned by his dad and later on he inherited the shop and the building which was attached to end of the shop (where the house and billboards are now). I do not know about the pub only that he owned the shop and at one time my Dad and Mum lived in the flat above the shop. After my Grandpa died, my gran sold the ground to Duncan's the scrap dealers who had the scrap yard behind the building.

Elizabeth Wallace: Bill, I can only remember that at one end of the building it was an ice cream shop, a few flats next, then a close to get access to the upstairs flats, then butchers, then Dougie's shop, a flat next to it and then an opening to get into the back of the building. There was a washhouse in the rear and allotments and to the back of them Duncan's scrapyard. Hope this helps.

Blantyre's Ain: Elizabeth Wallace this is all fascinating info Elizabeth, and it is great to have it recorded. Do you remember the other scrapyard across the road, called Ireland's?

Elizabeth Wallace: Yes, the workers used to come to the shop for their rolls as well as the men from the bolt works.

Elizabeth Wallace: Bill, there used to be a couple of houses down a wee bit from the shop where the small units are now. I remember that they got flooded at one time when the burn overflowed, and the family stored some of their furniture in the shop.

Enzio Caserta's Ice Cream Parlour.

Marianna Caserta said, "Pretty sure this building was owned by my grandparents, and they had a cafe and licensed grocers there when I was growing up. I remember riding in the vans often with my uncle and Granddad. And also pretending to work in the cafe when all the guys from the scrap yard came in for their rolls."

Caserta's Ice Cream van was orange and yellow and was driven by Angelo and Tony Caserta. Jim Frame worked with Tony in the late 70s on the Winton Crescent, Burnbrae Road, Morris Crescent and Small Crescent run, and Caroline Kilgour worked on the van in the 80s with Angelo on the Coatshill and Priory Bridge run.

Of the three Ice Cream vans in Blantyre at the time, Caserta's, Andy's Ices and Joe's Ice Cream van. Caserta's had the best ice cream and was favourite for its choice of sweets.

Robertson's Mineral Water Works at Springwell.

Five star soft drinks were served up at Robertson's of Springwells, established in 1870.

An advertisement in the Blantyre Gazette.

The factory was at this location because of the natural water spring, hence the name Springwell.

Famous for their 5 Star Old Scotch Ginger Beer...

Robertson's Ginger Factory was the Asda of its time, as far as employment was concerned, employing loads of people. My Mum, Rose Sim, nee Ward, worked in the Canteen for many years.

Jock Shaw and George McDermott were the drivers for Robertson's ginger delivery trucks. Jock Shaw and his van boy Tony, were a regular sight around Blantyre. Jock only had one arm but could throw and stack the crates with ease.

Robertson's
Ginger Cart

Jack Owens: Probably the two greys on the cart made it soooo special.

Sandy Wilkie: Aye, he and my father ALWAYS had a blether when I was on the horse drawn milk float with him when we passed them in Springwell!

William Ross: Jock Shaw lived in Parkville Drive.

Thomas Dunsmuir Hartman formerly Logan Street, now in Chicago wrote, "The Robertson ginger works, as we called them, was not the place to pass if you were a male, and it was at lunch time.

A lot of the women and girls especially during the war years just loved to get outside and sit down, with their backs up against the wall and have a smoke and heckle every man in sight, regardless of his age, all good clean fun. You were always guaranteed a good laugh of sorts.

A pal I knew was passing bye, and this woman calls out to him. Hey son where's yer bum did ye leave it in yer either trousers, and this other woman shouts out before he can answer, eh disnay have a bum, He's only got the wan pair o' trousers.

The Blantyre women were special, they had to be, among those Blantyre men".

Your Memories:

Hugh Lennon Tonner: Half of Blantyre worked there one time or another. A few stories to come out of that place

Steph Burns: Loved working there.

Peter Murray: This was my first job after leaving school 1977 great memories.

Tom McGuigan: Brilliant memories!

Liz Boxall: Auld scotch and cola quenchy cups!! Brill.

Alex Young: I started in 1975 was there when they knocked the old building down, sad day, not the same when Dunn's took over, Orange the best.

Melanie Baird: Omg I did my week work experience there loved it, happy days.

George Gibson: My grandfather was a Robertson. Awe remember it well! Loved the ginger especially the ginger beer.

Eddie Mcguire: Dogged school n try steal quenchy cups fae the back.

Helen Dyer: good old ginger factory... good old ginger factory...

Alex Graham: A few of my mates worked there years ago, Joe O'neil, Jim Lannigan and Billy Fairley.

Jim Walsh: I loved working there till they sacked me.

Anne Bell: Ur rite Alex went downhill used to get some laugh lol.

Christine Brown: Wee Rose Sim was the tea lady and her sister Ellen Robertson worked with me. Wee Rose was a lovely lady so was your aunt Ellen. My hubby and I met there and got married when we worked there, we had our 50th anniversary on the 12th July, this year x

Thea Borland Mcnamee: Work there on an off for years in the 70's as temp worker, April till Sept, then got full time. Loved it there. They were brilliant days… remember when a was in old bottling hall and wore my jammies under ma jeans it wis that cold. I went back and worked night shift when it was Dunn's.

Shuggie Whyte: I used to work there.

Alan Burnett: I worked there also, lost part of my finger on the machines in the Erca room.

Lynn Telfer: My Hubby, mother in law and his gran all worked there.

Melanie Baird: Did ma weeks' work experience there and loved it x

Bill says: My Mum, Rose Sim, worked at Robertson's for many years in the Canteen and my Aunt Ellen Robertson and Aunt Lilly Graham, worked in the factory. Our neighbour, George McDermott was one of the delivery drivers.

Mount Pleasant Building & Miners Cottages. (Sleepy Valley)

Known locally as Deputy Raw's or Dipity Raw's as some called it.
These cottages were primarily used for the Deputies who worked at the Whistleberry and Craighead Pits.
The cottages were built by Robert Watson Builders, Glasgow.

Your Memories:

Mary McGuigan: That's what they are called, never knew that all times I passed them or stared over fae bus stop x.

Andy Macphee: Used tae fire golf balls at them, and played the grand national in their gairdens, back in the day.

James Mclean: Ahhh it's the grand national lol.

Janette Brown: Aye it looks like them.

David Thomson: The grand national, every Springwell lads passage to rights lol.

Linda Halpin: We nearly bought one of those before we got married but lost out to someone else.!!

When you left Springwell and started traveling West along Glasgow Road, you passed under one of the two Railway Bridges  across Glasgow Road. In between the two bridges was the Whistleberry Road, parts of which are still there.

This road was popular with all the young courting couples from Blantyre, Burnbank and Bothwell. It was about a mile long and ran from Blantyre to Bothwell.

The Craighead pit was down there on the left and the road going past the old pit took you towards a Railway and pedestrian bridge across the river Clyde (Craighead viaduct) into Bothwell. You can just see Mount Pleasant through the bridge.

Craighead House

Craighead House on the outskirts of Blantyre, photo-graphed in 1870 by Thomas Annan.

Craighead House on the outskirts of Blantyre, photo-graphed in 1870 by Thomas Annan.
The house was situated on the Blantyre side of the River Clyde, just before Bothwell Bridge.

The seat of George Alston, Esq., is situated within the parish of Blantyre and county of Lanark. The house is placed on the left bank of the river Clyde and in a position commanding the most beautiful views of the surrounding scenery, that of the historic bridge of Bothwell being particularly fine.

The house was situated on the Blantyre side of the River

Clyde, just before Bothwell Bridge.

The seat of George Alston, Esq., is situated within the parish of Blantyre and county of Lanark. The house is placed on the left bank of the river

Clyde and in a position commanding the most beautiful views of the surrounding scenery, that of the historic bridge of Bothwell being particularly fine.

The house and estate were sold at the beginning of the 19th century to James Smith, son to a West Indies merchant in Glasgow, James Smith of Craigend (d 1786) After James Jnr's death c1815, his nephew sold Craig-head to another Glasgow merchant, Thomas McCall, who made considerable additions to the house.

Another Glasgow merchant, George Alston of Muirburn, acquired the property in the 1860s.

Following on from that, it went to an organization, "Jesuit Fathers" of the Roman Catholic Church and was used as a religious retreat and school of learning for young men entering into the Catholic priesthood. The mansion lay empty in the late 1990s until it was destroyed completely by fire on 18th February 2002. Contractors subsequently demolished the remains to make it safe.

Thomas Dunsmuir Hartman remembers, "There was also fairly sizeable brickworks off the Whistleberry Road. I remember this place with its great furnaces lighting up the area when the furnace doors were open, it was as if you could feel the heat, and you were at least 100 yards from the entrance to the works. I do believe it went under the unique name of, The Blantyre Works. "Catchy eh!"

Did you know? Sir Walter Scott was a regular visitor at this house. It is claimed he wrote parts of his work "Old Mortality" within that house and that his references to Fairyknowe, was actually referring to Craighead House.

Whilst transcribing the 1851 Census, I found the following record for Craighead House, the house was owned by two Spinsters, Mary and Jessie Brown, who had eight servants. (Living like millionaires and not knowing the fortune in Black Gold that lay beneath their land)

Mary Brown, 70, Jessie Brown, 59 – Landed Proprietors.

Servants: Charles Brotherton - Butler, 43,

Janet Syme - Dairy Maid, 33,

Marion Watson - Cook, 36,

Jessie Grewer - House Maid, 25,

Marion Lindsay - Laundress, 28,

Margaret Anderson - Ladies Maid, 25,

All of them unmarried.
James Dalgleish, Master Gardener and employer of one man, 39, was married with one son and lived in the Gardeners House.

A whole different world from the working-class weavers and miners of the village.

Craighead Pit

William Baird's Craighead Pit was opened in 1876.

Robert (Curly) Forrest
At Craighead Pit
Whistleberry Road
20th May 1920 19 years old

The photograph shows my Granddad, **Robert Forrest**, when he was only 19, working a horse, 'Roy', at Craigend Pit, off the Whisleberry Road, in 1920.

Robert Forrest, with his horse Hector

This photograph of my Granddad, Robert Forrest, with his horse Hector, was taken at Ferniegair, Hamilton around 1931, by a photographer who was fascinated watching Hector drink from a shovel held under a tap.

Granddad worked during that time for a building contractor called Wright. He was given several copies of the photograph, and it is interesting to note that these, like many photographs from the period, were printed on paper, which was printed on the reverse, to allow use as a postcard. I wonder if any of your readers know where, at Ferniegair, this watering point is.

~ George Park

Craighead Sports Ground

An aerial photo from 1950 looking down on Craighead Greyhound Racing track, later to become Blantyre Speedway.

The Dog Track was owned and operated by Frank Doonin, who bought the area and a house in Auchinraith Road in 1925 for a sum of £300. Originally used for Whippet racing, it also accommodated open air Boxing events.

Mr. Doonin was a pioneer in introducing greyhound racing to Scotland in late 20s. The track was widened and upgraded to accommodate five to six thousand spectators in 1965. The last grey hound meeting was April 1982.

Craighead Park, also known as Celtic Park is adjacent to Baird's Raws.

Jimmy Beaton, born in Blantyre, 1st January 1927, was a director and promoter for the Glasgow Tigers Speedway stars at Blantyre Greyhound Stadium 1977-81 and then Blantyre Craighead Park 1982-86.In 1977, through Jimmy Beaton, Frank Doonin introduced Speedway to the venue.

Speedway ran there from 1977-82 and closed due to building of the EK expressway. The last speedway meeting was on 18th October 1981, Tigers versus Bobby Beaton's Buccaneers.

The Speedway was home to Blantyre Tigers who gave us two local heroes, Scotland's greatest ever Speedway rider, Ken McKinlay 1928 - 2003 known as "Hurri - Ken" and Tommy Miller, "Atomic Tommy" who had a somewhat meteoric rise to stardom in 1950.

Speedway was staged at the Greyhound Stadium as the home of the Glasgow Tigers in the late 1970s / early 1980s before the new road build forced a move to Craighead Park which was closed down at the end of the 1986 season.

Craighead Park

Craighead Park, home of Blantyre Celtic F.C. from 1919, to the end of the 1986 season, when they went out of existence.

This photo of the Speedway was taken on opening night in July 1977.

Your Memories:

Stewart Campbell: Went to speedway back in 1982.

Evelyn Graham Shaw: We used to walk from Whitehill through the 'Bing' out to speedway.

Shug McNeill: Remember jumping the wall and sneaking in to speedway.

David Thomson: Used to love the smell of the red ash when the speedway was on, could smell it all over tyre, used to jump the wall to get in, the broken glass bottles that were cemented on top of the wall didn't deter us Springwell lads lol.

Michael Mogan: As a Coventry kid and a Coventry bees fan, I am also the son of two Blantyre natives (Tommy Mogan and Margaret McInally) and we used to come to Blantyre often. Going to the speedway was great up your way and gave me a way to support a team that related to my folks and my roots! Thanks for sharing.

George Mackenzie: This must have contributed to Blantyre's Ken McKinlay becoming World Champion?

Elizabeth Dobson Grieve: Loved going to the dog track with my dad.

Grant's Building

Grant's Building, which contained Owens Cycle and accessories, where you got your accumulator charged for your wireless (radio), Ella Little's Grocery, Sub Post Office, which was run by postmistress Miss Stewart and her assistant, Marian Kilgour. The shop also had Sam Douglas's Barbers in the back. At the end of the building there was a lane to Baird's Rows (Stainey Brae to Craighead Row's.)

Thomas Dunsmuir Hartman wrote, "If you crossed over Glasgow Road from Herbertson Street, this would put you just past the Cart entrance (Stainey Brae), going down to Baird's Raws.

Grant's Building c1970 looking opposite Herbertson Street and the start of Blantyre's Number One Co-op.

Grant's Building from Herbertson Street

Photo sent in by **Anthony Smith**.

Your Memories:

Len Northfield: Every time I see these photos it breaks my heart what they did to Blantyre. Ok, it wasn't exactly the prettiest town in the world, but it was a community with heart and soul.

Jim McDougall: Aye, I remember walking to Ness's School with my big sister back in the 1940's, passing by all those lovely old buildings, you're not alone Len, it is heart breaking to see them all gone, we had a Brilliant Community spirit in those days. A place I still call home, and still miss. Memories is what we have left.

Mary McGuigan: Aye deff Len, old buildings are better I think x.

Mary Summers: I feel the same Len.

David Owens: First time I've seen a photo of this. I barely remember being in the shop?

George Mackenzie: Used to get my haircut in Sam Douglas's which was IN the Post Office.

Mary Summers: Used to go into that post office all the time.

Tom McGuigan: It was called the wee post office. I think Alec Letham had the carpet shop for a while.

Shug McNeill: Asda tore the heart out of Blantyre.

Bill says: My sister Cathie, who worked for Blantyre Engineering, would visit the Post Office every morning to collect the mail.

Andrew Gilmour's Building, Glasgow Road

Gilmour's Building or Gilmour's Laun, as the locals would call it, was actually named Gilmour's Place and included Gilmour's Grocery, Black's Bakery, Gilmour Clothes, etc., Angie's Ice Cream Parlour, (The Victoria Café), Hawthorn's General Store and then Richardson's the Butcher. The Livingstonian Bar and the Blantyre Electric Cinema, also used by the Masonic Lodge, was opposite at the corner of Forrest Street.

Again, we have a tenement two storey type building, with stores at street level and through the close, upstairs to the second level.

Notice the horse on the pavement backed up to one of the shops. What could it be delivering? Something heavy, like sacks of vegetables, or butter barrels perhaps. What do you think?

From the left is Elizabeth Neil, Lizzie Jamieson, Agnes Dunsmuir, Tam Naismith (Manager), Mary Shanks and Agnes Kirkland.

The Gilmour family lived above this shop.

Andrew Gilmour's shops was a mini Co-op in its day as it offered all kinds of produce such as grocers, drapery, carpet and floor covering and almost everything else needed from your daily shopping list, as you can see from this advert of the time.

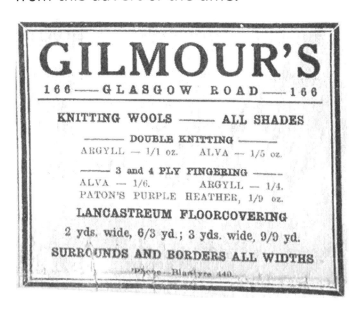

GILMOUR'S
166 —— GLASGOW ROAD —— 166

KNITTING WOOLS —— ALL SHADES

—— DOUBLE KNITTING ——
ARGYLL — 1/1 oz.   ALVA — 1/5 oz.

—— 3 and 4 PLY FINGERING ——
ALVA — 1/6.   ARGYLL — 1/4.
PATON'S PURPLE HEATHER, 1/9 oz.

LANCASTREUM FLOORCOVERING
2 yds. wide, 6/3 yd.; 3 yds. wide, 9/9 yd.

SURROUNDS AND BORDERS ALL WIDTHS

Phone—Blantyre 440.

Victoria Cafe, Glasgow Road

The Victoria Cafe on Glasgow Road, opposite the Co-op, was popularly known as Angie's Cafe.

Angie's Cafe, Glasgow Road looking East

Another View of Gilmour's Building or Gilmour's Laun as it was called, like all other buildings, being named after their owner or builder. Land was pronounced Laun locally, so this was Gilmour's Laun, looking east. The proper name for the building was Gilmour's Place.

The butcher's shop was run by Jock and Chrissie Richardson, who also owned a garage further up Glasgow Road, next to the old Community Centre.

Archie Peat commented, "Up above the shop (two windows) lived Wullie Park and his wife, he was a top member of the Labour Party, an International socialist and founder member of Blantyre Co-op.

I have it on good authority that this was a safe house for renegade Irish Free Stater's before independence in 1922.

Next door was my Grandparents, Archie and Sarah Peat. Archie was President of the Vics from 1933 to 1946. He was a Representative on the S.F.A and the Lanarkshire Junior FA. He also held the Military Medal and was CQMS (Company Quarter Master Sergeant) of the 6th Cameronians."

Archie Peat

John Dunsmore, aka, Wee Yanni said, "Me and Cathy Murray fae the Raws were at a Blantyre. Vic's match, the away team support always went into Angie's before the game for ice cream and whatever else. They bought Robertson's wee bottles of ginger and took them tae the match. Angie's bottles were stamped. At half time, me and Cathy lifted yins in the park, took them up to Angie's back door. Their van was being filled up but no-one was there. I went tae chap the back door. Wow a big dog had me by the leg and wouldn't let go.

Cathy done a runner, yer dad was passing and heard her shouts. Your dad came to my rescue, thank the Lord. Tain me doon tae my parents hoose and told my dad what had happened. My dad and your dad took me to the Doctors, can't remember the doctors name. Your dad and mine went into Angie's tae tell them what happened, they said me and Cathy had no right being there. Your dad said the dog should have been tied up. My dad just let it go and told Angie he was going to the

Police. The dog was put down. I'll never forget it, Bill, till the day I pass over."

Baird's Rows, Forrest Street

Forrest Street ran north from the Glasgow Road and ended at the railway line. Over the line was the Clyde Braes, most roads running north from Glasgow Road finished up or close to the River Clyde.

On the immediate right were Craighead Rows, known locally as Baird's Rows. I was born in the Middle Row, seven along from the Dog Track end.

This aerial photo shows Baird's Raws and bottom right is the Salvation Army Citadel on Forrest Street.

Top left of Baird's Raws is Craighead Sports Ground, home to Greyhound Racing and Speedway, which was owned by Frank Doonin. At the bottom of the Raws is the entrance to Craighead Park, home of Blantyre Celtic F.C.

Bottom right, opposite the Citadel is the entrance to Castle Park, home of Blantyre Victoria F.C.

Top centre right is Rosendale, leading off Glasgow Road where the bus is.

The building in front of the bus is Kelly's Corner on Henderson Building, at the bottom of Auchinraith Road.

To the left of Rosendale is Chalmer's Building, Chalmer's the Haulage Contractors was next to Caldwell Hall (Coffin Hall, so called because of its shape) which was used as the Stonefield Parish Church Hall.

Baird's Raws consisted of three rows of 108 tied miners' cottages belonging to Craighead Colliery. Purdie Builders of Coatbridge commenced construction of the houses in April 1878, in the area presently occupied by Park's Bus Company, between Forrest Street, Glasgow Road and the East Kilbride Expressway.

The houses were numbered but there were no street names, just being referred to as the Tap Row, Middle Row and Bottom Row.

You can perhaps imagine the community spirit that was enjoyed in the Raw's, everyone was Jock Tamson's bairns. As a child, you would eat wherever you happened to be at the time dinner was served, and your parents knew this, so there were no concerns about child safety in those days.

This photo was taken on June 1953 when the Raws celebrated the Queen's Coronation.

Photo sent in by **Ellen Clarkin**.

Queen's Coronation 1953 at Craighead Rows
(Baird's Raws)

Anthony Smith sent this photo in of his Uncle, a miner, on the bottom row.

Each Row had four Washhouses, each household having designated wash days.

The washhouses were also used to make soup on occasions, with each household supplying the ingredients.

They were also very popular with young "Winchers" or courting couples, as they were a haven when it rained, which was quite often.

A typical miners' cottage front room and kitchen. The family would sleep, bathe, eat and relax here. Mum and Dad would have the back room, unless of course they had

Front Room / Kitchen

rented it out to lodgers...

Bearing in mind there was no electricity, gas or W.C. to begin with. The sewerage was collected on a daily basis and waste water was thrown out, 'doon the sheugh'. The water was supplied by Craighead Pit. Candles were more popular than lamps, because they were cheaper to burn.

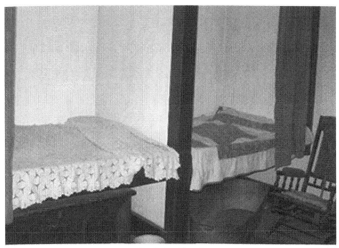

Set in Beds

Set in beds.

Underneath would be for storage or even coal. If the size of the family required it, pull-out beds would be kept there.

Some of my memories of Baird's Raws:

One day, I was given a Baby Rabbit by my uncle Johnny, who lived in the Bottom Row. By the time, I got home to the Middle Row, the Bunny was dead... I had suffocated it because I held it so tight. This was the subject of the Sermon the following Sunday at the Church of the Nazarene.

On a summer's day, I was sitting on the back-window sill and a boy from the Top Row facing us had a Goldfish in a bowl which he was stirring profusely. The Goldfish died eventually, and the boy left it lying on the ground. That experience had a profound effect on me.

I also remember sneaking up to our neighbour's window, Mrs Hamlin's, where she had put a plate of toffee apples out to cool for Halloween, and I pinched one. She caught me red handed and as punishment, she hung me up on the clothes line by my dungarees. I swung there until my Mum took me down, and then I got more punishment from her.

One day, I was out playing with half of a gun, and I fell on some broken glass and cut my hand quite badly. My Mum sent for Dr Jope, who put what looked to me like the handle of a spoon, into the hole in my hand. He was checking for any pieces of glass. And, because I didn't cry, he gave me a whole bag of sweets.

One of my favourite treats was when Mr. Scott, a neighbour would ask me to go and get a big tattie. He would then make some fritters, and we would sit on the front step and gorge ourselves with the fritters. The last time he made the fritters, I had a wee baby brother when I got home!

Salvation Army Citadel

The Salvation Army Citadel was a popular place for worship in the village, and you could hear their tambourines and trumpets as they gave praise at various locations around Blantyre. They had a Soup kitchen at the rear of Allen's Fish & Chip shop according to Betty McGaulley.

Opposite the gates of Blantyre Victoria F.C., the Citadel was demolished in the 1990s.

The Salvation Army Citadel c1960

The Citadel was demolished in the 1990s.

Thomas Dunsmuir Hartman, now in his 80s and living in Chicago, who was also a lifelong friend to my friend and Mentor, the late James Cornfield, tells this story:

"My little pals and I use to go down to the hall in a Sunday afternoon for our Ginger and biscuits all free, and you were encouraged to sing at the top of your voice, which I could not do in my own home. It was just great. We did not know what we were singing about but with biscuits and ginger who cared. We were all little tough guys, so girls always suffered. After we came out of the service, if you can call it that, we would immediately start making fun of the Salvation Army, like singing songs about them. One I can remember went,"

"The Salvation Army free from sin

all went to heaven in a corned beef tin.

The corned beef tin began to smell,

So, they jumped out and landed in h—l."

I have to-day the greatest respect for the Salvation Army, and in my book, they are the very best, in all that they do".

Just so that you can get your bearings, this is where we are at, Forrest Street, as we wander doon memory lane.

The Citadel is at the bottom centre, opposite the entrance to Castle Park, Blantyre Victoria's F.C. home ground.

To the left, is the start to Baird's Raws. The three-story building, Centre left, is the rear of Grant's Building with the lane separating it from Gilmour's Building.

Across Glasgow Road is the Burleigh Church, then Herbertson Street, then the Co-op.

© RCAHMS

At the top right of Forrest Street is the Livingstonian Pub with the top story demolished. This was the Blantyre Electric Cinema, nicknamed, "The Fleapit" where silent films were shown.

Your Memories:

Annie Murdoch Anderson Black: I used to go there. Thanks for the nice memories.

Laura Hamilton: My grandma used to worship there in the start of 1900's. She became a sergeant... think that's what they called them. Her name was Jane (Jeannie) Lindsay then to become Dunsmuir.

George Mackenzie: My pal Iain MacAlpine & I went there from Auchinraith Primary and handed over a 'jeely jaur' to get in to see cartoons. Great times.

Keith MacLean: Remember this place well...

Jacqui Williamson: I remember going to Sunday school in the salvation hall.

William Sommerville Oil Refinery

At the bottom of Forrest Street next to the railway line, we have William Sommerville Oil Refinery.
Known locally as the Oil Works.

You can see some men on their way to work at Blantyre Engineering at the bottom.

Here you can see the entrance to William Sommerville Oil Refinery at the bottom of Forrest Street, next to the railway line.

From the Oil works you hit a very rough man made path leading from Forrest Street and going over to the Village Railway Station 'A Shortcut'.

This was a great saving for the people who lived furthest east in Blantyre who had to catch a train.

Blantyre Engineering

Blantyre Engineering and Castle Park

Blantyre Engineering, a major employer of its time and Castle Park, home to Blantyre Victoria F.C.

Blantyre Engineering was started and owned by James Kelly of Glasgow Celtic and Kelly's Corner fame.

Forrest Street to the left and Clark Street just above Castle Park and John Street to the right. All of these streets were named after Col. John Clark Forrest, Grand Master of the Masonic Lodge. He was also the provost of Hamilton 1875-81.

Logan Street was named after his wife Janet Logan.

Jane Paterson: I started in Blantyre Engineering when I was 15 as an Office Junior had to pick up the mail every morning from the post office and then over to Little's for the rolls. I was later promoted to clerkess in the Buying Dept. Ahh happy days, remember Mr. Kelly well x.

Castle Park - Home of Blantyre Victoria F.C.

Castle Park - Home of Blantyre Victoria F.C.

Coming back up Forrest Street on the right is Castle Park, home of Blantyre Victoria F.C.

Blantyre Victoria was reconstructed as a junior team in 1902, playing in the Scottish Central League. The Vics were successful in winning the League Championship in 1935/36 and also contested the final of the Lanarkshire Cup in the same season.

The Vics won the Scottish Junior Cup (the highest achievement in junior football) in 1950, 1970 and 1982.

The building next to Vic's Park was Blind Wattie's Briquettes & Paraffin Merchant. His grey horse would pull the cart around the Blantyre Streets and stop on route where there were regular customers.

After Blind Wattie's was the Broken Hole - where you could walk behind the Tenements facing Glasgow Road, all the way to John Street and through the side entrance into the Public Park.

Blantyre Vics Football Club unveils newly-named KG Stadium.

Daily Record: 5 NOV 2016 BY LEONA GREENAN

Vics' also have huge plans to dig up the grass park on Forrest Street and lay a new 4G synthetic pitch.

Board members Kenny Gormley, vice president; Andy McDade, secretary; Bill Lowe, president; Jim Clelland and Ian Robertson, head of youth.

Blantyre Vics Football Club this week unveiled their newly-named ground and revealed their ambitious plans for the future.

The club, formed in 1890, renamed Castle Park the KG Stadium, following a substantial sponsorship from

Blantyre businessman Kenny Gormley, owner of Copy Stat Office Systems on Stonefield Road.

Former players included Lisbon Lion legend Billy McNeill, Leeds and Manchester United's Joe Jordan and the late Celtic manager Jock Stein. Bill continued: "It's all hands-on decks with our plans to move forward and create some great vibes in Blantyre.

We have this fantastic ground in a prime location and, in time, with a 4G pitch laid it is only right that we share such a facility."

The Livingstonian Bar & the Blantyre Electric Cinema

This is the Livingstonian Bar - Glasgow Road at Forrest Street, owned by McLachlan the Brewers. And referred to as The Tap Shoap.

The Blantyre Electric Cinema, nicknamed, "The Fleapit" was above the Livingstonian (demolished in this photo) and showed silent movies before the opening of the Picture House Cinema, The Doocot. The Cinema was also used for the first Masonic Lodge meetings in Blantyre prior to the Masonic Lodge being built further west on Glasgow Road.

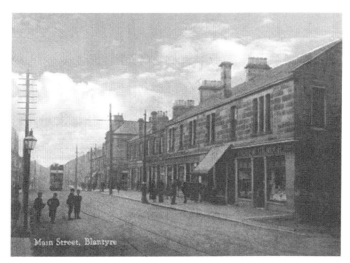

Here we can see the Livingstonian Bar at the corner of Glasgow Road and Forrest Street before the Electric Cinema was demolished due to fire. c1930.

Livingstonian - Front & Rear with the Blantyre Electric Cinema above demolished

The Blantyre Electric Cinema was operated by Richard Vincent Singleton.

When the Cosmo cinema opened in 1939, it was part of a chain of cinemas owned by the Singleton family.

The circuit, which now included some of the newest and most prestigious venues in Scotland, had rather more humble origins.

Mr. R. V. Singleton J.P.

It all started in 1910, when Richard Vincent Singleton, a printer by trade but a talented cinema pianist in the evenings, decided to go into the trade for himself.

He leased a Masonic hall in Burnbank, South Lanarkshire, and started advertising his show to the local miners. Along for the ride was his ten-year-old son George, who would grow up to become known as 'Mr. Cosmo'.

However, back at the Premier Pictures in Burnbank, young George's role was to help his father carry home the films and the sacks of coppers, on foot all the way home to Glasgow through the dark winter nights after the trams had stopped.

Hard work, but it bore fruit: By 1919, Singleton elder sold off his printing business, and the following year George was running his own theatre.

By then, the Singletons already controlled several venues, including the Paragon in Calton, the Blantyre Electric Theatre, and the Airdrie Pavilion.

An accounts' book for one of these cinemas also survives, for the year running up to the start of the First World War. It shows how difficult it was to thrive in the cinema business, at the mercy of fickle audience preferences that could result in significant profits one week and losses the next.

R.V. Singleton got it right, alongside making sure he selected the right films, and implementing an efficient way of splitting the cost of film hire between his venues. R.V. Singleton knew sure fire ways to build a clientele:

He engaged three musicians, printed thousands of half-price passes to slide under doors, and offered children's matinees on Saturdays, in which the young patrons would get ice cups and free liquorice.

While George Singleton became the best-known character of the family, his father continued to be a highly-respected figure in the Glasgow cinema trade.

So, next time you enjoy a cinematic treat at GFT, remember Mr. Singleton and the Lanarkshire miners of a hundred years ago, who with their hard-earned tuppences built the foundations of this family business and shaped Scottish cinema history.

The Co-op Hall, in Herbertson Street also showed silent movies. Both Cinemas were very popular in the First World War years for any news of the front. Charlie Chaplin was probably the most favourite performer at that time.

Partly sourced from: **Glasgow Film Org.**

The Livingstonian Bar, opposite the Co-op

Blantyre Co-op looking East from Jackson Street

The Livingstonian Bar on the corner of Glasgow Road and Forrest Street. The Blantyre Electric Cinema, nicknamed, "The Fleapit" was above the Livingstonian (demolished in this photo) and showed silent movies before the opening of the Picture House Cinema, The Doocot.

The theatre was used as a meeting room, especially for the local Masonic Lodge.

My Dad used to go to the "Fleapit" with the seniors and read the sub-titles for them. When he came to a word, he didn't know, he just said Glesca or Edinburgh. He was a bit of a lad, my Dad, Wullie 'Budgie' Sim.

Forrest Street to Clark Street

Glasgow Road looking West from Jackson Street - 1970

From Forrest Street to Clark Street, there was, 1st Masonic Temple, which was also the Electric Cinema and the Livingstonian Pub, Dr Jope's Surgery (which was painted dark green, and had benches in the waiting room and smelt of carbolic. Then a Chemist, Tempelton's Grocery, Clarkston Newsagent, Wee Don's (Valerio) Ice Cream, Marshall's shoe shop, a Butchers shop and the Wellington Bar, not necessarily in that order.

Thomas Dunsmuir Hartman wrote, "On this block from Forrest Street to Clark Street again all two storey type tenement homes, there were a couple of stores which I remember very well.

The first 'Templeton's this store was unique in that they would display a lot of their dry goods in shelves and canvas bags on the

pavement directly outside the store, and as you can imagine this was asking for trouble with us kids around.

I recall many a stolen mouthful of Oats, Pea pods, Biscuits. You name it; we stole and ate it.

In them there good old days there was very little of packaged goods, mostly everything came in bulk, and most of that were in canvas bags and wooden casks. The butter arrived in a cask probably weighing around 100 lbs it was hoisted by hand up on the marble counter top where the cask was stripped away. The butter was wrapped in cheese cloth, which had to be wetted down and stripped off.

The Cheese was in a rounded ball of about 50 lbs. This too was up on the counter. Outer layers of cheese cloth stripped off and duly cut into the proportions required by the customer.

Bill says, "One of my first chores on a Saturday morning when I worked as delivery boy for Norris, the grocer next to the Dookit, was to take the cheese cloth off a cheese, in the back room. Sometimes, this was easy and therefore quite enjoyable, but at other times, it was nigh impossible to get a start on the cheese cloth and frustration would take over. I think that was when I learned to throw a knife!"

The hand cutting of cheese was done with a piano type wire. The butter was hand cut and shaped with two wooden paddles, again into the size required by the customer. You have to remember that there was no refrigeration then and things could get rather sticky, so a fair amount of water was being used to counteract the stickiness.

The other store of note belonged to a family of Italian immigrants into Scotland, there name was Valerio.

There were three families of Valerio's Blantyre; all of them owned ice cream shops. There was Mickey's at the West end, Peter in the middle and Wee Don in the East side. They served up some great ice cream treats through the years, from their push carts and up to their motorized vehicles in the later years.

The family was so well respected that they have a modern street in Blantyre named after the family. They made a wonderful pea dish with lots of vinegar that all of us young kids loved to eat."

Bill says, 'During a conversation with Wee Mickey at his café on Stonefield Road, I asked him for a good Italian name for a Band, and Mickey replied, without taking his cigar out of his mouth, "Ah wiz born in Glesca son, I canny speak Italian."

The Wellington Bar – Glasgow Road at Clark Street

Glasgow Road looking east from Clark Street - On the left

Looking East from Clark Street, here you see a Tram coming from Motherwell, Trams were introduced to Blantyre in 1903 when this photo was taken.

On the left is The Wellington Bar – Glasgow Road at Clark Street. A pub often frequented by the Lithuanian people of Blantyre and Burnbank, because of its famous Dark Light Beer.

If you look beyond the tram car on the left-hand side, you can make out a piece of a cart, then two poles, right on the second pole, there is a window with a white blind drawn down. Turning left here would be the entrance to Forrest Street.

On the left is the entrance into Clark Street, which again was made up of the same two storey type tenement building with some detached bungalows.

At the end of the street was another entrance into the Blantyre Victoria Football Park, the football Park was running from Forrest Street over to Clark Street, again in between all the tenement type buildings, there was the common washhouse and drying lines for clothes with the coal bunkers for storage.

Looking West from Clark Street - Millar's Laun

Here we have Miller's Laun, Matthew Millar, cobblers known as Matha the Pole, the "Pole" description was given to everyone from Eastern Europe in those days, but the Millar family, who lived in Ivy Place, were actually Lithuanian. The Shop later became Millar's Sports Goods, after that we had Thorburn Hairdressers (George and Freddie), Agnew's Fish Shop, later to be owned by Willie & Jenny Douglas from the 1950s, until 1977, then Norrie Douglas until it was demolished in 1981.

Lightbody Cakes, British Restaurant later to become the Gas Board showroom, Batters Ironmongers, Boyd's Hall, (Bookies), Glencairn Laundry, Amerigo Russo, shortened to Rigo, the Sweet shop where Pasha Cigs were sold and finally Stepek's at John Street.

Iain Douglas said, "Just to confirm, the fish shop was owned by Willie & Jenny Douglas from the 1950s, until 1977. Then Norrie Douglas bought and owned it, until its demolition in 1981. Willie was my father's older brother, who died 1959'ish. Norrie also ran a fish & grocery van in Blantyre, until he bought the shop from his sister-in-law, Jenny.

Jenny's maiden name was Agnew. Maybe that's why the name has been mentioned."

Your Memories:

Thomas Barrett: We lived above Batters and the fishmonger was Douglas then.

Lynn Kelly: In between Rigo's & the bookies was Glencairn laundry my mum worked there!

Elizabeth Dobson Grieve: Big difference.

Jean Gibson: It was Douglas fish shop Norrie used do the van round.

Helen Dyer: Funny how we never thought of our home town as being Quaint... I do now, just love it.

Angela Mary McGlynn: Memories!!!

Mary McGuigan: I remember a Norrie's grocery van x

George Mackenzie: I remember Norrie Douglas coming around Kirkton Avenue (very busy on Friday's) & Batters Ironmongers reminded me of the shop in Open All Hours.

Moyra Lindsay: Norris Douglas was the fishmonger. Have to say I still miss Batters and I can still remember the smell in it.

Sylvia Wilson: I remember all the shops in the pic this takes me back wish I was still in that era.

Nancy McFadden: My mum used to clean the gas showroom

Mary Boyle: Fabulous photos! Love them, I remember Bunty from the Hairdressers, Mr Miller who owned the shoe store selling quality shoes. He regularly repaired my Nana's shoes, Mrs Mogan. Lightbody made the best morning rolls ever! Xx

Ann Ford: No, the best rolls came from Little's the bakers, ma da used to bring them in after doing night shift at the pit.

Norma Foley: These shops are the reason I signed the petition AGAINST ASDA, the worst thing that happened to Blantyre.

Batters Ironmongers, Glasgow Road

Just to clarify where we are in our journey from the East, on the North side of Glasgow Road. Stonefield Parish Church on the left with Walter Batters Ironmongers on the right. The turreted building on the right is the Castle Vaults at the top of John Street.

Every time I see the Two Ronnie's Sketch, I think of Mr Batters. Four Caunels... Naw Fork Haunels...

Stonefield Parish Church and Batters Ironmongery

69

Carol Crombie says, "Opposite the bottom of Church Street was Batters' Ironmongers, which was owned by my Great Aunt and her husband Walter Batters. My Dad, Kenny Crombie, remembers at around the age of eight being allowed to cut his first key! I think perhaps getting to use his hands so early on, planted the seed for him serving his apprenticeship with Harper's garage and then to Robertson's of Springwell. My sister and I were never allowed the 'ginger' or Kwenchy cups to make into 'jubilees' for fear, our teeth would rot!

Also, my Great Uncle Jack Brown was the manager at the 'Dookit' and Great Aunt Daisy held dancing lessons. Their daughter Joyce followed Daisy's footsteps too.

Many thanks for allowing me to ramble on."

Carol Crombie (39)

Here we see Forrest Street, on the left, in relation to Clark Street, in the middle and John Street on the right.

The Streets on the South Side of Glasgow Road are Elm Street (top middle), Church Street and Logan Street, far right. The football park is Castle Park, home of Blantyre Victoria F.C.

Besides the Shop and Warehouse on Glasgow Road, the Batters family owned 15 houses in Church Street in 1915.

You could get almost anything you wanted from Batters, little girl's scraps, paraffin, nuts and bolts, springs, ornaments. The list goes on.

They even branded some of their products like this chain pull, which is owned by Alison Walker-Hill's family who live at the old Board Room in the workers' village.

As you can see by your memories, Batters was a much-loved shop by the people of Blantyre.

Your Memories:

Helen Grieve: Their son was in my class at primary! They lived in Church Street then.

Amanda Palmer: Mrs Batters still lives across road from me in Church Street!

Helen Grieve: My scraps on a Saturday with my pocket money!

Margaret Mcculloch: Wish that shop batters were back, beats Asda any day.

Catriona Paterson: Best shop with the best smell, I bought my scraps from here when I was a wee girl, and I still have my scraps sadly the shop has gone... oh, the memories.

Rosemary Law: I remember sitting on the big chair next to the front door and the smell of the place.

Monica McFall Holmes: Yep Mrs Batters lives next door to my mum!! Loving all the old photos on this page. X

Amanda O'Neill Gwynne: I remember my mum taking me here to buy Scraps.

Fran Flavia McDermott Mcwalters: Remember the smell of the shop to this day x

Jeanette Izzett: Loved the smell in the shop.

Mary Boyle: I bought my Mum an ornament for Mother's Day from Batters when I was wee. It was an ashtray so being a non-smoker she wasn't impressed! Xx

Jane Barkey: Loved Batters even got my ornaments out of there. A lovely red glass dog, loved it.

Ivy Robertson: I still remember the carbolic soap smell.

Jan Ritchie: Great shop! You could get anything you needed! And Rosie! I loved the smell too! X

James Hunter: SMELL OF PARAFFIN.

Margaret Quinn: Bought my scraps there, spent hours deciding, could never afford thon big angels x

Helen Howe: Loved going to that shop for ma scraps cos they had good yins and a bit diff from other shops a still to this day love the smell in an ironmonger!

Jamie Boyle: I think the sketch from the two Ronnie's fork handles could been filmed in there lol.

Diane Cunningham: Loved the smell in it x

Marian Maguire: Best wee shop in Blantyre, you could go in there for one nail.

Maureen McGilligan Downie: The 2 Batter's Sisters lived in Church Street when me and Jim moved in they were lovely ladies that was (1988).

Marianne Timmions: It was like an Aladdin's cave things hanging everywhere.

Orlando Ancilotti: Best smell of any shop ever.

Carol Summers: I loved Batters, and used to go in with my Granddad. I also remember the smell and used to think they sold every single thing in the world there! Happy memories.

Amanda Price Campbell: I agree! The smell was fabulous!!

Sheena Thomson: I remember the smell when you walked in it sold everything.

Jane Barkey: Loved that shop bought a lot of ornaments in that wee shop a long time ago. Brought back memories.

Margo Haughen: Loved that shop...the Batters were my dad's cousins, I think!!

Jackie Croft: I remember this shop x.

Pamela Holland: It had two counters made of wood and depending what you wanted you went to that counter key cutting nails and school bus ticket was on the left counter.

John McCourt: Could get anything from a needle to an anchor, remember it went on fire.

Audrey Marshall: Thanks for this x

James Faulds: It was Matha the poles that did the soles etc., Willie Pate for papers, Bradly's for bottle Senatogen wine or four crown, Rego's for singles cigs, Annie Botterell's for fish and chips, Blacks the bakers, so many great shops and people.

Etta Morrison: Loved going in here just for the smell. All the wee drawers with every size screw and nails. No matter what you asked for they could go straight to it. I loved this shop, they sold everything, it had the two counters one on left side and one on right the smell in it was amazing!!

Sadie Dolan: Loved this shop sold everything, it had the two counters one on left side and one on right the smell in it was amazing!!

Hazel Krawczyk: He was my papa and lived in Church Street till he passed away just up from the original shop in Glasgow Road!

Pamela Bushell: Remember it well they sold everything under the sun you name it they had it I was also a paper girl for Willy pate loved my wee job delivered the Sunday papers brings back lovely memories.

John Murray: Was this that place that was on the same street as Pate's the Newsagents? Still have an Eveready torch that I got from there that was bought in 1979.

Laurie Allan Crothers: What a great wee shop it was. You're right Sadie, it did sell everything.

Nancy McFadden: Remember the Christmas window and buying scraps there.

Helen Gilchrist Young Baird: Loved that shop, especially for scraps.

Nadine Gallagher: Best shop ever often think of this shop. Never forget the smell xxx.

Carol Crombie: It was my great-uncle who owned it and I have only a faint memory of the shop – sadly.

Eleanor Duncan Nailon: loved going there for my scraps defo can remember the smell bring back great memories x.

Bruce Baldwin: One of the great wee shops Asda killed off. Loved it has been said. You could get almost anything here.

Joe Jones: Remember it well.

Jeanette Lee: I was a Saturday girl there many years ago and loved it.

Colin Balfour: Remember my dad sending me there for a pound of felt nails for his hut when I was a wee lad.

Joe Kane: Great shop it had everything the smell was amazing.

Andy Lynch: Walter Batters were Santa Clause.

Georgina Durnan Mackie: That was the best day's xx

Billy Mckinlay: Went to school with His son George.

John Crothers: They sold everything you needed.

Walter Batter's must surely rate as one of the most popular and favourite Blantyre shops... as your memories testify...

Stepek's Electrical

We can all remember the Stepek Electrical Shop at John Street on Glasgow Road and latterly, corner of Station Road and Glasgow Road, after all, most of our families got their first television and washing machine from Mr. Stepek.

Jan Stepek, a Polish Immigrant, was a carpenter to trade and learned radar during the War. When the War was over, he learned of a Grant to study Television and radio at Glasgow University, which he eagerly took, and came to Scotland in 1947 and settled into a room and kitchen in Cambuslang. He was often seen pushing his cart through the streets of Blantyre, offering to repair broken radios.

He only had one price for the repair, Ten Bob, but guaranteed that it would be repaired. He soon opened his first shop, then his second and eventually became the largest Electrical Retailer in Scotland.

He bailed out Hamilton Accies and became Chairman from 1969 up until 1987 when he stepped down. In

2000, he became Chairman once again until 2002.

Your Memories:

Andrew MacFarlane: A story which provides a great example of the social and economic benefits our community and country can gain from showing compassion and empathy towards refugees and our fellow human beings. Thanks for sharing.

Susan Flannigan Mayes: My mum knew him. She said he was a nice man and a gentleman.

Maureen Kelly Elliott: Brilliant. Worked in Stepek for 12 yrs... Good times x.

Alex Mcdermott: Only in Blantyre.

Ian Anderson: My mum and dad knew Jan Stepek, he came over during 2nd world war from Poland and started with a wheelbarrow fixing anything and everything nice man.

Catherine Travers Leslie: I used to work in Stepek's when I was still at school. Worked at the weekends and holidays - thanks for the picture, brought back memories - right on the corner.

Campbell Wylie: Very high HP terms.

Isobel Bolger: My dad was in the army with the guy Stepek.

Donna Timmins: Bought my washing machine from Stepek's, it's still in use.

Christine Brown: It defo is the top of John St, Rego's next to it then the laundrette pen-close then the bookies, Batters, Geordie the barber, fish shop, Matha the poles known as Millar's shoe shop.

Elizabeth Clelland: Think everybody in Blantyre remembers Stepek x.

Marie Cathcart: I think I still owe Stepek money lol.

Anne Mccreadie: I got my first telly out of Stepek's, paid it every Friday lol.

John Latta: Guy came to our house to empty the telly and forgot to do up the padlock, so I did and told ma da and got some doing that day.

Tracy Feelie: Who remembers bumpin Stepek? Pmsl x

Angela Tallis: yea got my first washing machine from there!! Paid it off then got my Betamax recorder lol, on my way home from work at Martin Murry the chemist.

James Faulds: next to Rego's and the bookies and the dry cleaners.

Betty Mcneill: They were the days when Blantyre had a Main Street.

Christine Brown: Geordie Thorburn had a Barbers just along from Stepek and his brother Freddie and you had Bunty for the woman's hair.

Christine Brown: I used to run down Elm Street to all these shops. Aye, and baseball boots cost next to nothing lol.

Glasgow Road Looking West from Church Street

Glasgow Road on September 17th 1937 with a hugely increased traffic flow – although no evidence of any traffic lights. The girl is Betty Morrison. Her daily job at school was to go to the Post Office for the School principal's mail. Details from **Margret Wilson**.

Betty is standing fairly close to the telephone box at the corner of Church Street and is looking across the road at a van just outside the Marshall's shoe shop (before it was Stepek's) on the other corner from the Castle Vaults.

Behind Betty, to her right would be Stonefield Parish Church (which burned down on 3rd September 1979 and was demolished in 1980). To her left would be the block which contained the Masonic Lodge, Craig the butcher's and on to the Priory Bar at Logan Street.

On the Corner of Logan Street, you can just see the Ironmongers store entrance, on the corner of Turner's Building.

Thomas Dunsmuir Hartman says, "On the east corner of John Street, there was a shoe store called Marshall's (later to become Timpson's and then Stepek's), which always displayed a fair number of shoes and Wellington boots hanging around the door entrance to the store.

As youngsters, we used to run by and see how many we could hit and unloosen from their hook so that they fell to the ground.

We must have had a great affection for this particular store or person that owned it, as we made up, a wee song that went like this:

"I hid a wee monkey. I feed it on Marshals Breed (bread)

Marshall! Marshall! stick it up your as! #%le ma wee monkey's deed." (dead)

We must have really loved that guy to have made up such a wonderful wee song, Of course it is easy to see that us Blantyre boys were influenced greatly by the Burns school of thought in our songs poetry."

The next store of any significance was the Labour Party store. This was situated in McAlpine's Building, a three-storey block directly attached to the two storeys. You can see McAlpine's on the right.

The McAlpine building was well known to everyone in Blantyre and more so to our family. This was where my Mum was born, and she lived here with her seven sisters and two brothers.

One of the stores in this block was a fish and chip shop by the name of Allan's. Everyone in Blantyre knew of this shop, as it sold the best Fish Suppers in Blantyre, and it was always used as a reference point in Blantyre, as in. "Yea that's three streets past Allan's, or it's across the road from Allan's."

The next shop was a Grocer by the name of Hugh's and next to them was another grocer by the name of Norris. I delivered the groceries for Norris for about two years.

Hi Bill,

At the right hand-side going up Church Street sat the telephone box and the tenement on Glasgow road housed the Masonic Lodge On the second floor. And from my memories of the ground floor shops (the 70s) there was a sewing shop, butcher and a Timpson's shoe shop. I also believe there was a pub which sat on the corner of Glasgow Road and Logan Street - this housed a particularly vicious Alsatian who used to slide down the back of a roof to go out to play with my Dad. 'The Dug Whisperer' or what!!!

These grounds have been going to waste for some years, the last cottage to be demolished there was latterly used by Blantyre Volunteer Group. The existing cottages on each side of Church Street start beyond the church grounds, where my Papa and Nana lived for over 60 years, the cottage now belonging to my Dad.

Behind this building was quite a large house, known to me as "The Braidwood's" - I believe the sisters who lived there were spinsters. Up until the 70s, there were garages and a wall surrounding the 'Braidwood' house'. Opposite the bottom of Church Street was Batters' Ironmongers, which was owned by my Great Aunt and her husband Walter Batters. **Carol Crombie** (39)

John Street, formerly called New Station Road.

Down John Street there was a side entrance to Stonefield Public Park, Toll Brae Stables, a Brick Quarry (where the football fields are now), the clay pits filled with water and this became known as the Lilly Pond which was out of bounds

for most children because it was so deep. This was filled in by Frank Doonin and became the two football fields in Stonefield Public Park.

Then there was Aitkenhead's Slaughter house, Willie McPhee's Piggery, a Lane to the Railway Station and underneath the railway tunnel to the right was Nicholson's Piggery. Once called Kirby's, Nicholson also had a Grocers shop in Station Road on the corner of Woodburn Avenue across from Farm Road.

Aitkenhead Slaughter house, used for butchering horse, cattle and sheep from the farms in the local area. You could hear the Gun Shots for quite a way along Glasgow Road.

Your Memories:

Jim Hunter: Johnny Aitkenhead was a legend when I was a kiddie in Blantyre. My father George Hunter who like myself was born in the house just past the wall in this photo (no 49) claimed he saw him smash a crossbar in a game of football, such was the power of his kick.

Len Northfield: That was my grandpa's slaughterhouse. He died before I was born, so I never knew him, but my Grannie was quite a woman!

Orlando Ancilotti: The Russell house was my uncle John Aitkenhead's. I'm related to the Russell's via him.

Stevie Fletcher: Len I heard John Russell speak of the Airkenhead's, were they the butchers in Blantyre, or even a famous footballer.

Orlando Ancilotti: That's right, my granddad owned the slaughterhouse down by the park, and Johnny Aitkenhead, my mum's cousin, played for Hibs and Motherwell.

Here we see Willie McPhee's Piggery, on the left going down John Street.

From McPhee's to Blantyre Engineering, the land was leased by the McAleenan family

who used it, mostly for Cattle grazing.

At the end of John Street, there was a fairly large close opening going under the railway lines which led out on to the River Clyde Braes, a good view of the surrounding area along the valley and the Blantyre Village area.

Railway Tunnel, John Street

This was the area that David Livingstone was born and grew up in.

Also, running along at the bottom of John Street was a continuation of the shortcut from Baird's Raws in Forrest Street to the Blantyre Railway Station.

Nicholson's Piggery, under the Railway Tunnel to the right. One time called Kirby's. Nicholson also had a Grocers shop in Station Road on the corner of Woodburn Avenue across from Farm Road.

Nicholson's Piggery over the railway line and next to the river Clyde with the sewerage bridge in the background.

Your Memories:

Helen Grieve: Been thinking about McPhee's going down John Street it was on the left and the house was in front of the piggery building if my memory serves me right. There was a grassy bank in front of the house. I played with Agnes McPhee when I was wee.

Jack Owens: McPhee's Piggery. Went there a few times with my dad.

Castle Vaults

On the other corner of John Street was the Castle Vaults. The pointed roof was a landmark in Blantyre whenever directions were given. A well-known pub and very well frequented place to drink. Unlike today when most pubs are owned by Breweries, the pubs in those days were privately owned, and the owners carried whatever types of beer he knew would sell in his particular area, but it was the same-old story after the third round of drinks, who cared what type of beer it was.

Blantyre Victoria's Castle Park was owned by The Castle Vaults and used by Blantyre Victoria F.C. as their home ground.

A good drink for a miner if he could afford it was 6 individual drams of whiskey with each dram followed with a pint of beer as a chaser. He would generally make this last from say 6 o'clock to 10 o'clock closing time.

The Castle Vaults opposite Marshall's Shoe Shop, was also known as The Black Diamond, and was owned by McLachlan the Brewers and known as The Bottom Shop.

From the Castle Vaults going West, we had Davidson's Emporium, who sold linoleum and such like, Hairdressers, Sandy Thompson's Newsagents, McWilliamson the butchers shop, after that, the McAlpine Building with Allan's Fish & Chips, (name changed to Andrews), Gibson's store, Hughes Grocery and then Alpine Street, where the McAlpine building continued.

To give you your bearings, the McAlpine building was opposite Logan Street.

Castle Vaults at John Street and Glasgow Road 1970, after the demolition of McAlpine's Building.

Photo sent in by **Anthony Smith**.

Marion Young: Ma auntie Helen was manager of the Castle Vaults.

Glasgow Road looking East from Logan Street c.1903

Stonefield, Blantyre

This picture shows a stretch of Glasgow Road from Logan Street in 1903 just after the trams were introduced. You can see a Tram, in the distance coming from Hamilton. There was a patch of waste ground beside Stonefield Church (pictured right with steeple) and then the Priory Bar on the corner of Logan Street.

On the left, we have the Castle Vaults with the pointed roof, a Blantyre landmark. Aka, The Black Diamond, which was a McLaughlin's Pub.

Jim Cornfield once told me that it was nicknamed, 'The Black Diamond,' because they used leather diamond strips that the Cobbler used, as kicking plates along the bottom of the bar.

Looking East from Logan Street. 1937

GLASGOW ROAD, BLANTYRE

By the 1930s, the Masonic Lodge, tenements and shops were built in three stages on the vacant ground, next to the Stonefield Parish Church and obscuring the view of the church from this position. If you keep looking along to the right across the picture at the roof line, where it makes a high point, and a flag pole sits on top, this is the Masonic Hall and directly across the road is John Street.

The facias opposite had all undergone refurbishment. The transport situation also changed radically, with cars and trucks gliding down a newly surfaced road, replacing the trams that had previously rumbled down the dirt streets.

The McAlpine Building is the three-storey tenement just visible to the left and opposite Logan Street.

The Man is standing outside the Ironmongers, J.C.

Sweet's cut price shop at the corner of Turner's Building, which became the Post Office in 1959.

Where it says, wines, is the Priory Bar on the corner of Logan Street.

McAlpine's Building

The next shop of any significance was the Labour Party Office. This was situated in a three-storey block directly attached to the two-storey known as McAlpine's Building.

McAlpine's Building

The building turned North at Alpine Street, and right again, facing Stonefield Public Park, forming a 'U' shape. The McAlpine building was well known to everyone in Blantyre and more so to our family. This this where my Mum lived with her Mum and Dad, eight sisters and a brother.

This was also where my Dad, Wullie Budgie Sim, got his nickname, because he used to whistle at the bottom of the stairs to attract my Mum's attention when they were courting, and her Mum would say, "There's that **Budgie** calling for you again."

One of the shops in this block was a fish and chip shop by the name of Allan's. Everyone in Blantyre knew of this shop, as it sold the best Fish & Chips in Blantyre and it was always used as a reference point in Blantyre. Betty McGaulley informs me that there was a Soup Kitchen behind Allen's. Anyone remember?

On the corner of Alpine Street, William Hugh's the grocer, Gibson's store, Allen's chip shop, McWilliamson the butcher shop, and Davidson's Emporium, where you bought your linoleum and such like.

Just to get our bearings, here we have the Rear of McAlpine's Building, after the west block was demolished, Brown's Building and the Dookit. Craig Street across Glasgow Road with Harper's Garage on the corner and at the top is the Miners Welfare and Calder Street School.

Thomas Dunsmuir Hartman remembers, "You will see that the McAlpine building makes a right turn down Alpine Street. (This was before the Alpine Street tenement was demolished) The homes down this street were the usual tenement type. The only thing unusual about this set up was that this whole block, the front of the block facing on to the Glasgow Road, and the buildings on the right-hand side of Alpine Street, plus a part of the public park all formed a square, and within this square, there were all these coal bunkers, washhouses, poles with lines stretched across them for drying the clothes that had just been washed, and the kids playing in between. I don't know if you can picture this like I can, but it is a memory I have, and I can tell you it was something to behold, especially when the wind got up and started blowing any sheets around and the whipping type of noise that was created"

The Dookit

Glasgow Rd. Blantyre

Next, we had Brown's Building, Cathy Pott's Fruiterer, Norris grocers, where I worked as a delivery boy for a couple of years. The Picture House (affectionately called The Dookit), later to become the Bowling Alley, Paterson's Chemist & Optician, Hogg's Newsagent (later Pate's), Little's the Baker, Paterson Painter & Decorator, Peter Craig Butchers and then Greenside Street.

The Picture House was opened in 1913 by a well-known circus family, Bostock & Sons and was able to show talkies by 1929. It later became owned by Jack Brown, who lived and breathed the world of cinema and show-business, was one of a disappearing breed of characters who toiled with all their heart in the ebullient, sometimes romantic but always precarious world of entertainment. Unlike many in today's profit-chasing and sometimes soul-less era, he was a dedicated show-person, working all hours to give value to his customers through the 1930s, 40s and 50s, and enjoying his job both front-of-house and backstage.

The Picture House (The Dookit), you will see that there are two-door openings into the picture hoose. The one at the right was the entrance to the cheap seats, and the one at the left was for the more expensive seats. The cheap seats were about half the cost of the more expensive seats, but there were about ten times as many cheap seats as there were of the expensive ones.

The Bus stop on the right where you could only get off the bus, but not on, presumably because of the Picture House, get off to go to the pictures and too many to get on when film finished.

Thomas Dunsmuir Hartman remembers, "The 'Dookit' Oh! what memories it brings back to me as a child and even into my youthful years. There was an enchantment about this wee picture hoose, which played a great part in our everyday existence. Saturday morning could not come around fast enough for us kids, so that we may go there and be thrilled and be educated with all the different ways of life, which was new and shown to us through this medium.

You have to remember we did not have any TV, or Entertainment was mostly during the week limited to the B.B.C. Radio. We didn't even have a Scottish radio station in those days. One Station and that was it. So, you can see why we so looked forward to our Saturday Morning Pictures.

We sure did get a lot for our money. They would start out by showing the Movietone News which was a synopsis of all the latest news from around the world. This showing was, although we did not know it at the time probably our first exposure to the world outside of Scotland, hence the education, I mentioned.

We would sit back and enjoy one of our series "FLASH GORDON' a then future space odyssey, or the 'LONE RANGER' with his sidekick 'TONTO' and that beautiful white horse 'SILVER' a great cowboy threesome.

They would then show a short Disney Cartoon, Bugs Bunny, or one of that type. Next, we would go into a full feature film which in those days would last just nearly an hour. At the end of this the lights would go up and the Ice Cream girls would stand up at the front of the cinema with their trays of Ice Cream for about 15 minutes, in which time the place was in an uproar.

Most kids had held back from going to the toilets, so there was always a queue formed to get into a space which was inadequate for the amount of kids in the cinema. A good few wee Jimmy's and Jessie's were getting up off their seats and looking for their pals to discuss the way that man got his face punched in, and he sure deserved it, didn't he!

There were ushers employed in those days whose job was to keep some sense of order in the Picture hoose. You also had to show them your wee stub of a ticket you had received from the pay kiosk in the foyer. They then in turn showed you to a seat or seats flashing their torches here and there, if the lights had been dimmed and the show already had started trying to find you a seat could go on all through the whole show and could be very interruptive. The chief usher for a long time was Brick McCallum. After the stop for refreshments and time for the projectionist to change his reels of film, the lights would go down, and the main feature would be shown.

There was many a time when something would happen in the showing of the film. The splicing of the various parts of the film would break apart. The speed would slow down or speed up because of some mechanical failure. Or the projectionist would fall asleep and not change the reels, or he would not change them fast enough for the crowd, so when this happened there was always the mumbling of angry voices and then the feet would begin to stamp the floor, getting louder and louder and then the cry would be taken up, BURN THE DOOKIT, BURN THE DOOKIT.

I would not have that guy's job for all the coal in the Blantyre pits, can you imagine this noise and this poor guy trying to feed or mend some old piece of film. A couple of break downs and the poor guy's nerves had to have been shattered. This was one of the ways we showed our displeasure at the interruption of our films, and it was manifested tenfold if it happened at a particular exciting part of the film, it was pandemonium and then an instant silence at the first flicker from the screen at the return of the film. Movie was not a word to our Blantyre vocabulary. It was, either we are going to the pictures or were going to see that new film with John Wayne. Another way we showed our discontent was to throw orange peel or wrappers up into the rays of light that was being projected on to the screen. For some reason, they always left the projection light on while they were trying to fix the fault of the interruption, this must have been for a quick re-entry of the film or could it have been just a safety measure of sorts, just try and imagine what would have happened if they had brought the main lights up.

If you were far enough back at the position of the ray's entry, you could always make with your fingers those rude gestures, and they would be projected on to the screen which would raise a good laugh throughout the Picture House.

Margaret I am giggling away with this memory as I type, we kid sure knew how to live it up when we got the chance. If you ever meet up with a Blantyronian, look him or her straight in the eye and say, 'BURN THE DOOKIT', if this does not bring on a reaction of hysterical laughter, then they are not from Blantyre.

If you take another look at the Gallery Picture of the 'Dookit' starting at the left-hand side of the picture (In Blantyre, everything was a picture to us the word photo was rarely ever used) you can see parts of the picture which would be showing sometime time in the following week, WHEN Irish EYES ARE SMILING.

This picture would receive more than the normal turnout, just because of the name and the life and whereabouts it was depicting, the reason being, that about 50% of the folks who lived in Blantyre at this time were of Irish descent. On the larger displayed billboard at the top it tells that the picture will be shown at 6-15 and 8-30 nightly. It also tells us that the picture now being shown is a picture featuring LAUREL and HARDY. You have a small type window in between and then another frame with about six small pictures displayed. These were taken from the main reel of the picture and displayed here as a synopsis of the picture which was now being shown. This was how the coming attractions of the 1930-1960 were shown.

Compare this to today's elaborate coming attractions now being shown in the Theatres. Today's coming attraction shows are a show within themselves with all of the elaborate sound systems and advertisements usually lasting as long as a small feature film.

Again, take another look and you will see that there are two-door openings into the picture hoose. The one to the right was the entrance to the cheap seats, and the one to the left was for the more expensive seats. The cheap seats were about half the cost of the more expensive seats, but there were about ten times as many cheap seats as there were of the expensive ones.

Above these two doorways, there is a long billboard or poster being shown, what the words read I have been unable to decipher and would appreciate any input of their intention.

On the right-hand side of the doors, here again are six wee pictures showing the coming attractions for maybe the next picture to be shown, which would start about Monday of that week and run until Wednesday of the same week, Thursday would then start another programme.

The Local picture halls in Scotland were never open on a Sunday."

The Blantyre Bowl

When the Dookit closed in 1958, two local carpenters, Ian Liddell and William Paul, converted the property into a 10-pin bowling alley, naming it 'The Blantyre Bowl" and opened in 1959, much to the joy of local youths.

My best friend at the time, Morris (Moses) Buchanan put me out in the Scottish Junior Championship final and went on to Olympia in London, where he won the British Junior Championship.

Unfortunately, the building was destroyed by fire and demolished in 1966. A porta cabin, housing the Clydesdale Bank, took its vacant place.

John Dunsmore, aka, Wee Yanni said, "Hi. Bill this story is one to behold. I got married 1st March 1968, I had just finished my trade as a monumental letter cutter. I was living with my father and mother-in-law in Fernslea Ave, Jimmy and Lizzie Holdsworth. I left the trade and was idle for a couple of months then got a job on the Bin lorries fae Auchinraith Road yard.

I loved the job as a front runner, wae a chap named Andy Sim his dad was Chuck Sim and Peggy (your Aunt and Uncle). The house I am in just now was theirs. I had done a swap fae Jerusalem, High Blantyre to here on the 29th of January 1969. The Bin lorry I was in done the pubs this day fae the West End Bar, all down Glasgow Road. Just at the Central bar, John. Fallon was the owner. The police stopped my driver of the lorry at the burnt-out Dookit which was now a Ten Pin Bowling Alley, prior to being burnt down. Police asked my driver if he would send me and my other friends, I worked with. They said two young boys were trapped inside the building. I just got into the place and heard wee boy shout out. He was behind a door. I went to his rescue and got about 40 ft. away. That's all I remember till I woke up in Hairmyres Hospital.

Part of the roof fell and clobbered my heed, I was out like a lark. The papers, Daily Express and Hamilton. Advertiser had photos of me lying there in hospital. Old Mrs Brown pouring sweet tea o'er my throat, I hate sugar. My dad went to a lawyer, J. Robertson, Muir Street, Hamilton to blame the Police for sending us in. Because I had two pints of beer in my body, as it was just after new year, some pubs gave you a half pint. All I got out of the case was a week's wages. I worked on the bins till 1974, just loved the job and was getting more money on the bins than being a. letter cutter, all water under the bridge noo. Mr. and Mrs Brown stayed at the back of the Dookit and went on tae own Hastie's. Farm in Victoria Street. I used tae frequent often as I knew the door men, big John Rodwell and T. C, your brother-in-law."

Hi Bill

Bill, you might remember me, I wrote to you a couple of years back. My name is Chick Frame from the old Buggie building. Now of Perth Western Australia. First, I want to congratulate you on the splendid job you are doing with Bla'an'tir's Ain Website.

I have just now, once again read James Cornfield's poem: Childhood Memories of Blantyre, and once again got that lump in my throat that it always gives me. The reason I am writing is because I know he doesn't use a computer, so I would like you to offer him my heart-felt praise for the job he did. I swear he stole the memories right out of my head, because that's just exactly what I remember myself.

I remember seeing a Tarzan picture in the old Dookit and there was Cheeta munching into a bunch of bananas, and for the life of me, I couldn't remember even what they tasted like. I remember going across the road to Bowie's fruit shop where right there in the window was a stooky bunch of Fife's bananas. I also remember one of the boys suggesting going into the chemist shop next door to buy a packet of chocolate laxative, because you didn't need any coupons. Probably lucky we had no money left.

Best of luck, **Chick Frame**.

Glasgow Road East

On the right is Turners Building and further down on the right is Logan Street and then the Priory Bar and the Masonic

Building with the pointed roof.

The three-story building on the left is McAlpine's, and after that Alpine Street then Brown's Building, which had Cathie Pott's Fruit & Vegetable shop, Norris Grocers, the Picture House, (The Dookit, just passed where the dog is), Paterson's Chemist & Opticians, Hogg's Newsagents (later Wullie Pate's). We then had Andrew Little the Baker, Paterson (Painter & Decorator), Peter Craig Butchers and after that, Greenside Street.

Wee Fat Wummin

This area is aptly described by an elderly cousin of James Cornfield, Peggy McGuigan, who at the time had lived in Coventry for some 60 years, as she described the Cornfield family house move from Dixon's Raw's to Logan Street.

She said to Jim, "Dae ye' mind when youse flitted? Ah mind as if it wur yesterday. It must have been the Monday that yir mither got the word that she had been gied a new hoose, fur she came runnin' roon the raw wi' her rubber apron an' yir faither's auld boots oan tae tell us the guid news, ye' see Monday wis' yir mither's day fur the wash hoose, so that's how ah 'ken".

The flittin' wis' oan the Friday, it being early lousing fur the men an' pey day furbye, so efter a bowl o' soup at oor hoose jist across the way, aw' oor men an' boys wir ready tae gie a haun' wi' the flittin', oor wimmin' folk hid been doon the nicht afore wi' thur pails, scrubbers, lye soap an' flerr cloths an' gied the hoose a guid gaunin' ower, so aw' wis ready…

"Tam Barclays horse an' cairt wis' hired at a cost of 2 hauf croons fur 2 hoors, an' it came right tae yir mither's

door wae' a bran' new waterproof sheet oan the back o' it, so that yir mithers things widnae git marked, fur ye see the cairt wis' yaised fur carryin' coal!

The cairt went up Dixon Street, turned right intae Stonefield Road, passin 'Jock Millers piggery, Murdoch's pub, Trayner's wee shoap, Chucker's jeans an' the Independent Co-op. Then right intae Calder Street an' doon past Carfin Street, Govan Street, Millar Street an' Burnside Street. Then past Maggie McAleenan's shoap, across fae Tam Barclays yaird, an' the new clinic across fae McAlpines-in-the-Park (Netherfield Place) tae the Clay Road (Victoria Street) an' the polis station across fae Calder Street school an' the new Miner's Welfare an 'the wee Congregational Church at the junction of Craig Street (Slag Road).

The horse an' cairt then turned left down Craig Street past Carlton Terrace an' aw' thon lovely wee cottages, especially the wan (Poplar Cottage) yir auntie Lizzie Paton wis boarn in, tae ye' came tae Harper's Garage at the corner.

The cairt then turned right on to the Glesca Road, past the Cosy Corner pub, Greenside Street, Arbuckle the butcher, Andra Little the baker (dis he still make thon lovely wee rolls?)

Hogg's paper shoap, Grimson's wireless shoap, Paterson the chemist, the Dookit picture hoose, Norris the grocer,

Cathy Potts fruit shoap at the corner o' Alpine Street, opposite Hugh's the grocer, Gibson's store, Allen's chip shoap, McWilliamson the butcher shoap, an' Davidson's the drapers, which wur aw' right across the road fae the Turner's Building, wi' J.C. Sweet's cut price shoap oan the corner, then the entrance intae Logan Street, wi' the Priory Bar oan the ither corner.

Before they started building, Logan Street wis jist a wee street wi' Turner's Building oan the right haun side wi' a park next tae it, where aw' the brass an' silver bauns in blantir yist tae practice, while oan' the left haun side, wis the Priory Bar an' Priory Hall (where aw' thon' doo' men yist tae meet), alang wi' the new Drill Hall."

Your Memories:

John Pollock: Brilliant This!!

Wendy Wilson: Lovely story.

Helen Dyer: Classic reading... heart felt emotions.

Isabell McGinty Cain: Excellent. Karen Nicoll: Brilliant this.

Marianne Stark Aitken: This is an account of my gran and papa's flitting way back in the first half of the last century I remember this story from my mum who wasn't born then so def before 1936, told by my uncle James ... faimily x.

John Ryan-Park: That description of Blantyre was really good, one could travel from Dixon's Row to Logan Street past all the side streets and shops all named with this wonderful family as they flit from a miner's house Dixon's Row to a council house in Logan Street Blantyre.

Etta Morrison: Loved reading this. In tears also thinking of old Blantyre and its miner's raws and relations long gone. Thanks for the memories xx.

Maureen Wood: Really enjoyed this. Both my parents, Naismith and Murray were from Blantyre.

Sheena Thomson: The Lizzie Paton in this story is my Gran, she married Charlie McGuigan, and one of their family was Mary who was my mum.

Marianne Stark Aitken: Oh, looks like we're related Sheena xxx.

Sheena Thomson: Wouldn't be surprised Marianne, Grandpa McGuigan was one of I think about 8 children.

Raye Kelly Robertson: Enjoyed reading this thank you so much for sharing.

Margaret Stewart: Thank you so much for sharing this. It has created an amazing picture of very hard times and very strong people.

Jean Andrew: Bless the Peggy's of this world. Grandfather Alfred Nimmo would have known this lovely lady and suddenly I am closer to her.

Helen Lawson Taylor: Loved reading the story, it took me along all the streets as I was reading and brought back memories of my young days.

Betty McLean: Something lovely about those days and the friendly neighbours, so touching.

Hugh McDade: My parents used Tam Barclay also for our flitting in 1939 to timber houses.

Dallas Carter: Genealogical gold dust, this.

Stuart Oneil: Great read Bill. Thanks for sharing OOR TOON.

Andrew Little's - Bakers

Andrew Little's - Bakers of 200 Glasgow Road, which opened in 1928 and closed due to redevelopment on 17th February 1979.

The bake house was at the rear of the property.

The photo from the early 1930s shows Isa (Isabella Little) in the doorway of her shop in Glasgow Road.

Little's bakery, and Black's bakery were both famous for their delicious rolls and the discerning customers were known to walk past one of the shops to get to the other. They were known to do the same thing with the Butcher's in order to get their preferred square sausage or cut of meat.

The late James Cornfield wrote a poem about:

Andrew Little's Rolls

No matter where I go,
no matter what I see,
My hearts always in Blantyre,
where I long to be.

Some things I've forgotten,
but one I've never forgot,
The smell o' Little's rolls,
especially when they're hot.

Young ones nowadays,
don't know what they've missed.
Why eating Little's rolls,
is better than being kissed.

Whenever I saw Isa standing,
outside their front door,
Then round the back I would go,
when we wanted more.

The aroma form the Bake house,
especially from the ovens,
Was enough to make you think,
of buying another dozen.

I know things are not the same,
everything up the poles,
But as long as I'll live,
I'll never forget Andra Little's Rolls.

Your Memories:

Betty McGaulley: I lived above Little's the Bakers, 200a Glasgow Road... a very famous Baker! Wullie Pates? Brown School of Dancing, the "Dookit" all in the same block.

I remember the bread strike of 1968. Oh, My God?? The shop was beneath my bedroom! They were lining up the stairs from 4.00 a.m. in the morning.

J.D.S. Domestic Services had their first shop in what was Little's, until it was demolished, according to **Drew Semple**.

The Cosy Corner Pub - Glasgow Road at Greenside Place Street

The Cosy Corner, were winners of most of the Darts and Domino competitions they entered in the mid-1950s, and these are all the Trophies won. They are celebrating their victory with a fun day out, to some Miner's Club in Fife, which was a favourite of theirs. - James Cornfield

Some of the families who lived above the Shops were Lynch, Hawkins, Guy, McMahon, Cumminsky, Valerio, McGarvey, McQuade and Davidson.

All these small buildings with similar names were called after either the Owner, the Builder or the Factor, to distinguish them from the similar buildings which made up the facade of Glasgow Road.

"Hi bill, looking at the Drew Semple video, Aint No Characters Anymore, the picture at the Cosy Corner pub, the big guy at the back is my dad. I think the one with the cap on. We lived across the road in Craig Street number 45 then moved to 4 Belvoir Place behind the Parkville. I think that was Dr Gordon's house at one time. My name is **Gibby Mooney**, brother David, dad Jock worked at Robertson's as did his dad David Mooney".

Co-incidence or what? Gibby was instrumental in introducing my sister Cathie to her husband to be, Ian Miller. Now they are back in touch after all these years!!

Standing, Left to right: John Tamson, Patrick McGonigal, George McDade, Frank Urban, Patrick McAleenan, Terry Bute, James McCallum, William McLinden, Wullie Allan, Philip McGuiness, Andrew Alan, Jock Mooney, Shug Murphy, Robert McNamara, Walter Park, Hughie Fitzpatrick, John Fullerton, Bobby McKay, Dave Houston, Pat McAleenan, James McAleenan, Thomas McGarvie, Brian Soper.

Front: Jim McAlister, David Ellis, Steven Robertson, Frank Brown, Honey Glen, Tommy Allen, Robert Clarke, Thomas Kane, Pat McCleary.

Miss E. L. Davidson was the proprietor of the pub at that time and lived in the house above it.

Names supplied by: **Gibby Mooney, James Cornfield, Karen & Rena, Caroline Cunningham, Helen McAllister, Sheena Mason, Betty McGaulley, Stephen Kelly and Lisa McLelland.**

Your Memories:

George McAllister: Hey that's my dad. Wee Jimmy. After the demise of the Cozy and moving to High Blantyre, he made the original DOON INN as his local. Amazing to see this.

Margaret Duncan: The McAleenan's are my relations - my gran was Margaret McAleenan.

Mhairi McGaulley: My Gran was Mary McAleenan and my great Aunt is Rose McAleenan.

Margaret Duncan: If I'm correct Rose McAleenan lived at the bottom of John Street in a wee cottage. My gran had a sister Rose who went to America, Mary who was a spinster, Matt who lived in Craigneuk, Wishaw and George who never married. I've got a family tree.

Anthony Smith: The off-licence hatch was around the corner at the right side.

John Dunsmore: Yip. Tony, I used tae get my carry oot fae the wee hatch before I went tae the Co-op dancing on a Friday nite.

John Dunsmore: The man in the centre of the door way white shirt x tie is Bobby McNamara. He stayed next door tae my parents in Lime Grove, Coatshill. He moved tae wee pensioners Hoose across fae Parkville hotel.

Harts Land or (Herts Laun) as they say in Blantir, was a two-storey stone built building with shops on the ground floor and homes above which stood on Glasgow Road, corner of Greenside Street.

This area taking in Greenside Street was known locally as the Stud, because of the profusion if children who were born and lived there!

From the Cosy Corner Pub which stood on this corner, later to become Devanney's store, we had McGarvey the Barber, which became Jimmy Cleary's Hairdressers, Peter Valerio's Ice Cream Cafe, Bradley the Cobbler, Mrs Guy's wee sweetie shop and finally the Central Bar Pub, (AKA. Sullivan's, later to become Fallon's).

Guys Sweet Shop, Glasgow Road, Blantyre

A little picture of Susan Guy who was the daughter of Hugh and Catherine Guy, who owned the shop on Glasgow Road. Susan died in 1950 aged 62. Unsure of how old she was in this picture. It may latterly have been the Guys sweetie shop referred to in previous posts.

Sent in by **Alison Morgan**.

Mrs Guy used to make some of her own sweets. She would turn the wheel on one end, and the sweets would drop out the other end into a cone-shaped paper bag. She always had trays of toffee and fudge on the counter and a small silver hammer for breaking the toffee. There were sweet jars stacked on shelves with everything from chocolate raisins, sherbet lemons, liquorice sticks, bonbons, jelly babies, love hearts, liquorice allsorts, you name it, enough to make all children's eyes as big as saucers.

Hart's Land (Laun) 1979 Just before Demolition

Joe Murphy said, "That's the Cosy Corner pub at the corner of Greenside Street, the entrance into the public park. At the other side of Greenside Street was McLennaghan's electrical and paint shop. This picture from right to left is the Cosy Corner, Jimmy Cleary's barbers, Peter Valerio's ice cream shop, (Peter was the brother of Micky Valerio, who had his own ice cream shop at the bottom of Stonefield Road), Next was the TV repair shop, which was previously Bradley the Cobblers then became Joe Russell's chippy. Mrs Guy's wee Sweet shop, Fallon's pub, (previously Sullivan's pub) all the way down to the Gazette Office.

Across the road from the Cosy Corner, at the corner of Craig Street and Glasgow Road was Harper's Garage. Next door was Whyte's the plumbers in the Central

Building, later to become Orestie's Chippy, Haddow's the Dentist, then the Head Master's House and the auld Ness's school down to the corner of Victoria Street. Ness's school was the "BROO" when I was a kid."

Photo by **Jim McGuire.**

Jimmy Cleary's, Ladies and Gents Hairdressers

Jimmy Cleary was a successful boxer in his time and also owned and operated Ladies and Gents Hairdressers with his wife Ella at various locations around Blantyre.

Your Memories:

Sadie Dolan: Did his ex-wife Ella not work with him at one point?

Margaret McGuigan: Jimmy, Ella Cleary that's where the aunts and uncles went.

Christine Brown: Always went to Ella, lovely woman x.

Margaret Slaven McSorley: Got ma hair tipped as they called it in Paton's for ma sixteenth birthday, got ma hair done for ma wedding Ella Cleary done it and Lena Scully worked in it.

Sadie Dolan: Ella done my feather cut.

Mark Rock: With the famous shaky Shug, as well.

Annie Murdoch Anderson Black: Ella did my feather cut also xx I am getting home sick now!

Paul McGivern: Jimmy short back and sides.

Leigh Hynds: Ma dad said that cars a Datsun 1200 A or a sunny anyone know?

Sharon Burt: Lol, Ella gave me my first ever perm. Omg think I cried for days. Lol

Andrew Mccluskie: Lol old shaky Shug a can mind him when a wis a wee whipper snapper.

Monica Whelan: I got a 'Purdy' off Ella... lol

Morag Campaigne: Jimmy Cleary and Ella Farrell best hairdressers in their time, I remember them well.

Paul Gilligan-Black: Didn't matter what you asked for... you got a short back & sides!! Many a time I walked out of them with shaky Shugs digestive crumbs all over my head & shoulders!!

James Donnelly: Jimmy Cleary's wae shaky Gordie! And the auld ashtrays about a meter tall! And the stained wood panelling way the smoke. Oh, how I loved getting ma crew cut ARMY STYLE! Lol

Agnes Hynds: Leigh your uncle Tom said it looks like a Datsun 140 j. Look how quiet the roads are, compared to now, thank god, I was not a driving instructor they days lol.

Marc McAuley: Jimmy 'n Ella are my gran 'n grandpa, legends, wee Jimmy still going strong.

Liz Hughes: Jimmy and Ella did work the gither.

Barrie Pentney: It was alright at Jimmy's for a haircut unless you got old shaky Shug, everybody used tae say na ur awrite m8 al just wait for Jimmy lol.

Allan Love: I remember when Jimmy started doing Flat tops, everybody got one even if you didn't ask for it, as he couldn't help himself with his new flat topper gadget. He also had a picture of Bros next to his seat. Lol.

Grace Watson: Used to take my wee boy for his cut, then over to St Joseph's nursery.

James Faulds: Jimmy was a good barber, and his shop was next to the only crossroads in Blantyre, Craig St, Glasgow Rd leading into the public park and the side door to the Cosy Corner.

Janice Cja Clark: Had my hair "set" there on my wedding day.

William Allan: Ma favourite words there were, I'm waiting on Jimmy. Shaky shug gave me an inch line one side and a metre line the other lol.

Marc Moran: I remember getting sent to get ma hair cut for ma first communion and coming back with a skin heed and ma Mum going mental LOL happy days.

Stephen Mcgowan: Jimmy got shakey Shug back in shop on Station Rd, that's when I said **** it I'm buying clippers ha-ha!!!

Steven Johnstone: Aye a remember shaky Shug lol, Jimmy was wan of the nicest people you could meet, had to take Shug most times cos Jimmy was busy, ma eyes were shut every time he cut ma hair.

Ma heart wud go when a heard the clippers goin on.

Billy Purse: Cleary's, they wur the days.

Joey Campbell: Jimmy's fir a skinhead.

Aileen Farrell: Used to take my son there from when he was a wee boy, he had a mop of hair, is only 22 now and has hardly any hair lol x I still see Jimmy and Andy coming in to my work a lot, they still remember me xxx.

Danielle McClymont: My wee papa Jim lol, bless x.

David Andrew Hilston: Used to get my haircut there.

John Latta: Jimmy Cleary and got my hair cut there many a time or Andy McNamee if Jimmy was busy, but avoided flash.

Peter Valerio's Ice Cream Café

Peter Valerio's Ice Cream Café, pictured here on the left, across from Harper's Garage at Craig Street, on Glasgow Road.

Thomas Dunsmuir Hartman remembers, "The other store of note belonged to a family of Italian immigrants into Scotland; their name was Valerio. There were three families of Valerio in Blantyre, all of them owned ice cream shops. There was Mickey at the West end, Peter in the middle and Wee Don in the East side. They served up some great ice cream treats through the years, from their push carts and up to their motorized vehicles in the later years. The family was so well respected that they have a modern street in Blantyre called after the family, 'Valerio Court.'

They made a wonderful pea dish with lots of vinegar that all of us young kids loved to eat.

Peter's special was a double chocolate side covered wafer with his special flavoured ice cream (each of the b rothers hadtheir own type of flavour) he also did a great snowball ice cream. YUM!! YUM! I sure did like that one."

Bill says, "Peter's Cafe was one of my hangouts, and I can remember one Sunday; we were messing about, and I was thrown against the inside window and smashed it."

Peter was not amused. But, because we were regular customers, he let us off with a warning.

Edith Bulloch: Remember Peter Valerio's cafe across from Harper's garage, worked in both.

Ann Millar: Aye Sylvia, Wee Mickie 'n Peter Valerio were brothers only Peter was a crabbit man n Wee Mickie was the opposite. Mickie could hardly see o'er the counter; he was that wee.

The Central Bar

The Central Bar – Glasgow Road opposite The Ale House, owned by Bernard's the Brewers. Also, known as Sullivan's a former Manager, then latterly known as Fallon's after John Fallon of Celtic F.C. fame, who owned it.

Former Celtic Keeper John Fallon stands outside his bar (Fallon's Bar) on Glasgow Road, Blantyre posing for this photograph, taken in 1978.

In the NEWS 1976...

Ex-Celt's, John Fallon, Pub Hit by Blaze.

Strathclyde CID were today probing a blaze which badly damaged a pub owned by ex-Celtic goalkeeper John Fallon.

Police called in the fire brigade early today after an explosion blew out a window at Fallon's Bar in Glasgow Road, Blantyre. A fire tender had to be sent from Motherwell because the Hamilton brigade was fighting blazes in Uddingston and Hamilton.

Several fires had been started throughout the pub.

Just before opening time today Mr. Fallon, who left Parkhead in 1971, went through the charred lounge with his staff, collecting Celtic pennants, which decorated the walls.

MIRROR

As he cleaned up a mirror which marked his days when Celtic won the European Cup, Mr. Fallon owner of the pub for the last seven years said, "I couldn't believe it. We have suffered a number of broken windows in the past, and when they told me there had been an explosion,

I immediately thought that one of the gas cylinders had gone up.

"It appears that the premises have been broken into and several fires started, but there is no sign of a robbery.

The money I left in the till is still there. "It will be several days before we get the place opened again."

As staff cleaned up, workmen moved in to start the repairs.

Patrick Sanaghan: My dad's favourite haunt when we lived in Craig Street.

Stewart's Building

As we continue our Wander Doon Memory Lane on Glasgow Road, we had the Pub called the Central Bar (Fallon's) which was at the end of the block, right about where the telegraph pole is. The three-storey block on the left was a private one owned by the Stewart Family. Old Mrs Stewart owned this block and had her Apothecary Store down stairs, right where you can see the old truck, and the canopy pulled down. This building also housed Peter Craig's Butchers and Adam's Furniture Store.

Thomas Dunsmuir Hartman wrote: "Now!! To us, here was a place of awe and mystery, one walked into her store, and the smells were out of this world and alien to anything else you had ever encountered. She had those large magnificent shaped jars with a lid on each, which I have never seen anywhere else in my travels, each and every one holding a specific herb or Chemical, and everyone neatly labelled. One always approached this store with a certain amount of reverence. It was as if you were afraid that she may have the power to cast a spell on your being. I know that we did sometimes refer to the lady as being a witch. You could purchase Cinnamon Sticks here. Another favourite item from the store was the Liquorice Root.

Glasgow Road looking East c1900

A recognized cure for all that ails you, Sidlitz powder!

This was wrapped up by Mrs Stewart in a white parchment paper as were all purchases made at her store. In Blantyre if you had a Headache, Hangover, Stomach Pain, Toothache, Backache, you name it, the cure all was the Sidlitz powder".

Stewart's Building on the left before the Gable Fronts were added.

McAlpine's three story Building on the bend, Tram coming from Motherwell, Stonefield Parish Church steeple on the right and Central Building where the Coach is passing. Also, called Hill's Paun building, which included The Ale House – A Public House opposite The Central Bar, which served only ale, hence its name. Closed in the early 1900s then opened as Hill's Pawnbrokers.

It had living accommodation upstairs and in one of the homes lived a very prominent boxer who had fought Benny Lynch, the world flyweight champion, on Oct 24th 1933 – Boy McIntosh – KO – Round 4.

I don't think he had much fight left in him after he met Benny.

Blantyre Gazette

Next to the Stewart, Building was Brown's Painter & Decorator, and then the printing works of Clifford the printers, who published the weekly Blantyre Gazette, anything and everything that happened in Blantyre was published here, whether it was good or bad material.

John Clifford. Final Edition, Blantyre Gazette. Jan. 1964.

December. 1925 - January 1964.

The Gazette was first published in December, 1925, by John Clifford Snr. assisted by his two sons, Andrew and John. Mr. Clifford died in 1950 at the age of 83.

His eldest son Andrew died at his home in Edinburgh in 1958.

The business was continued by his second son John. Throughout the great strike of 1926 and the world war 1939-1945, the paper missed only one issue (thought to be during the strike period.)

Now for reasons of indifferent health: being no longer a young man and after the tragic death of his only son, John Jnr, and having no one to hand over the reins to, Mr. Clifford is reluctantly forced, in the Paper's 39th year, to cease publication.

"The journey has been long, eventful, satisfying, happy and good company, but now it is to be good-bye. We have come to the end of the road......"

The above paragraph, was written by John Clifford himself and appeared in the last issue of the Gazette Newspaper in 1964.

The Paper Cost One Penny when first published in 1925, and cost only tuppence halfpenny in 1964 Edition! It was obvious that he did not set out to make his fortune by publishing and providing this small, popular, and newspaper at a very 'Reasonable Price' throughout the 39-year period, that he was in charge of the Gazette.

 John Clifford also served as a member of the Education Board and Parish Councillor and was one of the Councillors that were involved in the creation of Stonefield Public Park in the 1930s. John has to be applauded for his contribution to the People of Blantyre and to its History and Heritage.

The location of the Gazette building on Glasgow Road opposite Victoria Street, was formerly an Ice Cream Parlour owned by Jimmy Capaldi & family, which was a well-known meeting place for men, at the turn of the 19th / century, because it contained a full-sized Billiard table! This site was known locally as "Hope Hall" because of 'The Band of Hope Hall' (A society similar to the Salvation Army) was the first building to be erected on this site, in 1800s.

James Cornfield 2009

Next door was painters' yard then a plot of land next to the toilets. In the 1940s Duncan Slater's dad rented this plot, he had chickens and ducks for eggs and special events.

Marion Robertson: Mr. Clifford, 2nd left, with hat on and cigarette, he owned the Blantyre Gazette. I Lived next door to him in Station Road back in the 60s, nice memories.

Bill Graham: I met Mr. Clifford when doing charity works, and he was living in the nursing home across from Smith's shop in Main Street. High Blantyre.

He would sit and tell us great stories about his life and the newspaper he owned. He used to try to get us to go to the off licence for him, but we were only 14 or 15, so we could not do it. He also used to ESCAPE (his words) to the pub, much to the annoyance of the Matron as he would come back very merry. A lovely old gent.

The Gazette

Have you heard of the Blantyre Gazette?
It was the old way that news was spread
Whether it be a broken window,
Or an obituary for the dead.

John Clifford (Snr.) was the proprietor,
With a first edition in '25
The Village of Blantyre could keep in touch,
Their only contact to survive.

With local lads plying their trade,
Keeping Blantyre up to speed
A penny a paper, who could complain,
A truly fantastic local read.

John (Jnr.) worked real hard,
No siblings left to take the reins
Sadly the last edition in '64,

The last time the press did strain.

J.J. Whelan 2011

The Toll Brae House

This is an etching of children crossing Glasgow Road going to school at Stonefield Parish School, affectionately known as Ness's.

The Toll Brae house was the white cottage on the left. A Toll was paid to climb the Toll Brae from here to Station Road. The Toll was not for the use of the road but for the hire of heavy horses to pull the carts up the brae. They only paid going up the Brae.

Shire horses would be used to pull the carts up the Brae. The horses were stabled in John Street.

My Dad and his mates would offer to push the smaller carts up the Brae for some coppers in the way of payment.

Stonefield Public Park

The Archway at the entrance to the public park is a Memorial to Dr Cowan-Wilson.

Renamed in 2006 to McAnulty Park after the legendary Andrew McAnulty, "the old war horse" of the early 1900s

Entrance to Stonefield Public Park

Stonefield Public Park

Stonefield Public Park – 1950

Stonefield Public Park, 1950 from John Street with Boating Pond and Old Man's rest, middle right.

Exit to Station Road and the Prefabs just off Farm Road and the Glasgow Road entrance on the left.

Looking east down the Toll Brae from the entrance to the public park.

Entrance to Stonefield Public Park on the left of Glasgow Road looking East, just before the Public Toilets. This is halfway up the, 'Toll Brae.' Annfield Terrace. A two-storey tenement, is on the right with Gibson's shop, grocery & provisions on the corner of Victoria Street. You can just see Ness's School, and the junction of Victoria Street passed the tenement.

Glasgow Road looking East

Glasgow Road looking East Today

Same view today.

Glasgow Road looking east from the Entrance to McAnulty Public Park.

Your Memories:

Len Northfield: Glasgow Road was great before they demolished it and built in the park here. In my opinion, it ripped the heart out of the town.

Elizabeth O'Brien: Doesn't it look good? Looks much better than it does now.

Lynn Kelly: Remember the Park well. I used to pass through it going to my granny's house in John Street. I always picked a bunch of flowers for her, xx.

Yvonne Watson: Looks soooo much better here than it does now!

Ann Crossar: I loved our fab park when I was wee - there was loads to do - putting, boating pond, paddling pool as well as swing park. Soo loved our park - wish we had that now! X.

Len Northfield: My uncle, Bill McKillop, was responsible for all the parks, and he did a bloody good job.

Jim Caullay: Just thru the arch were stones you could make a wish on..., so my gran said & I believe her.

Michael Docherty: Now it's a dog's toilet.

Stuart Oneil: Cracking pic.

Stuart Oneil Walters: looks lovely x.

Marc Moran: I remember that arch way and also how nice the park used to be "The Big Lounge "on a Friday and Saturday night.

Ann Ferguson: I remember this so well, walked through the park most days going to school.

Bette Conner Houghton: My dad worked in the park.

Sheona Thomson Brennan: I remember it looking like this in the late 70's... why and who is responsible for the state it is in now... can they try not get some of that glory back... though suppose you can't just go knocking houses down nowadays!

Mary Meekat: I remember the arch too, oh stop your making me homesick, it's a great photo by the way.

Margaret Barnes: Loved the park, my granny lived on Glasgow Road backing onto the park spent many hours playing there.

Caroline Lee: No gates or railings, were they removed during the war? In the sixties you had flowers, rose beds, etc. and bushes were shaped. Now grass is a mess, no flowers, bushes cut in a square shape, why? Have u ever seen a square bush! Then weeds dog mess, litter.

Robert Henderson: I used to play on the putting green and used to swim in the pond.

Annie Murdoch Anderson Black: I remember this so well, I spent many a summer in there with the wee paddling pool and my pieces in jam, a bottle of water and have great memories, thanks for this xxx.

Marc Moran: Saturday night after the YMCA disco with your girlfriend LOL.

Caroline Lee: Len, the park was there way before Glasgow Road was demolished, it was Asda who ripped the heart out of Glasgow Road... Worst thing to happen to Blantyre, and who would rather have empty units than reduce rent!

Stewart Willis: My gran had the fruit shop at the top of the road next to the paper shop, spent nearly every Saturday as a child either in the shop or in the park. Putting green, boats, pond, swings happy days. Now it's a complete mess in comparison.

Marc Moran: I think I remember those stones or someone telling me about them.

Eileen Clark: Just like I remember when I used to take a shortcut to school every morning to get to Ness's School. Great memories they were.

John Fallon Jnr: As I've said on this site before, the local councillors let the people of Blantyre down, look at our public park, Greenhall and Kirkton Park they should hold their head in shame!!!

Sandra Mckeown: Loved this photo we used to get chased by the parkie if he thought you were dawdling from school. Lol Xxxx

Saxonrose Law: The wee guy at the front looks like he needs a pee x.

Alan Baird: Surely no, he's just passed by a public lavatory.

Gord Fotheringham: this is the way the park always was... why did it decline... someone should ask their M.P... This parkland was never to be sold... get after your M.P.'s.

Eleanor Duncan Nailon: Remember it so clearly. Lol. It really was a beautiful park. Used 2 love going on the boats, number 8 come in. lol xxx.

Sharon Kerrigan: This is how I remember the park... in the good old days.

Liz Allan: The local councillors did let us down and are still letting us down. I do remember the park this way the massive slide the small paddling pool and the horse it was a great park but no longer. The same as Blantyre deteriorating.

Tom McGuigan: It was ASDA that started Blantyre's demise.

Liz Allan: There was a bus stop almost where that person is standing.

Christine Robertson: All the kids used to go there after their first Holy Communion and get there. Picture taken under the arch and all the flowers were in bloom. It's a shame it can't be reverted back to its former glory.

Willie Rouse: Dae ya mean it's aw changed noo? We left Blantyre to come to Ozralia in 69.

Jane Dunleavy: Park was always gorgeous and that end had beautiful flowers but all parks had wardens then to ensure they weren't vandalised.

Michelle Brankin: I do, black n white b4 my time. Remember park when the good summers 'n the boats would be out. My dad lived in village.

Janice Clarkin: Yes, played in it when it looked like that ha, ha, giving my age away now.

Jeanette Allardyce Ward: I do, it was lovely. All the brides went there to get their wedding photos taken. It has been totally ruined along with Blantyre's main street.

Patrick Gaughan: I Walked through Blantyre main street today, hard to believe the park used to look like this, then when I passed Asda I couldn't help but think, if you let your house go into the state Asda has made Blantyre main street, the council would evict you, why don't they make Asda tidy up the run down empty shops or demolish them.

John Fallon Jnr: Here, here, Patrick, we must make a stand against the local councillors, they're still railroading us!!

Wendy Dalgleish: That is a superb pic! Xxx.

Mary Davies: When small we had oor picnics here, jam pieces' n bottles o water, good ol days, lol.

Gord Fotheringham: The last thing I heard about this huge park was there are houses built on it? After the Stewart's building was demolished in the village? Whammy... they took the play park away? All there is, is houses. Not really for me to Judge the M. P's but what happened here? Did the villagers vote on selling this play park?

Liz Allan: No as usual the councillors made that decision without asking the people who the park was supposed to belong to. The people of Blantyre.

Bobby Dunsmuir: I can remember, the gardens were well maintained.

Jim Brankin: They were always well kept and you were not allowed to walk on grass.

Jimmy Hislop: I think a Mr. Crow was the Park keeper here when I was a lad.

Vincent Lombardi Building

Duncan Slater says, "This photo was taken from our front door at 1 Priory Street, the white car V.W bug at Station Road was my dad's and the store across the road before Mauchline's was Annie McVey.

Before the chip shop, a store sold Surplus Army items, I got my first scout kilt from it, and also mum purchased used parachutes as did a lot of women to make dresses from it. When the store closed, Vince's moved into the larger store, and Agnes Hamilton took over the old chip shop.

Norris was Agnes Hamilton's, which was a fruit and Veg. store. Before they opened the Post office at Logan Street, they had one opposite the Bethany Hall.

So, there was a Bakers, Norris Fishmonger, Annie McVey, Mauchline Newsagent, Vincent's Fish restaurant, Robert Craig's Grocery, later to become McWilliam's and then Gallacher's."

Glasgow Road at corner of Station Road

Photo by **Jim McGuire**

At one time, the old turnpike road toll house stood at this corner which was also at one time a cotton works.

Placed strategically on the corner so that no-one could sneak past it. The toll house probably targeted traffic going to and from the Mill Village and Railway Station.

Road tolls were abolished in the 1850s.

The tenement block with the crown feature which replaced it was built in 1902.

Carmen McGuire wrote: I attended St. Joseph's primary and Elmwood Convent 1965-1971. I am a farmer's wife. My father was Jim McGuire, trumpet player. My mother was Clelia Lombardi, whose father had "Vincies" fish and chip shop on Glasgow Road. Her uncle was Mickey Valerio, who owned the, 'Café de Royal,' on Stonefield Road.

Our journey now takes a turn down Station Road with, what was, Anne and Betty McWilliam's became Gallagher's Grocery, later to become Stepek's. Charlie McGuigan's bookies, Frank Cassidy's, Andy McNamee's Barbers. Jimmie Cleary joined Andy when his shop closed in Glasgow Road.

Vincent Lombardi Building Today

Your Memories:

John Ryan-Park: Corner of Glasgow Road & Station Road, Blantyre. To the left of Station Road was once The Broadway Picture House, it was burned down, various offices replaced that site.

Frances McDonald: I worked in Vince's in the early sixties.

Jeanette Allardyce Ward: I grew up in Priory Street, remember it like this before they closed it off. Was always busy with everyone going about their day. My mum worked in the Co-op when she was young too x.

Emma Trevethan: I remember Vince's great fish and chips, we used to have them Friday night for a treat. X.

Alison Walker-Hill: Look how busy it is!!!… Changed times!

Jean MacKie: I was bright up in Clyde Crescent, just off Station Road, remember it all.

Joan Baird: used to go there every weekend x brilliant chip shop.

Jane Barkey: That was a great fish supper, not like today, all batter and hardly any fish in it.

Jane Barkey: I only remember the chippie when it was Double D fast food, as I am only 30.

James Mcguire: Chip shop was brilliant always lovely aromas from there and that coffee shop cafe was excellent, proper Italian atmosphere and is that not Jimmy Cleary's barber shop? Great guy, lovely family… it does bring back memories indeed, starving as per… can see people enjoying their coffee as I pass by and hated the short back 'n sides every time I went there hated it… lol Oh yea and always walking about bored to death especially on the way home from school, always seemed like miles 'n miles…

Helen Stewart: Loved Vince's chipper, always got a laugh with him, brings lots of good memories x.

John Ryan-Park: Yes, Vincent Lombardi's Chip Shop was a great Restaurant.

Graeme Smith: Jimmy, Andy, Shaky shug worked in the barbers, it was the best in Blantyre.

Thomas Izzett: You had a 1 in 3 chance of getting Shaky Shug and having a shite haircut for a few months.

Wullie Mourning: Jimmy, Andy's barber's wiz known as Jimmy Cleary's, even though Andy owned it. Lino on floor, wood panelling on walls, 3ft ashtrays overflowing wi' doubts and Clyde 2 on the tranny. Happy Days....

Station Road 1910

Station Road connected Blantyre Mills to the main Glasgow – Hamilton Road.

This picture was taken around 1910, looking towards the Livingstone Memorial. The space on the left has been filled in with another house and the whole of the right-hand side has been rebuilt with modern dwellings.

A picturesque Postcard of Station Road, early 1900s.

Nicholson's Shop, McLaughlin's Building, Station Road. c1960

Nicholson's Shop

Looking North on Station Road, we have Nicholson's Shop on the corner of Woodburn Avenue across from Farm Road. They also owned the Piggery in John Street at one time. Every house in the village had a bin for the piggery, called a broke bin, which would be filled with food scraps and anything that would rot. Nicholson's lorry would come on a certain day to collect.

There was a short cut into the Public Park through the fence behind the Building, very useful for the children to pop through the fence to get their sweets.

This shop was the hub of the village.

After the Nicholson's, the shop was owned by Anne and Jim Barbour, who got Dougie Fraser's wife, Ann, to manage the shop after her husband Dougie died in 1971, and she sold their shop in McCaffrie's Building, Springwell. She retired in 1977, and the shop closed shortly after that. The building was demolished in the early 80s.

Your Memories:

Marion Robertson: My sister Fiona Glen lived upstairs in the corner flat above the shop, Karen Glen your bedroom paper had teddies and caravans in this flat lol, great memories and of course great wallpaper x.

Fiona Glen: Marion, it was Wind in the Willows wallpaper in Karen's room above the shop. I remember Mrs Fraser and the Barbour's who had the shop below. X

Jeanette Allardyce Ward: I mind of this wee shop on Station Road. Used to get sent here for the Sunday papers. There was a wee shortcut through to the public park where u nipped through for your sweets when you were in the big park.

Olive Rawlings: Lived in this building till the age of 16. They were great days.

Marianne Timmions: I remember the Barbour's that had the shop my dad was friends with the dad. I used to walk people's dogs that lived in the building and I remember the derelict land behind it, we used to pick the raspberries that grew there, fun days????

Fiona Glen: Hi Marianne, I knew your mum and dad from Station Road. We were the Weir's from Station Road. I also stayed above the Barbour's shop who were Anne and Jim Barbour. It's a small world. Xx

Marianne Timmions: Loved that wee shop, yeah small world, unfortunately my parents are no longer here but loved living in Station Road. X

Blantyre Station 1900

In 1849, the Caledonian Railway opened its Rutherglen – Hamilton route which included a stop at Blantyre. Although originally intended as a goods line for Lanarkshire's coal and iron output, passengers soon became an important source of revenue, and Low Blantyre Station was rebuilt in the picturesque form seen here around the turn of the century.

Steam Train coming from Glasgow

Steam Train coming from Glasgow via Newton on 4th June 1949. It looks like a School outing, probably to the David Livingstone Centre. In 1974, the route was electrified and the appealing brick and timber station buildings removed and replaced by modern British Rail fittings.

More recently, the station has been the subject of a revamping project involving landscaping and the installation of works of art. Nowadays, on a site at the far west end of the station, two silver men clutching a pole between them can

be seen heading in a determined fashion leading the train traveller from the station to the nearby David Livingstone Centre.

Aerial view of Blantyre Station c1950

A poem from my friend **Lon McIlwrath**, now living in Vancouver, Canada.

Broadway Train, 1967

Oor Mum gave us a ten-bob note,

Tae see the Saturday mat'nee,

So, me an' ma wee sis and bro,

Went aff tae the Blantyre Broadway.

It wis sae nice, the summer heat,

We'd raither be ootdoors insteid,

Then walkin' doon Victoria Street,

An idea came intae ma heid.

We'd get oorsels aboard the train,
Fae Blantyre tae Glasgow Central,
A rerr day oot for us three weans,
And oor Mum wid never tipple.

Ah telt this plan tae ma wee crew,
Ma wee brother thought it wis grand,
Wee sister wisnae quite sae sure,
But she said okay in the end.

We bought some sweeties fae a shop,
Tae begin oor big adventure,
Then quick we flew, a skip and hop,
Straight past the Broadway pictures.

But haufway doon auld Station Road,
Wee sister she burst oot greetin',
The tears they flowed and froze she stood,
Despite oor soothin' and pleadin'.

Ah said tae her, "C'mon noo sis,
Oor Grampa takes us tae the toon!"
Ah held her haun, gave her a kiss,
And whistled a wee Grampa tune.

That wis just the thing she needed,

Tae put aff her apprehension,

And oor wee gang then proceeded,

Tae the Blantyre railway station.

Ah gave ma best big brother face,

For the man ahint the wicket,

"Three cheap returns please, toon's the place,"

And wi' that we had oor tickets.

The train came soon alang the line,

And stopped wi' a screech and rattle,

Ma heartbeat fluttered, like a sign,

As we barged on in a prattle.

The carriage lurched, gave a shudder,

When the train man blew his whistle,

Moved slowly first, then much quicker,

Pulled by the noisy big diesel.

Newton, we passed, then Cambuslang,

We were wide-eyed in sensation,

The railway tracks a-rat-tat sang,

As we neared the Central Station.

The train slowed doon, a sudden halt,
But we didnae hit the buffers,
Off we got in that mockit vault,
Made black by the auld steam puffers.

Just we three, in crowds of people,
Their wee hauns Ah held sae tightly,
Ah stretchit tall, like a steeple,
But could see the boards just slightly.

Wee sis and bro, excited noo,
Were askin' too mony questions,
Ah answered them as best Ah knew,
Zig-zaggin' through the congestion.

"Look way up there," Ah said oot loud,
"D'ye see that, platform seven?
That train'll take us oot this crowd,
And back tae the Blantyre station."

So fast it seemed, the back-hame train,
Wi' relief Ah steppit aff it,
We crossed the bridge, went up the lane,
And the long walk hame wis startit.

The two wee wans were tickled pink,

Their day oot had been a riot,

But walkin' back Ah had tae think,

How tae make them keep it quiet.

"Listen youse two, we had great fun,

But we cannae let mummy know,

So, if she asks us whit we've done,

We'll say a Broadway movie show."

Mony years later, Mum wis told,

The big secret we'd kept sae well,

She said she knew, but didnae scold,

She'd done the same thing twice hersel.

Lon McIlwraith - Copyright 2011

The Village Bar

The self-sufficient mill community facilities included a public washing house, bleaching green, graveyard, school, post office and farm, counting house and General Store, which was next to the Post Office.

The Village Bar - Formerly Blantyre Works General Store...

In the early days, the workers were paid in tokens that could only be spent at the General Store, a win-win situation for the Mill owners, the Monteith's.

Village Bar, with side loading door for loading goods off carts.

The General Store later became a Public House, known as The Village Bar, in the early 1930s and is situated in Station Road, Blantyre.

The Village Bar continues today to be a popular part of the village community life.

Margaret Quinn: Remember going to the family bit and the barman opened the window between the bar and the snug to serve you, imagine that happening now lol.

The Pey Brig

Footpath Bridge from Livingstone's to Bothwell.

The bridge shown in this photo was referred to locally as the "Pey Brig," as there was a toll paid to the brig toll keeper (Jake McBain).

The bridge was built in 1852 by the Monteith's of Blantyre Works. It later changed hands and became the property of William Baird and Company, Coal masters, who leased the toll collection rights to the highest bidder.

It is Blantyre folklore that if you were on horseback and carrying a sword... you were not charged the ha'penny toll.

At its peak, the brig toll was collecting between four and five thousand ha'penny tolls every week!

The old "Pey Brig" was closed on 26th April 1949 to be replaced by a new bridge in October, 1952. This new bridge, the "David Livingstone Bridge" was somewhat shorter-lived than its predecessor only lasting 50 years before being demolished in May 1999 and the new one opening fully on 18th October 1999. The first person to walk over it was the late Blantyre historian, **Neil Gordon**, who also had the pleasure of opening it.

Here is an aerial view of the new Livingstone Footbridge, built in 2002, in relation to Shuttle Row and the Blantyre Weir.

My Dad told the story of one foggy winter's night, when he was crossing the Bridge, coming towards him was a very tall man in a Top Hat and Cape carrying a Cane. As they met in the middle of the Bridge, the tall man said, "It's a fine night for a Murder!" My Dad reckoned he broke the four-minute mile on the way home.

Hydro Power Station - River Clyde

In 1993, a small hydroelectric plant was built to take advantage of the head of water at an existing weir at Blantyre.

The single turbine is capable of producing 575 KW. It is operated by RWE Npower Renewables Limited.

The original 1790 dam was 16.5m wide and extended in 1796 to 63m, in 1814 to 109m and in 1836 to 127. 5m

Because of legislation, a fish pass had to be constructed. This was completed in 1994 and since then salmon numbers have been on the increase in the mid-section of the river.

Anthony Smith and his Mum in dry weir, summer 1950.

Photo by **Anthony Smith**

Blantyre Mills established in the 1780s

David Dale and James Monteith established Blantyre Mills in the 1780s for the spinning of water twist yarn.

The mills were a major employer in Blantyre and expanded steadily throughout the first half of the nineteenth century and more so with the introduction of Turkey red dying in 1804 (the second such factory in Scotland), and a weaving factory in 1813.

However, in the latter half of the nineteenth century the cotton industry began to fail due to various aspects such as under investment, foreign competition, difficulty in obtaining raw materials, and the break-up of the British Empire and Monteith & Co. finally went into to liquidation in 1904.

Workers Village c1830

A workers' village was built around the mills c.1830, and by 1836 its population was approaching 2000.

Blantyre Mills c1860

Blantyre Mills c1860 from Bothwell

Dale & Monteith had difficulty recruiting local people to work in the mills, and on one occasion apparently recruited around 200 would-be Highland emigres whose ship was stranded at Greenock, persuading them to accept Blantyre instead of going to Canada.

The self-sufficient mill community facilities included a public washing house, bleaching green, graveyard, school, post office and farm.

With the decline of the textiles industry and the Company in liquidation, the houses making up the village were allowed to fall into disrepair and were condemned in 1913, although it took another twelve years for the local authority to begin demolishing them.

Shuttle Row tenements and the surrounding grounds were eventually bought by the founders of the Livingstone Memorial in 1927.

Workers Village Gates

Workers Village Gates which were closed at 10.00 p.m.

The old Gate Pillars were acquired and renovated by the new owners of the Calderwood Estate in 1904 and can still be seen today at the entrance to the main Calderwood Lodge at Stoneymeadow Road, Blantyre.

Dear Bill,

I'm wondering if you would happen to know where in Blantyre, this home is, and if it's still standing

or any history on it, on the back of the photo it's marked gate cottage.

The woman by the gate is my great grandmother Martha McLaughlan-Reid married to John Reid.

Thank you very much and look forward to hearing from you!

Debbie Cochran-Reid

Hi Deb,

The Gate Cottage was one of two at the entrance to the Workers Village in Blantyre, unfortunately no longer there. The Village Gates were last occupied by the Semple family on the left-hand cottage and the Strang family on the right-hand one.

Best regards,

Bill

Mill Village Post Office

This c.1903 picture shows the edge of the mill village, now the approach to David Livingstone's Memorial Centre.

The village gates stood on this road near the bridge, and were closed every night after a 10.00 p.m. curfew. The round building on the right is marked as the site of the post office in maps of 1899, but has long since been demolished, along with its partner across the road.

Of all the buildings in this shot, only the one that houses, now known as the Village Bar remains today. Both sides of the road are occupied by modern housing schemes.

The above is a water colour painting by Blantyre historian, **Neil Gordon**. (Deceased).

David Livingstone Memorial Centre

Livingstone's birthplace and childhood home, is the Centre's museum. It opened in 1927.

The Centre is a biographical museum in Blantyre, South Lanarkshire, Scotland, dedicated to the life and work of the explorer and missionary David Livingstone.

The centre is operated by the National Trust for Scotland and is housed in a category A listed building.

The centre depicts Livingstone's life from his early childhood working in the mill, to his African explorations. These are illustrated with the aid of various pieces of his journals, letters, navigational and medical equipment, as well as dioramas of significant events in his travels.

David Livingstone's birth room in Shuttle Row.

It is located in the former mill buildings which once housed 24 families, including Livingstone', and where he was born on 19 March 1813.

Former Counting House, Blantyre Mills

This view shows the former counting-house of the mills, also known as the Wages Office, with its external turnpike stair. Such stairs became popular in the early

1900s, when this building was built and was originally attached to one of the mills.

The counting house was the place where the business of the mills was conducted, customers and suppliers interviewed, and wages counted out. The counting house was the place where the business of the mills was conducted, customers and suppliers interviewed, and wages counted out.

The Glasgow Herald - Mar 19, 1984

Charming and historic Tower House listed Grade B attractively situated on the wooded banks of the river Clyde, offering six principal rooms and outbuildings.

An unusual opportunity for imaginative restoration and conversion.

Offers over £6,000.

This view is taken from the Footbridge and shows Shuttle Row at the top, the Counting House on the left with the New Flats which were discerningly designed to complement the other buildings, and The Board Room on the far right.

Mill House

Bottom Row, Workers Village c1900

This photo of Mill House, taken in 1900 shows the start of the dilapidation of the Bottom Row which by this time was used as workers' accommodation. The building behind the Co-op cart is the Board Room before the rest of the building was demolished.

Mill House, known as the Board Room, which was part of the Bottom Row in the Workers Village. Built of local Sandstone and is currently the last house on Station Road.

At the time of writing, Mill House, is owned by **Alison Walker-Hill's** family. Alison said that she uncovered a sign within the building saying, "Jolly's Stables." Jolly was one-time Manager of the Mills who lived in the Lodge.

Livingstone Memorial Grounds

A popular location for School, Church and Club outings, and the playground is a memorable place for children. Set in parkland and gardens overlooking the River Clyde, there are plenty of picturesque woodland walks around the area, including along the Clyde Walkway to Bothwell Castle, making it the perfect place for a family day out.

 On 16 February 1844, Livingstone was working in the ditches of the watercourse when some natives were screaming to him to help them kill a

lion that had just dragged off some sheep.

As Livingstone put it later: 'I very imprudently ventured across the valley in order to encourage them to destroy him.'

It was not Livingstone's only mistake; he went with only one gun and with no armed native at his side. He fired both barrels at the lion but only wounded him.

As he vainly tried to reload, the lion leapt on him and catching him by the arm, shook him 'as a terrier dog does a rat'. Livingstone's upper arm was splintered at once; the lion's teeth made a series of gashes like gun-shot wounds. Livingstone was only saved by the sudden appearance of Mebalwe, an elderly convert whom Livingstone had brought from Kuruman as a teacher.

Mebalwe, seeing that his master would be dead within minutes, unless he acted, snatched a gun from another native, loaded and fired both barrels.

The gun misfired, but the lion was diverted at this crucial moment and bounded off to attack his new assailant.

The luckless Mebalwe was badly bitten in the thigh and another who tried to help him was in turn bitten on the shoulder.

At this stage, however, the lion suddenly dropped dead, killed at last by the wounds initially inflicted by Livingstone.

Livingstone was extremely ill for weeks... It is hard to imagine the agony he must have suffered without anaesthetic and without the help of another doctor. He had to supervise the setting of the badly splintered arm himself.

Nevertheless, he made an astoundingly fast recovery and within months was working cautiously on the lighter tasks involved in building his house.'

Livingstone's Lion Designed by Famous Film Animator

Ray Harryhausen may not be familiar to everyone but to those who do know it, his name stands as a landmark in the history of a genre and cinematic art, the art of dimensional stop-motion animation.

His crowning achievement in this field occurred in 2004. Because Diana Harryhausen is the great-granddaught er of the missionary and explorer, David Livingstone.

Ray designed and oversaw the casting in bronze of a one and half times' life statue of the great man being attacked by a lion. The statue can be seen in the grounds of The David Livingston Centre in Blantyre, Lanarkshire in Scotland.

Ray proudly stands in front of the huge bronze statue to David Livingstone in Blantyre, Lanarkshire with the sculptor Gareth Knowles. It was erected here in April 2004.

Photo: **The Ray & Diana Harryhausen Foundation**.

This is an illuminated water fall representing Livingstone's Travels, a fountain in the form of a half globe over which jets of water are projected.

Livingstone sailed for Algoa Bay, South Africa, in December 1840. His first stop was a mission station in Kruman in what is now Botswana, and it was there that he met Mary Moffat that he married in 1845. After Mary died in 1862.

Livingstone was commissioned by the British Government and the Royal Geographical Society to locate the source of the Nile.

Model of Straw Hut

Here we have a Model of Straw Hut where Livingstone died. The journalist Henry M. Stanley came across the explorer in Ujiji at Lake Tanganyika in 1871. Despite being too weak to continue his expedition safely, Livingstone refused to return home and died two years later in a hut in Chambito's Village, similar to this replica straw hut. (Photographed in the 1950's).

Model of Straw Hut

(**Bill says**, "This hut was built by my Uncle Jock Sim."

Photographed at the David Livingstone Centre in the 1950's).

1874 wood engravings Joseph Nash by Jacob Wainright of Livingstone's Coffin on ship.

His body was disguised as a package (corpse was considered unlucky) and carried on a nine-month journey to the coast before being returned to Britain.

Station Road

Going back up Station Road, who remembers when the streets were this quiet?

This is the old entrance to St. Joseph's, Infant part of the School!

Can anyone identify the girls, perhaps it's you or your sister? If so, maybe you can date the picture.

Hello Bill,

I'm **Gordon Fotheringham**. I believe the young lady going up Station Road to be my sister Anna, the year would be about 1950 or 1952.

Betty McGaulley from Toronto, who sent in the photo asks, "I wonder whose car that was?" If you know, share it with us.

Hi Bill, I think the car may have belonged to my late grandmother's doctor – his name was Cowan-Wilson, and she told me he was the first person in Blantyre to own a car. There is a street named after him and a monument. Just a thought. Regards, **Paul Hunter.**

Your Memories:

Donna Baird: Aww Station Road at St Joseph's School xx.

Karen Baird: Station Road at the original entrance to St Joseph's school.

Marion Robertson: I lived at no 38 Station Road, seen in the pic with the car outside, I lived in no 6 as well, next to the barber's shop (51 yrs. ago) lol the barber before Andy, was a guy called Frank, remember him too, Jimmy Cleary moved into the shop with Andy, when his shop closed in Glasgow Road x.

Linda Helping: Yea Station Road, going down to David Livingstone's where my mum still lives... and I lived from the age of 21, but originally from Coatshill Avenue, number 52...

Carolyn Patterson: Station Road, I went to the Joe's this was the primary part of the school, they were happy days 1966 WOW.

Jean Gibson: Station Road. My first marital home was on the right out of picture.

Anne-Marie Clarkin: If you're stood at Stonefield Park Gardens looking down to the village, this is definitely Station Road, the gate on the left where the kids are being still there and the semi-detached bungalows (where the bead used to live, then Tom Weir, (son of Wullie Weir the bookie), is just past the lorry that's parked on the right. Frank Cassidy was the Barber or Frank 2 slash as he was better known. So, says my other half, Chic.

Marion Robertson: Anne-Marie, tell your other half Chic he's spot on, I'm Tommy Weirs daughter (the bookie) my maiden name is Weir.

William Rae ~ The Pilgrimage Postcard

PubMed.gov reported:

The Blantyre bonesetter: William Rae's rise to fame and the popular press.

William Rae (1841-1907) was a bonesetter in Blantyre near Glasgow, who quietly practised and treated the local people from the region in relative obscurity.

In 1904, the popular press became aware of his work, and after they printed stories of his skills and cures, Rae was flocked by patients from the surrounding regions.

The stories were then copied by newspapers in England, the USA, Australia and New Zealand, and Rae became internationally known. This article gives a historical look at Rae, his patients and his methods of treatment, as well as the medical views on bone setting and this individual.

The Postcard Message reads: We are having time of it. Will write tomorrow. We are now waiting to see him, with love, Annie'

The name of the house is Raploch Cottage. Which was the residence of Mr. Wm. Rae, Bone Specialist. The house is in Station Road, and remains virtually unchanged as can be seen by this photo.

A second postcard reads: He found 7 bones out of place that had been out 7 yrs. but he died before he could complete his work. August 28th 1907

On Sunday 28th July 1907, after being confined to bed for 3 weeks with Bronchitis, William died in his own bed aged 67.

MIRACLES IN SCOTLAND.

269 CRIPPLES IN FOUR DAYS.

"MINER EARNS £100 DAILY.'

(Interestingly, if he did earn £100 per day, which the numbers seem to stack up, then that would be the equivalent of £10,191.81 in today's value Just Awesome)

Recently, we published a reference to the, wonderful cure effected by Mr. William Rae, a Scotch miner.

The London Daily Chronicle of June 21 contains the following account of the man and his work, written by a special correspondent:

I have just met for the first-time William Rae, the Scottish bone-setter, who is revisiting Blantyre, a small village about seven miles, outside Glasgow. Curiously enough, in the city itself not a soul appears to have heard even of the wonderful man, for wonderful he is, whatever one may think of his achievements.

Mr. Wm. Rae, the Famous Blantyre None-Setter

However, once within the village, his name is, as it were, written on the very walls. The little place is full of pilgrims, mostly from Lancashire and Yorkshire, bringing with them, almost every description of deformity, cases that have baffled the doctor for years. In their simple-hearted faith, these lasses and lads crowd around the "doctor's" door patiently waiting for their turn.

There was no need to ask where he lived. I simply walked along until I came to where a crowd stood around the gate of a humble cottage, and as I pushed my way through what might have been the out-patients' department of a London orthopaedic hospital, they looked at me with pitying eyes, wondering what could be the matter, or as they would put it, "what was up wi' me."

The door was open and along the tiny, passage stood two rows of patients waiting until their turn. The front parlour was full of them: they lined the staircase, and as I entered the waiting-room, two little boys were tying up their crutches in a bundle, so as to carry them away the easier.

"What, cured?" I cried.

"Ah. thee may say that, mester," they piped, and then. "'Eh, but he's a wonder."

And the man of whom Lancashire is talking to-day; what of him? He took not the slightest notice of me as I slipped into his surgery, and as he was sitting in an armchair, his head bowed upon his breast. It was some moments before I was able to catch a glimpse of his face.

An Impression.

When at last he did look up, I saw in "the twilight such a rugged mobile face as one meets upon the moors. A shaven upper lip seems almost to clinch the lower. Both lips are compressed, but the expression is not unkindly. The eyes are set far back in the head, sheltered beneath a pair of shaggy eyebrows, and as he bids me a gruff "Guid evening " he almost thrusts himself at me, blinking curiously as if to exercise some hypnotic power.

By his side stands his son. And whilst the next patient gets ready, the bonesetter talks in the broad Scots, he first spoke at Larkhall, in Mid-Lanark, sixty-seven years ago.

"Humph," he said, with a shrug of his shoulders, "awm getting tired."

"Had a heavy day?" I shouted.

"Umph. Yes," still looking at me curiously as if to assure himself that my intentions were bona-fide. And then, "Vera lang day indeed. They're comin in frae all parts, maistly frae Bolton. Since Saturday, aw've seen twa hundred and sixty cases more or less, and drawing himself up with pardonable pride-"aw've done something for all and every one of them."

"Do you then guarantee to affect a cure in every case?"

"No, not every case. Those aw can du nothing for aw leave-alane, but maist time, something can be done.

"Doctors. Yes, it's always doctors. What do they know about these things, eh? What do they know?

Tell me. Nothin'. Listen to these boys and girls as they come in. What du their faithers tell me? -hip disease, bone disease, pshaw! That's the doctors for ye. Did ye ever see a diseased bone in a living man? I never did. Ye can see it when he's dead. 'I canna pit that right, na, na. Ye canna pit together a leg that's been cut off, but ye can tak the thing in the beginning."

"How, then, do you explain all these diseases?" I asked.

Theory and Practice.

He was quick with his answer. "Bluid, mon, the bluid. Where that's wrong aw the rest's wrong. An' then, apairt frae that ye hae careless mithers lettin' their children fall, ye have old standing injuries that have niver bin lookit to. A've had cases here that ha' bin wrang fur thirty years, an' then have done something fur them."

So, saying, he brought his fist down upon his knee, and turned to a patient who had just entered. It was a youth of about 16, whose appearance proclaimed curvature of the spine. The "doctor's" assistant ran a critical eye over the case, and the case stood there in its Sunday clothes, blushing, like a girl.

Everything was rough and ready. There was a sofa and two or three cushions. A couple of siphons of soda water, and as many tumblers were close at hand. Appliances there were none. It will, therefore, be readily understood than an operation was a most primitive affair.

"Pull up your shirt, and let me see your back," and suiting the action by the word the bone-setter's assistant disclosed the deformity, and the great man at once began an extempore lecture on his subject.

"Now, look at that," was his angry comment. "No man in this world need have a humpit back if it was only taken early enough." And he began to run his hand carefully along the spine.

Mr. Rae then began a practical exhibition of his peculiar gift, which something told him he possessed when he was but 17 years old.

This boy came from Bolton, and had been attended by a doctor, so he said, for many years. He was now directed to lie breast to breast with the setter, who began to handle the spine apparently with the object of pressing it into place. This process he continued for quite five minutes, directing the patient all the while to lie perfectly at ease.

When at length the lad stood up, he declared himself better, and then, encouraged, presented a thumb that had been damaged with a ball in a cricket match. The doctor felt it, pulled it, there was a click, and hey presto! The boy's face lighted up as he bent it to and fro.

"Gum! It's a' reet," and paying his half-sovereign he dragged on his clothes, and his mother presented herself to take him away.

There was something of pathos about it all. That very morning an early train brought about twenty families from Bolton, fathers, mothers, children, infants, old men and bent women.

Alighting from the train, they first secured lodgings, and then made their way to the bone-setter's cottage, where they were given a number and directed to await their turn.

A Pathetic Case.

One mother brought her two infants, both helpless little mites, swathed almost from head to foot with bandages and surgical appliances. They, were suffering from hip and spine disease. 'As she carefully made her way among the crowd other women turned aside in pity, and then waited anxiously whilst she sought the "doctor."

In half an hour, she came out radiant, the bandages all gone, declaring that the little ones had been cured.

Another case was that of a young woman, who readily related to me her experiences upstairs. She came from Bacup, she said. For years, she had been suffering from hip disease, one leg being shorter than the other. Doctors she had tried, without relief, and at last her friends advised her to go to Blantyre.

"It didn't hurt me a bit, not one bit. He just got hold of my leg, gave it a pull, then pushed it right back, and it was all over. Of course, I walk just a bit lame still, as you see, but it feels, oh! so much easier. I am to bathe the joint every morning in cold water, and walk as much as possible. Eh, he's a clever man. He is."

The day long one could hear similar stories, but it should be said that in no- case was the cure instant. There always seemed to be a certain amount of lameness after the operation, though the verdict was always the same.

As far as the figures are concerned, the statistics for the four days are, at all events, startling. In all 269 persons have arrived, and the 'doctor" worked all day on Sunday (June 19).

The little village is crowded. Every train brings pilgrims to the Scotch Lourdes, and so great has been the press that quite 60 were turned away on Monday.

His visit to Blantyre, he says, is a record. Roughly speaking, it means at the least £100 a day not a bad income for a rough, unpolished man, who might still be to all appearances, a workaday labourer that is, if no one saw him handling his patients.

Whitstable Times and Herne Bay Herald - Saturday 02 July 1904

William Rae, the Blantyre bloodless-surgeon has received from London, an offer of £10,000 if he will straighten the applicant's leg.

If William Rae had been successful in straightening the leg, he would have earned the equivalent of £1,120,000.00 in today's money.

The Broadway Cinema - Looking East

Monday 18th September 1939 by the Blantyre Picture House Company. It got off to a shaky start as World War II had broken out just 15 days before and limited what films were shown. News reels were popular in the immediate years.

On the Grand Opening, the first film shown was, 'The Dawn Patrol,' starring Errol Flynn and Basil Rathbone.

Front Stalls: 3d – Stalls: 6d – Back Stalls: 9d – Balcony: 1/-

Also, very popular on Sunday nights when local bands played and put up prizes for the best singer from the audience, the X-Factor of the day. Bands from all over, would do a 15-Minute Audition for Free, and if they were liked would get a booking for a future show.

When the Broadway Cinema opened in September 1939, there were small iron railings around the corner of Glasgow Road and Station Road, protecting public from traffic, just as in the above photo.

However, as with most iron railings all over the UK, they were cut and removed for the war effort. Sadly, this had a devastating outcome for a Blantyre family. In 1946, after a Matinee, the children swarmed out into the daylight, and a little girl named Netta Valerio, sister of Velma (whose father was Mickey of Mickey's Cafe) was killed at the corner of Glasgow Road and Station Road.

My friend, the late **James Cornfield** recalled that the family shortly afterwards, paid for railings to be reinstated at the corner.

The last film played at the Broadway in the 1970s was the 'Jungle Book', according to Ian Guy Lecturer in Nursing in New Zealand.

The Broadway was owned and operated by Jack Brown, cinema and theatre manager-promoter; born Millport, November 28, 1909, died Hamilton, February 11, 1997.

The Projectionist for 25 years was Bobby Campbell.

Sadly, the building was damaged by fire in the early 70s and instead of being turned into a Bingo Hall, the Broadway was demolished and a modern two storeys building for Blantyre's Housing department built upon its site. The building is now the home of Blantyre Credit Union.

Your Memories:

Linda Halpin: Was the dentist not there as well, Hugh Biggins, he did a gold crown on my back tooth, and it's still there after all these years!

Pat Cunningham: I can remember going to the Broadway on a Sat afternoon, we used to walk from Whitehill from my grans house to the Broadway and we bought a jubilee with the bus fare. It cost 9 pence to get in.

Linda Warner: I remember the 1st time I went to the Broadway matinee and saw Greyfryer's Bobby & broke my heart I think I was about 7 at the time. Loved the jubilees and penny whoppers and lucky potatoes.

Jean Gibson: It's a long time since Blantyre had 2 pictures halls. The Broadway was on the corner and it had a balcony and in those days the programmes changed 3 times a week and you saw 2 films at each showing, plus the news and trailers. Gone are the days!

Marion Murdoch: My sister's boyfriend used to play in the Broadway. It was called go as you please I think, he later became her husband. Great memories.

Alan Smith: The Broadway used to have a Saturday afternoon showing of old horror movies for kids. I'm sure they were x rated!

Glasgow Road – 1920

Glasgow Road looking west. The Broadway Cinema would eventually be built on the right where the gas lamp is situated, some nineteen years later. The Stonefield Tavern and the No: 2 Co-op are on the left.

Bethany Hall 1908

Glasgow Road, photographed in 1908. The primitive Methodist Church, on the left-hand side of the picture, originated in 1893 when it only had a handful of members. By 1902, services were being held in Dixon's Hall (built by the coal-master of the same name) and the decision to build the Glasgow Road church was taken the following year.

The new church opened in 1905, the same year as St. Joseph's R.C. Church, further along Glasgow Road, and was in use until the First World War. After lying vacant for a time, it was bought by Stonefield Independent Co-op in 1925.

It later became the Bethany Hall and was run by the Christian Brethren, who have been active in Blantyre since the first decade of the century.

More recently, the church has been taken over by 'The Word of Life Church', an American based Christian group and even more recently, a Children's Nursery.

Joanna Terrace, Glasgow Road, Looking West

Joanna Terrace 1903.

Entrance to St Joseph's School on the right, Chemist on the corner, formerly Dr Harkin's surgery, Livingstone's Church Steeple in the distance. McSoorley's big barra on the left.

Hi Bill,

From what I remember the building on right is Joanna Terrace. I lived nearby at 265 Glasgow Road and the Tram Terminal was at Stonefield Road, gone when we moved into 265 in 1940.

An old woman had a sweetie shop in Road, and she made a clooty dumpling every Saturday and sold big slices for a shilling, just great and like my grannies.

Yours Aye,

Ellen Nimmo Pickering

Canada

Joanna Terrace 1970s

Photo by **Anthony Smith**

Tram Terminus 1903

The Tram Terminus at the bottom of Stonefield Road with David Livingstone Church Steeple in the background.

Note that St. Joseph's Church has not yet been built.

St. Joseph's School which doubled as a Church on Sundays and Holy days, prior to the new Church being built in 1905.

As with all metal work, the railings on both sides of the road were surrendered for the war effort.

St Joseph's Church and School 1905

St. Joseph's School situated in Glasgow Road opposite

Stonefield Road. Built in 1878 and was used weekdays as a school and Sundays and Holy Days as a Chapel, replacing the Hall of Worship in Dixon's Rows which was four house units converted into a church hall. The Church could accommodate 620 sittings.

I was surprised that there are no more photos of the two buildings together.

The present-day St. Joseph's R.C. Church was built next to the original in 1905 and can be seen in the background of this photo in relation to one another.

It was our friend **William Ross**, who pointed it out to me when I previously posted the ploughman photo of Russell's Farm. You can see the two buildings together.

From the left we have David Livingstone Memorial Church, St. Joseph's R.C. Church and next, the St Joseph's Church and School, seen here, just behind the plough horses.

However, after a long and intensive search, I came across this unique photo, which clearly shows the old Church alongside the new one.

Thomas Hamilton-Hailes: St Joseph's was where I had my first day at school in 1959 ... and I was a prod. It took till dinner time before the Police could calm my mother by saying they'd found me: I'd got fed up waiting for her to get ready and wandered off from Fernslea Avenue to the only school that I knew about; and where all my neighbourhood friends went to.

I still have a perfect recollection of that wonderful first morning at school... and of the two "Blantyr Polis" comin' in to take me home to my frantic mammy.

After the term break, the catholic school started back a week before the prods and so there I was sitting outside the door in my wce Royal blue short trouser suit ready for my first day at school ... which should have been the Ness's.

Probably thinking I was a big boy now that I was going to school, I joined my mates and walked off down to school with them. In their classroom, the teacher wanted to know who I was and various answers such as "That's wee Tom from downstairs frae us," didn't help her much.

A priest was brought in to help sort out who this strange wee boy was but he didn't recognise me as one of his flock.

The desks were amazing; you could lift the desktop up and, lo ... there was a wee blackboard with chalk: I'm loving this.

We had to close our desks and put our heads down on our crossed arms on the desktop; to keep quiet while the teacher and the priest left the classroom to try and sort this out with the head master ... who might have been responsible in the end for getting in touch with the police.

I took me a long time to get used to the Ness's... mainly because their wee desks didn't have that great wee blackboard but rather a fixed top with a silly wee shelf under it.

I will always have treasured my first day at school.

Dixon Street, Hall Street and Park Street made up the three of Dixon's Rows; My Grannie and my sister both lived on Dixon Street, but I never knew the origin of the "Hall" in Hall Street ... till now.

Thomas Hamilton-Hailes

St Joseph's R.C. Church Build

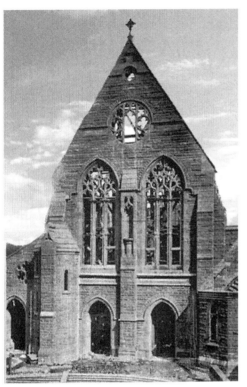

In 1889, the ground of the existing St. Joseph's School and Church was extended by some 80 feet to the west in order to accommodate a new Church. The go ahead to build a new Church in 1898 was given by the Archbishop of Glasgow, and work began on the Gothic Style Church, which can accommodate 1,000 people, in 1904.

The Church was designed by Messrs Pugin and Pugin of London at an approximate cost of £10,000, (£1,075,000 in today's money). The opening sermon was preached by Rev John a Maquire, Archbishop of Glasgow on the 10th June, 1905. Father Hackett was appointed priest in 1888 at the old-School Church, next to this new build and served in the new Church until his death on 5th March 1921.

Affectionately known as "The Doc," by his faithful parishioners, they built a new High Alter, which is still there today, in his memory.

Source: **Diocese of Motherwell**

Neil Gordon's Blantyre An Historical Dictionary.

St Joseph's R.C. Church

St. Joseph's School situated in Glasgow Road opposite Stonefield Road. Built in 1878 and was used weekdays as school and Sundays and Holy Days as a Church.

William Ross wrote: "The layout of the school in the 50s was that building known as the old school building a gap and the new building. To the right, you had boys and girl's toilet block. There was a gap and small building. Behind this was the prefabs, this was the junior secondary. The primary school was three sides of square of wooden huts situated at the right of the toilets and before the prefabs. The head mistress of the primary was Miss Duffin, and everything was done to the sound of her clicker."

Father Hackett was appointed priest in 1888 at the old-School Chapel, opposite Stonefield Road and next to this

new build, and served in the new Church until his death on 5th March 1921.

Affectionately known as "The Doc," by his faithful parishioners, they built a new High Alter, which is still there today, in his memory.

St Joseph's R.C. Church - 2010

Your Memories:

Mary Crowe: Remember Miss Duffin with her clicker.

Morag Campaigne: Miss Duffin had black hair and bright red lipstick. Remember her clicker well, she used it to get us all into our lines in the playground.

Anthony Smith: I started school in the wooden huts of the Primary school. I can still remember when St. Blane's opened and everyone who lived on that side of the road moved there. I can also remember moving into Primary 1. Which was the HALF CIRCULAR room on the new building.

Marian Maguire: Such a shame this was demolished.

David Livingstone Memorial Church

David Livingstone Memorial Church, Including Hall, Boundary Wall and Manse is a listed building Category: B, Date Listed: 4 May 1994

Historic Scotland Building ID: 6589. An ecclesiastical building in use as such.

The congregation began with meetings in domestic premises in 1876, a wooden church being erected on this site in 1878. The name Livingstone Memorial United Presbyterian Church was adopted soon after (Livingstone having died in Africa in 1873), becoming the Livingstone Memorial United Free Church in 1900, and then the Livingstone Memorial Church in 1929.

The manse is situated to the rear of the church.

Aberdeen Journal - Monday 17 March 1913

UNVEILING OF STATUE AT BLANTYRE, LIVINGSTONE'S BIRTHPLACE.

The Livingstone Centenary was celebrated in Blantyre, the birthplace of the great missionary explorer, on Saturday. The special feature of the celebration was the unveiling of a bronze statue in the tower of the Livingstone Memorial U.F. Church in Blantyre.

When the church was being built, some thirty years ago, the family Livingstone was asked if they would be agreeable to the church being given the name "Livingstone Memorial." The family readily consented to the request, and being shown the plans of the church they suggested that a tower should be added as a specific memorial. The suggestion was acted upon by the congregation, and a niche seven feet high was reserved for the purpose of erecting a statue to Dr Livingstone at some future date.

The matter was more heartily taken up two years ago, it being then considered that the statue would be an appropriate memorial to the occasion of the master missionary's centenary. The statue stands fully seven feet, high, and had been produced at a cost of nearly £400, which sum has been wholly contributed by public subscription.

At the ceremony on Saturday, there was a large and representative attendance. Fred L. M. Moir, the African Lakes Corporation, and chairman of the Committee, presided,

THIS STATUE ERECTED BY PUBLIC
SUBSCRIPTION TO THE MEMORY OF
DAVID LIVINGSTONE
BORN 19TH MARCH 1813 AT BLANTYRE
DIED 4TH MAY 1873 AT CHITAMBO-ILALA-AFRICA
UNVEILED BY HIS DAUGHTER MRS LIVINGSTONE WILSON 15TH MARCH 1913

and introduced Mrs A. M. Livingstone Wilson, youngest daughter Dr Livingstone, who gracefully performed the unveiling ceremony. A presentation to mark the interesting occasion having been made to Mrs Livingstone Wilson by the Rev. T. A. Hugh, minister of the congregation, a number of addresses were delivered, including appreciation of Livingstone by the Rev. James Wells, D.D., ex-Moderator the U.F. Church General Assembly.

Amongst those who took part were the Rev. R. Ward law Thompson, D.D., of the London Missionary Society; the Rev. R. Rutherford, Calder head, representing the Presbytery Hamilton; the Rev. James Mackie, Bothwell, representing the U.F. Presbytery of Hamilton; the Rev. G. Allan, representing the Congregation, George Pate, general manager to the Canon Company, representing the subscribers: the Rev. Robert Mackenzie, Allow, first minister Blantyre Livingstone Memorial Church; and Provost Smellier, Hamilton.

Source: **britishnewspaperarchive.co.uk**

The Dandy was a Bridal Path and right of way from Glasgow Road all the way to the Mill Village and the Clyde, and was a popular walk for families and  young couples. The tree-lined Avenue had some prestigious homes as mentioned above, and I can recall the banks either side being filled with Bluebells.

Poor Clare Monastery – Blantyre

Former Nunnery at Thornhill Avenue, Blantyre

The Nunnery was in Thornhill Avenue, down the entrance to the Dandy.

Formerly known as Thornhill Villa, a Mansion at the time, was once owned and lived in by James Kelly of Celtic F.C. Fame, who also owned the Kelly's Corner Bar and Blantyre Engineering.

A close neighbour at Priory House in Thornhill Avenue was John McCaffrie, owner of McCaffrie's Pub in Springwell.

The mansion, as it was then, was purchased by the Doonin family in 1973 when the Poor Clare Order moved to a purpose-built monastery attached to St. Bride's Parish Church in Bothwell.

I don't know the circumstances of how Thornhill Villa became the Poor Clare Order Monastery, but if I were to hazard a guess, James Kelly may have bequeathed the Property to the Order.

In 1952 our Monastery in Cork, Ireland, was bursting at the seams so it was decided to find a new monastery in the Diocese of Motherwell, Scotland.

Five Sisters from Cork were warmly received into the Diocese after a long overnight sail on the boat from Dublin. Their first house was in Blantyre where, over the years, the community gradually increased.

In 1973, we moved to a new purpose built monastery attached to St. Bride's Parish Church in Bothwell where we participate in the daily mass of the Parish. Two of the Sisters who originally came from Cork, Srs. Paschal and Jarlath are still with us, regaling us with stories of 'the good old days,' when the hardship involved in a new Foundation was lightened by joy and laughter.

Pictured here in 1972 is a wonderful, happy photo of the Poor Clare Nuns in Blantyre, a year or so before they moved to Bothwell.

In 1973, Bishop Thompson (of Motherwell) decided it was best that the Monastery be moved next to St Bride's Parish in Bothwell because he could foresee a time when he would not be able to spare a priest to celebrate Mass.

As a boy, I used to deliver groceries in the early Sixties and had to put them in a 'half-barrel' and ring the bell. The barrel would be swivelled inside, and the groceries removed and then returned with a sum of money to pay for the groceries and my tip. Never was there a word said.

The property was acquired by the Doonin family in 1973. Gary Doonin remembers a couple of graves being removed from the bottom of site about 1998/1999.

Photos by **James Brown** and **poorclaresscotland.**

The Parkville Roadhouse – Glasgow Road.

After the Dandy, there are some private houses, two of which, next to the Parkville, were owned by Aggie Bain, of the oldest house in Blantyre fame, in 1915. Then we have The Parkville Roadhouse, formerly the home and surgery of Dr John Cowan-Wilson, which opened in 1959.

Voted one of the top 100 bars in Scotland by The Dram and winner of Scotland's Best Community Pub of the Year in 2014 in the Scottish Entertainment Guide.

The Parkville Hotel in Blantyre, has everything to offer. With its warm inviting decor, you can relax in the lounge where you can sample a great selection of wines, cocktails and array of whiskies, complimented by the stylish restaurant.

The elegant private event space, The Park Suite is perfect for hosting all kinds of parties and celebrations and of course is famous as a fabulous wedding venue, holding parties and celebrations up to 230. With 5 new stunning Hotel Bedrooms, it is a home from home.

The Parkville in Blantyre was the heart of the community 60 years ago, and it is still as big a part for the community now as it was then.

Your Memories:

Jim McDougall: Brilliant Memories of a time gone by of a lovely place called Blantyre. Sandy Wilkie: School days, Round Table meetings, EKYFC dances, weddings, 21st's, McGonagal Night, Paterson family, Jim Mullen, Robert Craig doos - so many memories in that building!

May Young Breen: Many a family wedding in there x

Sandy Wilkie: School days, Round Table meetings, EKYFC dances, weddings, 21st's, McGonagal Night, Paterson family, Jim Mullen, Robert Craig doos – so many memories in that building!

May Young Breen: Many a family wedding in there x.

Margo Haughen: Going tonight!!!

Bars and Superstars

Its Sunday morning, the smell of ham is travellin' up the
stair
Can still taste last nites bevy, and pizza thro ma hair,
We set aboot oor Saturday nite, just the back o 8
That was us till closing time we ended in a state.

Two pints in the Parkville, the West End for a jar
Back to Craig's, then the Cozy, or maybe the Priory Bar
The Smiddy it was timeless, the smell was in the air
Fags, pipes and dugs, wi sawdust on the flair.

Headin tae Matt Boyles, the crowd was pretty mixed.
The usual cry fae big Peter, wee man how u fixed.
Andy Kelly is holdin' court, with 'burn your playhouse
down'
Pipe Armstrong telling stories, funniest guy in town.

The Village bar or Teddies, the Knights or Union Jack.
We headed to the Hoolet's, just to hear the crack.
We staggered past the Doon Inn, then down to the Vics,
Then James Mcguire shouted 'hey boys am takin' pics'

All the pubs have changed now, and some are even
gone,
The superstars in all the bars passed their stories on
At the height and on the day these guys were the best
Sadly here no longer, and mostly laid to rest.

Drew Semple (May 2011) Copyright grecodisc.

Glasgow Road looking East -1925

A peaceful time on Glasgow Road between the wars with a Tram coming from Motherwell.

Glasgow Road looking East c1925

The Tramlines have been extended from the Tram Terminus at Livingstone Church in 1907, to the West End where passengers would change trams to go to Cambuslang, Rutherglen and Glasgow.

The homes in Glasgow Road were mostly semi-detached properties with dormer roofs and built of local sandstone.

They had gardens front and rear although the front gardens were reduced in size when the road was widened. Electricity was not supplied until 1936 so these homes were lit by gas lanterns or oil lamps, heating, of course, was by coal fires.

Tram Crossing Priory Bridge

The Priory Bridge, also known as the Spittal Bridge spans the Rotten Calder on the A724 to the West of Blantyre.

It is, in fact, fact three bridges, which were widened to accommodate the growth in traffic.

The original Bridge was of medieval structure and widened in 1844 by unemployed weavers.

It was widened again in 1907 in order to accommodate the Glasgow Tram Company tramline with the Lanarkshire Tram network by adding a metal structure.

The three bridges are clearly seen in the above photograph.

The bottom dark arch is the Medieval Bridge, the lighter arch of the 1844 reconstruction above it.

Calderglen – Blantyre

Calderglen was one of the Blantyre mansion houses, which managed to survive after its heritor residents (including John Richard Cochrane in the late 1880s) it was compulsorily purchased by the Coal Board as the plan was, I believe, to have opencast mining there.

The family were very sad to have to move out.

As it happened, the Coal Board changed their minds eventually, and re-sold the house.

By the 1950s, it was opened by a greyhound racing company, later being taken over as the Calderglen Nursing Home.
Photo by **James Brown**.

A Gift from Blantyre

During World War 1, in a response from an appeal by the British Red Cross for donations to fund ambulances,

Blantyre Gift

a Committee of influential ladies, including Miss Moore of Greenhall, Miss Jackson of Bardykes, Miss Bannatyne of Milheugh and Miss Cochrane of Calderglen and other ladies from the Parish, worked tirelessly to fund the ambulance.

A sum in excess of £500 was raised through various means, which ably covered the cost of £450 for the new ambulance.

And on Saturday 1st May 1915 a brand-new ambulance was presented to the Blantyre Branch of the British Red Cross and proudly toured around various points in the Parish, including here pictured at Calderglen House.

Terry Hughes says, "In WW1 the Red Cross society through The Times newspaper ran an appeal in 1914 for donations for ambulances. 512 were supplied to Allied Forces. I think this could be one of them.

I found the date to be 1915 when this Blantyre Ambulance was photographed at Calderglen.

The Ambulance was most likely a Talbot-Darracq.

Blantyreferme Pit – Caldervale – Fin-me-oot

Fin Me Oot was the name given to a small miner's village located along the banks of the Rotten Calder, a tributary of the River Clyde.

The village's formal name was **Caldervale.**

However, in its latter years, after the demise of mining in the area, its location meant it was not easily found by visitors, and this may be how the name Fin Me Oot came to be associated with it.

Anecdotal accounts relating to the name suggest its use only began after mining ceased.

Mrs McGuire, Mrs Millan, Mrs McGowan, Mrs Nicol

By repute, the village was still extant in 1959, but the date of last occupation, or of its demolition, are unknown.

Caldervale 1950s

The records of AG Moore & Co, owners of the Blantyreferme Mine near Uddingston (which employed 456: 386 underground and 70 above), show that the mine owners' houses in Blantyre Parish were located at nearby Blantyreferme, and Caldervale, which had 40 two apartment houses with sculleries, occupied by 56 miners, at a rental of £9 2s (£9.10).

The village was described in a condition report of 1910:

Erected under the Building By-Laws – Two blocks – two storeys in height – Walls hollow built-plastered on solid – Wood floors,

ventilated – Internal surface of walls and ceilings good – No overcrowding – Apartments good size.

No garden, ground available but not fenced – no wash houses – have cellars.

At Caldervale, a water closet has been provided for each house, placed inside the existing scullery, and pail privies have been abolished – Inside sinks, with gravitation water – Drainage treated at a private purification installation – Scavenged at owners' expense.

- The Housing Condition of Miners. Report by Medical Officer of Health, Dr John T Wilson, 1910.

A gated access road leads to the site off Blantyreferme Road, and can be found south of the Clydeway Golf Range, after passing through a railway bridge with a narrow underpass controlled by traffic lights. The access road slopes down to the area shown on the approach picture, where the bench and sign can be seen in the vegetation on the right. The bench faces the area where the houses would have been found, accessed by the road leading off to the left of the picture. The sign pictured on the pole can be found down this road.

Visiting the site also explains the adoption of the name Fin Me Oot. From Blantyreferme Road, the access road curves downhill and to the left, giving no view or indication about the existence of the houses. Even when approaching them down the track, their location down another road upon the left (opposite the bench) means they remain invisible until you draw level of the road, and turn to face them.

The main track is actually part of the Clyde Walkway, and carries on past the bench, through a rail underpass, where it takes a sharp left turn and carries on to the Rotten Calder, which feeds the River Clyde. A restored pedestrian bridge crosses this tributary, leading on to a stone and brick path which continues up the banking to emerge in a clearing. Nothing of interest remains, other than a small Bing (pile of waste material or spoil from the former mining operations).

The bench and signs pictured to have survived for a number of years, and appear to have been unaffected by the works. The sign on the seat was noted to have been updated after the works were cleared, when seen again in 2009.

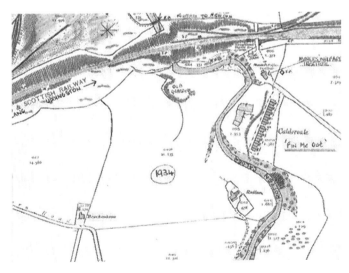

Period maps

The map of 1934 is particularly significant, as it clearly shows the arrangement of the two lines of tenement buildings, allowing the two lines of ten dwellings to be counted in plain view. This corresponds with the earlier description which referred to "40 two apartment houses."

Additionally, noted in this map is the existence of a Miners' Welfare Institute, just to the north of the houses, which had a snooker table on wheels, so that it could be wheeled under the stage when not in use. The Welfare was a 'dry' house.

Mapped in the 1960s

In the area along the west, down the hillside between the houses and the Rotten Calder, as a marked area of ground, next to an item marked "Tank." The marked area is believed to have been allotments

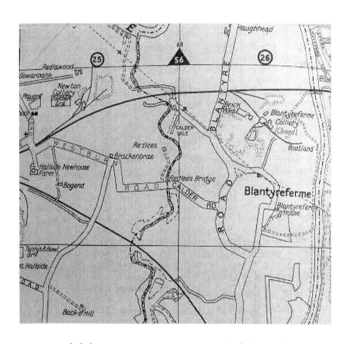

where the miners would have grown vegetables, but may also have been used as drying area for clothes. The area is at a significantly lower level than the houses. Therefore, the Tank is assumed to have been part of the "private purification system" referred to in the 1910 report by the Medical Officer of Health, referred to above. This area is now overgrown and wooded.

Found in a street map dating to the 1960s, this scan shows the location of Caldervale along its access road off Blantyreferme Road. The building detail seen upon the map is also in general agreement in the description of "Two blocks – Two storeys in height."

Your Memories:

Marie McDermott: My Mums Family the Eadie's lived there.

Michael Connor: Me and ma mates found it in the late 80s. We were told to follow the Calder River from the Wimpey houses.

Robert Cairney: Fished it oot wae ma uncle.

Margaret Steven McAuliffe: I used to know a fellow called Eddie Gilhooley, he lived in fin-me-oot. His mother went to school with my mum.

Berty Booster: A friend of mine lived in Fin-Me-Oot her name is now Mary Irwin, she was then Mary McGinty. She is in her mid-60s now and her then boyfriend (now husband) used to walk down the Blantyreferme Road to go and court her. I am not sure how they met, and Mary may be able to say when the demise of the village was, I will ask her and get back later.

Michael Connor: My wife's father Robert Eadie lived in Northway in Blantyre her name is Marie as well, any connection? Marie McDermott.

Blantyreferme Brick Works, near Uddingston
c. 1924 – 1947 – Blantyreferme Colliery

There was a large brickwork on Blantryeferme Road, which was on the right as you travel towards Uddingston from Blantyre immediately adjacent to the

Blantyreferme Colliery, just before the wee arched railway bridge. The Brickworks served the Colliery with the kilns being located in the colliery itself.

The site was one of the first industrial sites to be spruced up and landscaped, with trees and walkways, although there's not much else to it – last time I went, a board gave the history for the site, which adjoined Blantyreferme Collieries, part of which are still in industrial use.

Of course, as with all other Brickworks in Blantyre, they each had their own branding.

Blantyreferme AA – A.K.A. The Whins

A World War II anti-aircraft battery and army camp was sited at Blantyreferme, near Blantyre to the southeast of Glasgow, west side of Blantyreferme Road. It was decommissioned in 1945.

Not a round was ever fired in anger, just practice.

The Whins, as they were called, consisted of wooden huts, which were completely refurbished in 1948 by the Council in order to house some fifty plus homeless families due to the shortage of housing. They paid a rent to the Council and had water and power. They would have a Dance on a Friday night.

The AA Battery and surrounding area are part of the Redlees Park, which is a new urban park that has been created from 27 acres of derelict scrubland on the site of the disused clay quarry in Blantyre, a Lottery Heritage Fund Project, incorporating walkways and information boards, which were part of a school project. The Redlees site goes back to the 1800s when it was part of the Calderbank House Estate.

It was a great Playfield for us kids, playing soldiers and explorers...

Great Memories..

Your Memories:

Hari Docherty: This is the first place I lived, we were squatters, then moved to Dechmont Camp before getting a prefab. There were wooden army huts that were used for accommodation.

Berty Booster: Redlees urban park as it is now called – well worth a visit.

Colin Balfour: Used to play down there as a kid.

Michael Connor: I used to play here as a kid.

Alan Young: Stayed right across from them my dad told me all about them.

Helen Grieve: There were a couple of kids in my class at school from the Whins!

Orchard at Boat Jock's

Come on, how many of you poached apples, pears and plums here?

And do you remember the mink farm?

Boat Jock's was a must visit during the fruit picking harvest. We would fasten our belt over our shirt or jumper and fill it up with the forbidden fruit.

The Boat House

'Twas in that year of 1866 that John Scott a well-known Fruit Grower from Carluke, leased Boathouse Farm. The holding is beautifully situated on the south bank of the

Clyde, some 200 yards upstream of Haughhead Bridge (The Rid Brig) in Blantyre.

The name was given to the farm because of its close proximity to the Ferryman's Boathouse, next to the steading. The whole is part of Blantyre Farm or Blantyreferme, (a corruption of the old name, Fremblantyre) which was owned at that time by Patrick Scott, (no relation of the lessee) and is thought to be part of the original orchard planted by the Augustinian Monks from the nearby Priory, who originally came to Blantyre, from their Mother Abbacy in Jedburgh, in the early part of the 13th century.

The ferry operated between Blantyre and Uddingston and was one of two ferries on the Clyde, the other being at Blantyre Works Village. No mention is made of the fare for the ferry, but I suppose it would be similar to the charge paid for crossing the Suspension Bridge (Pey Brig) at Blantyre Mills; 1 Ha' penny single, 1 Penny return.

For years, I thought that the name 'Boat Jock' by which this area of Blantyre was known, referred to the orchard,

but in fact, it was the call given by persons on the Uddingston bank to attract the Ferryman's attention, by calling, 'Boat Jock, Boat Jock,' whenever they wanted the ferry to cross the water of the River Clyde.

Jock was a great big Hie'lander, named John Munro, ferryman and general factotum of the owner to the property, Patrick Scott, a Laird of the old school, who was known to be frugal with his bawbees, (careful with his pennies). He kept a barrel of salted herring in his kitchen and was reputed to dish out a daily portion to his employees himself! Lest the fish became done too quickly! Big John told John Scott, the Laird gave him a salt Herring for breakfast each morning on a broken (cracked) plate, and when he complained, the Laird replied "Ye' shid be gled 'tis a hale herrin' Ah' gie' ye' oan the broken plate, an' no' the ither way roon' aboot! There's many a wan who wid be gled tae' take yir place, herrin' or nae herrin', plate or nae plate" nevertheless; the Ferryman seemed to make a good living ferrying people across the river.

His brother Hugh who was a ploughman at Priestfield Farm, High Blantyre, often boasted about his brother's prosperity, in

his strong Hieland accent saying, "Yess, John has sousand's and sousand's, aye an' hunner's o' sousand's, forbye the coppers he has in the drawer," Such was life of the Scott and Munro families in this beautiful part of Blantyre, that year of 1866.

Ackn; A MacCallum Scott M.P. (Son of John Scott.)

Photo by **Jim Brown**.

Boat House Blantyre.

'Twixt Clyde and Calder near Haughead,

'tis where our Native people did tread,

as did a man by the name of Blane,

who once passed bye and left us his name.

One day perchance, should you pass bye,
you too might hear a plaintive cry
of voices calling for the Ferry boat,
"Bo-oat Jo-oak. Bo-oat Jo-oak"…

You'll turn, perchance to see,
this ancient site near Blantyre Priory,
as Boat House appears from out the gloom,
like the mystical village of Brig-a-doon.

The call is heard within his Cottage,
by the Ferryman who leaves his pottage,
rising swiftly from his chair,
makes his way down towards the pier.

To where his Skiff is safely moored,
making sure it is properly oared,
he launches forth onto the Clyde,
and rows towards the Uddingston side.

To ferry travellers to and fro,
is the job of Hie'lander John Munro?
At which task he is the best,
being strong of arm and broad of chest.

Should you be fortunate to behold this scene,

you may think it all a dream

but stranger wait, be not be afraid,

'tis written and of times said.

Those of us from far and wide,

are chosen to walk this path by Clyde

to bear witness just like thee,

as you pass by these things you see ...

Near this place some Monks did dwell,

upon this place didst cast a spell

'tis not a spell that one should fear,

but rather a spell one holds dear.

These holy men from days of yore,

his guardians be for evermore...

tho' they are gone, yet still remain,

to show that this be Gods domain!

So, stranger have no fears,

it only happens every hundred years!

James Cornfield. 2008.

The Priory – Blantyre

The Priory, dating from the thirteenth century or earlier, was situated upon the banks of the Clyde opposite Bothwell Castle.

One Victorian commentator said of the scene: '... what with the stags that bounded through the woods and the salmon that swarmed in the rivers, the jolly priests and peaceful villagers of that old Blantyre must have felt that verily their lives had fallen in pleasant places!'

Records state that Friar Walter of Blantyre Priory was involved in negotiating a ransom for King David Bruce when he was a prisoner of the Battle of Durham in 1346.

The Priory from Bothwell Castle

William Wallace is said to have performed a swashbuckling leap into the Clyde from its walls when interrupted on a visit by some hostile English soldiers.

The Priory became the ancestral home to the first five Lord Blantyre's and of course, Teresa Francis Stuart, Granddaughter to the first Lord Blantyre, who modelled for Britannia.

The ruins of the Priory can still be visited, although judging by this 1908 sketch, it seems unlikely that there is much left to see.

Priory Impression by Blantyre Artist, **John McDermott**. The coloured original can be seen at the Blantyre Miners Resource Centre.

Rivers Meet

Meeting of Rotten Calder and Clyde... with Haughhead Pit in the background. This is the western perimeter of Blantyre.

Well, that is the end of Our Wander Doon Memory Lane, Part One ~ Glasgow Road, North Side.

We started at Springwell and journeyed along Glasgow Road taking in all its arteries, Forrest Street, John Street, Clark Street, all of which are in the Parish of Stonefield.

We then journeyed down Station Road to the Workers Mill Village where we could have delved much deeper with all that is available upon this subject. And finally, down Blantyreferme Road to the Rivers Meet.

~~~

A Wander Doon Memory Lane – Part Two – Glasgow Road, South

We now start Part Two and begin our Wander Doon Glasgow Road on the South side which will be from Springwell to Barnhill, taking in Glasgow Road, Rosendale Place, Auchinraith Road, Herbertson Street, Jackson Street, Church Street, Elm Street, Logan Street, Craig Street, Victoria Street, Calder Street, Stonefield Road and Bardykes Road ending at the Hoolet's in Barnhill.

We start with **Robert McDougall Fruit & Veg** yard and Market Garden. Remember his big Maroon Van delivering to your door? Robert would deliver what he thought we needed throughout the week and always the necessary vegetables for soup on a Friday.

Next, we had **Lawson's Building** with a shop, small grocer & baker, owned by Meg Lawson, and then...

Charles Ireland Scrapyard and Foundry

As kids, we used to get some scrap through a hole in the fence and take it around to the entrance, the man would give us a few pennies. We thought we were the bees' knees, but he probably knew exactly what we were doing.

Your Memories:

Peter Murray asks: "When was the explosion in Charles Ireland's foundry at Greenfields Foundry?" This is where the Bus Station is at Springwell. Can anyone shed some light on this?

Moira Lees: Hi Peter, explosion happened 21st November 1973. A guy tried to open a safe and blew his legs off x.

Bill Hunter: Remember it well I was a Painter working at Robertson's, Springwell 25 feet up a ladder when there was this explosion and my ladder blew back from the wall about 2 feet. I later met the gentleman on several occasions. The safe was locked with no key and he had to burn it open with an Oxy Acetylene torch. Unfortunately, dynamite was in the safe but no one knew this. He lost both his legs.

Liz Doonin: Mr. Hannaway lost both his legs in that explosion.

Janette R Minto: Apparently, there was ammunition found there at one point from Second World War.

Blantyre's 9 Hole Golf Course

Blantyre Golf Course was a Nine-hole course situated at what is now Springwell Crescent, the Clubhouse being at No 32/34 in the Crescent. The Blantyre 9 Hole Golf Club was founded in February 1913, and its course was on land owned by Merry & Cunningham Ltd. the mining Company.

The Membership fees were £1.1s for men and 10s 6D for women. In today's value that would have been approximately £105 for men.

My friend, James Cornfield, now deceased, had the metal, 'No Trespassing sign'.

The club was then voluntary would up in1918, probably due to lack of membership and the war effort.

The records show that a notice was posted in 1918 asking members to remove their

possessions from the clubhouse.

I believe that the course ground was eventually taken over by the Council for much-needed housing.

Some of this information was furnished by Alan Finlay Jackson who is in the process of researching old Scottish golf clubs, which no longer exist. Alan was born in the western outskirts of Uddingston, and his grandfather's

GOLF CLUB.—A special general meeting of Blantyre Golf Club was held in the Lesser Co-operative Hall on Thursday evening. The captain, Mr John Sharp, presided. Owing to the present conditions there was only a small attendance of the members. The Chairman, in the course of his remarks, pointed out that it was becoming increasingly difficult to keep the club going, and that in the opinion of the committee the club was in a better position for being wound up than it had ever been. After the secretary had read the statement of affairs, it was moved and seconded that the club be wound up voluntarily. The attention of members is directed to the advertisement re members' clubs, etc.

house, where he lived during the war, looked straight over the Clyde Bridge across to Dechmont, and to the left of Blantyre. His grandfather was a miner. Alan moved to England some 55 years ago.

Caldwell Hall

This 1950 aerial photo of Glasgow Road is showing Chalmers Laun, so called because

Chalmers Haulage Contractors had offices in the building.

Adjoining Chalmers Laun is the three-story Caldwell Hall which was owned by the Rt Hon Sir James Caldwell, P.C. Member of the Faculty of Procurators, Glasgow, 1864,

Deputy Chairman of ways and means and Deputy Speaker, House of Commons 1906-10, Liberal M.P. for St. Rollox Div. of Glasgow 1886-92 and Mid-Lanarkshire 1894 – 1910, J.P. Lanarkshire and Glasgow.

The Caldwell Hall was used by The Blantyre Holiness Mission for worship prior to 1910 when they purchased a Nissan Hut and erected it in Jackson Street. The Hall was later used by the Stonefield Parish Church for all Church functions.

The hall was nicknamed, "The Coffin Hall," because of its coffin shape. The road to the right is Rosendale Place and then Rosendale.

The building at the bottom of the photo, just in front of Baird's Raws, was Baird's Company Store.

Rosendale

Rosendale

Rosendale, a three-storey red sandstone building built in 1890. This picture was taken in the early 1970s after the Chalmers Building, and Caldwell Hall was demolished.

The Auchinraith Club is at the far end of building and was a spit and sawdust "Men Only" Club, even the cleaners were all males. A well frequented place by the miners. Opposite on Glasgow Road you can see the entrance to the Horseshoe Bar known locally as 'Kelly's Corner' after the owner, James Kelly, of Celtic F.C. fame.

Rosendale was quite an impressive-looking building as you entered Blantyre from the East. Most people remember it this way and some even think that it was parallel with Glasgow Road.

It was, however, mostly obscured from passing traffic on Glasgow Road by the Chalmers Building and the Caldwell Hall before they were demolished in 1959.

Everyone in Blantyre had an occasion to visit Rosendale

when the Shows (FUN FAIR) as we called it, came to the village.

It was parked in a piece of the wasteland directly behind the Rosendale buildings, to the right of the photo.

Thomas Dunsmuir Hartman remembers, "Rosendale Place was the name given to a large three storey tenement type buildings with the first-floor entrance from the Main Street. The other entrance for the other two stories was around the back of the building or with an attached tiered stairway, as a child when I originally saw this stairway at such an angle it was frightening. That stairway looked scary to me."

The bottom of the photo is the Top and Middle Row of Baird's Rows.

Rosendale

(A Magic Place When We Were Young)

Ah' remember the tenement called Rosendale
in Blantir toon fae whence ah' hail,
an ancient place, a bit o' a dive,
but somehow magical, when yur only five.

Ah' remember ma pals an' thur cheeky wee faces,
thur wee short troosers held up wae braces.
Playin' ootside was always a must:
Kickin' a baw in the stoor an' the dust.

Ah' remember the outside toilet wae dread,
is it any wunner we peed the bed?
tae go doon there made me awfy unhappy,
thir wur times ah' wished, ah' still wore a nappy.

Ah' remember the close wae hardly a light
the ghosts oan the stairs that gave ye a fright,
an gaun tae bed when the time wis just right,
tae wait fur the Daleks, that came in the night.

Ah' remember ma da' wae his jet-black hair,
young an' handsome an' fu o' flair,
a Blantir Dandy some wid say:
but a gentleman always, come what may.

Ah' remember ma mother, a young Snow White,
always there tae make things right,
tender, lovin' an' fu o' care,
wae a heart fu' o' love, for us tae share.

The family remembers those childhood days
in auld Rosendale in oor different ways,
an' as we remember, happy or sad,
we'll always be grateful, tae oor mum and dad.

Brian Cummiskey Co/BC/2004

ROSENDALE

Just a wee note on my poem, 'Rosendale'. It was the first poem I ever wrote. I wrote it for my father's 70th birthday.

It was he who said he has seen the ghost of an old woman on the stairs. The Daleks that came in the night were inspired by a life-size Dalek that sat in the Co-op window on Glasgow Road. I'm sure it was the Co-op, opposite the old post office. The mither tongue gratefully added by Mr. James Cornfield.

Rosendale residents Protest at County Buildings

Angry Protest: These furious residents from Rosendale Place in Blantyre went to the County Buildings in February of 1968 to protest against the delay in re-housing.

Mothers of young children complained that chimneys were ready to fall, there was no toilet in one close,

ANGRY PROTEST: these angry residents from Rosendale Place in Blantyre went to the County Buildings in February of 1968 to protest about delay in re-housing. Mothers of young children complained that chimneys were ready to fall, there was no toilet in one close, rain was leaking into rooms, and a roof had a tarpaulin over it.

rain was leaking into rooms, and a roof had a tarpaulin over it.

Source: Hamilton Advertiser.

Sent in by **Gerry Kelly**.

Your Memories:

Hi Bill,

I lived in Rosendale as a nipper from 1948 to 1954. My mum, Cathie Callaghan (nee Fagan), was a teacher at St Joseph's and my dad, Joe Callaghan, was a miner at Cardowan. They lived in Rosendale for some time before I was born on 7th May 1948.

We lived up several different closes, and I remember it as a very happy place with not much money but loads of community spirit. Everybody knew everybody and looked out for each other's weans. We had plenty of freedom, and the only flies in the ointment were the Springies (Springwell kids) who used to invade across the railway line at the far end of Rosendale. This always resulted in a battle with stones (using the ballast off the railway) before we moved to close quarters with sticks and stuff. These battles regularly resulted in injuries to even small kids. I left when I was 6, by which time I'd already had my arm broken by a stick, and my head split by a stone. Happy days eh?

Andy Callaghan.

Hello there Bill,

My name is **Don Barkey**. I remember living in Rosendale as a kid. I was 4yrs old then, and my little sister was born in May of 1968. This was my first memory of a child in Scotland. We moved to Hazelwood Drive in Blantyre for a short time then my dad and mum (Donald and Rose) with my little sister, and I moved out to Australia in 1972. I hope this brief piece of info has filled a small piece of the jigsaw.

Regards, **Wee Donald**

Christine Allan Brown: There was a building on the Main Street in front of Rosendale.

Blantyre's Ain: Yes, it was Chalmer's Building and then the Caldwell Hall, known as Coffin Hall because of its shape.

Christine Allan Brown: Thanks, can remember it lol

Jeanette Bryan: My Mum lived in Rosendale.

Martin Smith: I lived at the top of Baird's Row. On Glasgow Rd. Can't remember the number.

Sadie Dolan: My aunt lived in Rosendale, hated the outside toilets, x.

Jean Orr: Oh, I just vaguely remember it, we (Watson family) moved to Coatshill when I was 3, I remember the "flitting" on the back of a flatbed lorry! I also remember the fair & the dog track in later years!

Moira Macfarlane: I lived in Kelly's building, it was great when the shows came.

Mary Mcguire: It's great to see Kelly building in background Moira x.

Joan Adams: Remember these and the shows used climb fence set back off our house down bank old railway lived Springwell right opposite. Old bridge half way along old railway happy days.

Marie Mc Millan: the garage was cross the road john x

Marie Mc Millan: I lived in 2 Rosendale and my cousin Margaret Rouse lived in 4 Rosendale x.

Gerry Walker: Did Margaret move to the West End.? If so we were at school together. We swapped houses with her granddad about 1974.

Jeanette Bryan: My mum lived in Rosendale.

Margaret Quinn: Frances mc Donald your granny stayed in Rosendale whit wan is her hoose x.

Susan Walker Graham: I lived at No. I and my cousins lived in No. 2.

James Faulds: the greyhounds were tired just lost the race in the dug track Rosendale was a great place to live that and Springwell.

John McCourt: I was born in number Two Rosendale place, remember as a wee boy fighting the Springwell squad across either side of the Railway.

Maggie Tonner McVeigh: We Lived in No1 (The Tonner`s) in 1957 and my mum worked across the road in John O'Neil's Garage.

Gerry Walker: Is this the same Tonners that moved to Devondale. Brothers Mick, Chris and I can't remember the oldest one's name. (Apologies).

Maggie Tonner McVeigh: Yes, Gerry, tis I Maggie Tonner of brothers Lex Michael and Christopher. Sadly, Michael passed away 2000, and also Russell Burns has passed...from Craigton Place and a few others from Michael's age group. I vaguely remember The Walker's. X

Margaret Slaven McSorley: A was born in Rosendale.

Elizabeth Ann Ward: My mum lived in Rosendale x.

Agnes Flannigan: My husband was brought up in Baird's raws.

Martin Smith: I lived on Glasgow Road at the top of Baird's Row. Loved it there!!!

The Buggy Buildings

Buggy Buildings, was the name given to a three-storey tenement which was situated on Auchinraith road, between two smaller tenements.

No one knows why it was given the name as it was no 'buggier' than any other buildings, but it was probably due to the builders using reclaimed timber, which was already riddled with bugs.

The three properties were owned by two Australian brothers who gave the proper names of, James Place, Melbourne Place (The Buggy) and Radnor Place.

The road to the left is Elm Street.

This is a great view of the Buggy Buildings on Auchinraith Road.

The road leading to the Buggy Buildings is Elm Street.

The Church of the Nazarene is the second from the bottom right.

At the top of the photo, there are prefabs located in High Blantyre, which was the largest prefab scheme in Blantyre.

Bill,

I have copies of these photos that were inherited from my late grandfather, William Dobson.

Although I don't know who any of these people are. I think that they are associated with the "Buggy" buildings, so if any of your readers could shed any light on them, then I would be obliged.

Thank you so much and keep up the good work.

Kind regards, **Elizabeth Dobson Grieve**

Gran Dobson's Women's Guild

The above lady posted a labelled "Gran Dobson's Women's Guild" and asked if anybody could identify them.

I don't know how long ago it was, but I can help.

This was a snap of St Joseph's Catholic Women's Guild in 1950s on their September weekend trip to Blackpool. My Mother, Mary Peat is in the back row left, framed by the door.

The lady kneeling on the far left was called Lizzy Reilly and the lady on far-right standing with the bag was Cummiskey, who had a son and daughter Alec and Morag and is the grandmother of your Poetic contributor, who talks about the Whelan's and the Cummiskey's.

Archie Peat, Liverpool

Auchinraith Primary School

This was the opening day of Auchinraith School on 31st August 1900 at 3.00 p.m.

The Glasgow Herald reported the event stating that on the invitation of the Blantyre School Board, a party of some 70 guests, representative of all the local public bodies and neighbouring school boards attended a ceremony.

The school was opened formerly by Dr Grant, chairman of the School Board. When the guests arrived, they were served with tea and cake, after which Dr Grant addressed the group with an inaugural ceremony concluding by inviting the company to inspect the new premises.

Notice how the Ladies and the little boys were dressed, as though they had just come from a Quakers Meeting.

Architect Mr. A Cullen designed the school in the similar fashion to the 1875 schools at Stonefield Parish Primary (Ness's) and the Primary at High Blantyre (Hunthill Road Annexe).

The building cost approximately £7,500 (£825,000 in today's value) and was one-story in height, capable of accommodating 650 primary scholars.

There were 10 classrooms each able to accommodate an average of 60 pupils (teachers nowadays would perish the thought!).

A large multi-function hall stood in the centre of the building for drilling the scholars and later for use as a theatre.

The building was finished and furnished in a most modern style of the time and connected to gas heating.

After the inspection, the company enjoyed a meal and wine banquet in the main hall. Dr Grant presided, and Messrs Menzies and McQuarrie were croupiers. A number of toasts were made, and the pupils were permitted to school the first Monday after.

Auchinraith Silver Band celebrated the occasion and everyone dressed up in their Sunday best. What a day!

Head Master, Mr. John McNish.

Staff: Miss Rennie, Miss Johnston, Miss Grant and Miss Bremner.

Auchinraith Club

The Auchinraith Club, was situated at the top of Craig Street and Auchinraith Road, where Auchinraith Primary School used to be.

Auchinraith Club

Although the building would not win any design awards it was a very popular Club in its Day and unlike the original Auchinraith Club, the Committee allowed women in. It was mysteriously burnt down September Weekend, 1998.

This is what you had to say about it:

Alan Baird: I think it burned down in the summer of 1998. I actually stood and watched the excavator demolishing it. I often would frequent it on a Saturday night.

Margaret Bell: Oh my, remember hearing all the singing. After the club was out. X

Janice Frank: OMG... that was a part of my life for many years. My mum worked there behind the bar and cooking for a while as well as being a waitress, and my dad was on committee and drank a lot there lol. I also waitressed and served at the bar there since I was 16.

And like you Jade, had so many family nights and parties there. Xx

John Cornfield: My mam worked here. I had many a good night here too, good club.

Wendy Monaghan: Worked in the bar 'n did my stint as a waitress, nobody cud beat wee Winnie at the waitressing. Xx great memories. Xx

Janice Frank: Don't think we appreciated the community spirit among us all back then. Many great memories in there. Xx

Margaret Bell: All great memories Janice. Think it was Jock McCaroll and Lynda Ward lol. Wish it was the same now. Xx

James Minto: Lol Dee I think there was a lot more jobs going on up there 'n no just bar ones lol. X

Linda Halpin: I sang there, every weekend, great club.

Janet Saunders: Passed it every time going down tae ma grandparents' house.

John Allan: I got barred at one time.

Stephen Hasson: Long time ago the "Auchie."

Liz Anderson: Had many great nites in Auchie, mam and dad and family. Only club we didn't need to get a taxi to, as we stayed in Logan Street. Dad was on the committee for years.

Janice Frank: Wee Winnie lol she would walk up and down with one pint on the tray most of the night. X

Jade Sloey: My grandpa ran Auchie, spent a lot of time there when young, many family parties and annoying the bar staff lol. Gees how time flies William Monaghan.

Dee Mcewan: Omg it's been a while since I saw that place 'n can't believe it's gone now. I had my very first bar job in there lol long time ago now though xx I totally lied about my age to get the job as well. X

Paul Hudson McGowan: I remember it well, at least the building anyway. I was only a young lad in 70's. Looking at it now you would think it was a nuclear bomb shelter or a fort or something.

Alan Baird: many a good night was had in there, I watched it getting demolished the night it went on fire.

Jim Tallan: still got my shareholders card.

Robert McLeod-Wolohan: I was a committee member there for a couple of years, seems so long ago now.

Catherine Burnett: that was a good club. X

Mary Odonnell: My mum work there Linda Ward.

Janice Fullerton: My wee dad George Paterson [pie] was on the committee, loved the club, he liked the old one as there was no woman allowed in, God bless you pie.

Natalie Ward: I was gonna tag u mum… Jeanette Allardyce Ward. Ma wee granny Bridie would be babysitting me… Ma maw n da were at the 'Auchie'… X

Jeanette Allardyce Ward: Lol aye that's rite, a then shed b babysitting u a Cheryl coz we were still going to the Auchie lol. Used to phone home to check uze were ok. X

Jeanette Allardyce Ward: I started going there when I was 16 lol, every weekend, loved it, everyone in it was so friendly and it was the same people who went there every week, which made it a great club. Had many a good laugh in there during a lock in lol.

Liz Nelson: I used to go there when I was 16 lol.

Lorraine Mcguire: My mum Flora worked in the club for a number of years.

Margaret McGuigan: My dad lived there well that's what my mum said.

Jean McSorley: I think ma mum an dad ran the auchie, I think a was about 2 it 3 at the time I was told. This was b4 they went on to manage the Blantyre Vic's... bring bk the gd old days. Xxx

Margaret Lappin: A good family friend worked here for years, Ellen Nicoll, god rest her. Xx

Liz Mcginty: Worked in the club fae a was 17. My dad Pat Barrett was club manager then. Great club n many a good nites in it.

Liz Cutts: My mum Ellie O'neil used to go there every time we came to visit family Hugh Rodgers and the crew happy days. Xxx.

Stephen Mcgowan: I had ma very first pint in it wae ma dad!!

Mary Davies: Many a good night I had in there, one night I dropped in to pick up my late husband, I was pulled onto the dance floor, for a pass the parcel. I won the prize of a bag of coffee, and gave it to an old couple who were sitting. Great memories of this club.

John McCourt: Worked behind the bar with Ellen McGovern, Big Pat Phairs a great club.

Eleanor Duncan Nailon: Went there when I was 16 loved it, thought I was so growing up. Xx

John Mcadams: Where I had my official over 18 pints with ma da.

Ricky Forrest: Had my first legal pint there.

Mattie Taggart: I worked in the club lounge with Mary Meechan first and then Ellen Phairs or Nichol, God rest the 2 of them R.I.P. who were also great friends and I also worked with Iris Cornfield R.I.P. they are all gone so my time must be near. We all got on great and the lounge was always packed. You knew what they wanted to drink as soon as they walked in. I worked in it for about 7 yrs. Amanda your mum worked behind the bar as well it was a great club then and good tippers lol. Xxx

No5 Co-op Bakery – 1930

This imposing five-story brick building was situated at the junction of Craig Street and Auchinraith Road and at six o'clock in the morning it was rather a scary place.

I used to deliver milk from here in the early 60s and helped to load the Milk Float at the side of the building, while the top four stories were busy with their ovens, baking bread, etc., which gave the building an eerie glow in the dark mornings. I remember thinking it was like a medieval workhouse, with all the noise and clatter being made by the workers. I was always relieved to get on the Milk Float and leave for my milk run. The building dominated the Auchinraith skyline, as only the nearby Auchinraith Pit Bing could compete on size. The greatest ever Scottish Speedway rider, Ken McKinlay made deliveries from here on his bike.

Your Memories:

James Faulds: My brother Robert delivered the milk around Springwell and Dunsmuir brothers were the mechanics in the yard Duncan McDougal from Croft Park was the driver on the milk float and Hammy had the grocer van.

Moira Mulvaney Pacheco: And he lived just down the road in the Timber houses, Ken McKinley.

Robert McLeod-Wolohan: I also worked here in the 60's delivering milk in the morning and then bread, milk cakes, etc., and my driver was Rab Shearer, good memories.

Jean Boyd: I remember this building well.

Margaret Slaven McSorley: Their tips at the fair and Xmas where brilliant, money to ma mum and clothes that were in style bought themselves ah memories.

Jean McIntosh: The building could pass for a church, very fancy for a bakery etc. Look at the workmanship in it.

Aerial View of Timber Houses

A photo taken from Merry's Pit Bing of the Timber Houses circa late 40s. Taken by Tracey McDougall's grandfather, John Cameron – who was born in 1924 in Watson Street beside High Blantyre Primary and also lived in Birdsfield Timber houses and also Calder Street with his wife's family the Campbell's, then Fernslea Avenue beside St. Blane's Primary and later in Winton Crescent.

Look out for the Bus, Railway Line, Cemetery, Tractor, Bike, Family walking, Couple gardening, Prams and Air Raid Shelters. A picture tells a hundred stories.

Sent in by **Tracey McDougall.**

Found the Bus yet?

Your Memories:

Gary Doonin: Great photo notice the big field in left of photo between rear of houses on Auchinraith road and rear of timber hooses. That field is still there and used for equestrian purposes, a lot of people in Blantyre don't know that field exists.

David Aitken: Man, I never knew that field was there, must check that out.

Elizabeth Weaver: I still can't get my bearings – how do you get to that field?

Gary Doonin: James is correct the Kelly's, a well-known family in the area, had a timber hoose on Auchinraith Road but their house seems to be hidden by the timber hoose in the Birdsfield cul de sac. Talking of jumble sales James, it's obvious you couldn't move that Icelandic jumper.

Jim McDougal: We moved in to the prefabs Main St across from the factories after in 1947, everyone in those days had lovely gardens, all the garden paths were laid in red ash from the Bing, my brother Duncan and I after school with a barrow had to fetch load after load so dad could lay his paths, the Bing also great for playing cowboys and Indians, aye those were great days growing up in High Blantyre, Brilliant photo Tracey.

Maggie O'Brien: Is it not Murray's Bing?

Gary Doonin: Locals called it Murrays but Merry's was name of the pit owner. See my maws house on Auchinraith Road at top right of picture.

James O'Donnelly: I was going to mention that I recall you actually got the majority of your current clobber from the sale that day!

James O'Donnelly: I'm sure the last big house on the right was Kelly's house (Kelly's coal) where my mum's family grew up. Ma aunty Celia and uncle Pat kept on the house after my grandma died. I remember my cousin Celia and I, when we're about 10, organised a big jumble sale out the back garden in the late 70s… It was really busy and we donated to an old folk's home. It's difficult to imagine something like that happening nowadays.

Christina Frame: Climbed that Bing a few times and skinned my knees on the sharp red stones!!

George Mackenzie: We lived in the pre-fabs at the foot of Murray's Bing and I got the only leathering I ever got from my faither when he caught me sliding all the way down the Bing on a shovel!

The Horseshoe Bar

Back to Glasgow Road, and facing the corner of Rosendale and the original Auchinraith Club was The Horseshoe Bar, at the start of the Henderson Building. The pub was also known as Kelly's Corner Bar, after James Kelly of Glasgow Celtic F.C. fame, a former owner.

The legendary James Kelly was blessed with the honour of being the first ever Captain of Celtic F.C...

J Kelly 1890

He acquired the tenancies of pubs in Blantyre, Hamilton and Motherwell within a decade of joining the club as an amateur and an apprentice joiner.

The success he enjoyed with running these three businesses ultimately smoothed his path into public life as a Justice of the Peace, County Councillor and School Board Trustee.

He was Capped 6 times and was Captain of Scotland. At the end of his playing career, he became Director and Chairman of Celtic F.C.

He started and ran what was known locally as Kelly's Engineering but was actually called Blantyre Engineering in which was in Forrest Street.

He lived at Thornhill Villa, Thornhill Avenue, down the entrance to the Dandy.

The former 30 roomed mansion later became a Nunnery of the Poor Clare Order.

I don't know the circumstances of how the Poor Clare Order started using it as a Monastery. If anyone knows, please share it with us.

This photo is from the Horse Shoe Bar on the corner of the Henderson Building on Glasgow Road, looking west,

Glasgow Road Looking West 1902

which had Clark's Funeral Parlour, a Solicitors office. Botterill's Fish Restaurant, a Watch Repairer and a Barbers – the old post office is on the right at the telegraph pole, and next was the lane to Baird's Rows.

The Burleigh Church is on the left with the dyke around it, then it was Herbertson Street and the Co-op – across the street was Black's, the bakers and Angie's ice cream shop and then Forrest Street.

Thomas Dunsmuir Hartman remembers, "There was a barber shop for men. Very few of us boys went to the barbers; it was sit doon in the chair, bowl on your heed and all that stuck out from the bowl was chopped off.

There was a watch repairer, and he had this huge clock hanging outside his shop which a lot of people used as their own time piece, large enough that one could see it a block away, if you were sitting on a bus passing the shop, you could see the people just by habit take a glance at the clock. It was much used in those days."

Your Memories:

James Mcguire: I was born in Kelly's building thought I'd just let you know that.

Blantyre's Ain: James, do you have any photos of the Pub inside or out?

James Mcguire: Gosh unfortunately not wish I had, there is some photos of my father, sorry I can't provide you with some I barely remember it, but lots of miners singing...

James Faulds: Kelly's pub, Bookies, Archie McKay's, lawyer's office, Botterill's, Church, Herbertson St, then the Coop.

Grace McCaffery: Botterill's first shop was on the left a bit further down.

Mary Mcguire: Brilliant Moira x

Moira Macfarlane: R U the Jim that lived above the pub, and ur dad was Eddy, if it is let me know please.

James Mcguire: yes.

Moira Macfarlane: I was brought up in Kelly's building.

James Mcguire: Hey Annie my dad owned that pub.

Mary Mcguire: No Jim he worked in the pub.

Moira Macfarlane: Annie Botterill's chips lovely jubbly, then next door was Nancy Botterill's.

Martin Smith: The watch repair shop, was that called Lehmans?

Jim McAllister: Kelly's building, that's where I was born June 1960.

Herbertson Street

Herbertson Street just before demolition in 1979. This was the No 1 Co-op Building which stretched from Herbertson Street to Jackson Street and has obviously seen better times. The entrance to the Co-op Hall, next to Wheels, is where the Co-op Hall was upstairs and besides dances on a Friday night, wedding and funeral functions were held and in the early days, silent movies would be shown.

And of course, this was also the entrance to where you would collect your 'Divi'.

On Glasgow Road was John Reid's Printers, before he moved to his new premises which is now Gavin Watson Printers, and further along Glasgow Road was the Chinese Restaurant, the Lucky House, where my brother-in-law, Tam (T.C.) Campbell was one of the doormen.

The Kawasaki Motorcycle Dealership, Wheels is unknown to me, perhaps someone can remember who owned it.

Photo by **Jim McGuire**.

Roberts building at the top of Herbertson Street, and the old police substation built around 1900 being demolished with the Co-op Building.

Blantyre East Free Church Mission Hall

Blantyre East Free Church Mission Hall in Glasgow Road at Herbertson Street c1890, with old Police Station on the right.

The main church was built in front in 1892 and the Mission Hall becoming the Church Hall, all later renamed Burleigh Memorial Church post 1945.

Services began in 1878, and the Mission Hall erected in May 1878. The memorial stone for a permanent church was laid on 12th March 1892, and the church was opened on Saturday, 3rd December, 1892 at a cost of

£1,620 (about £250,000 in today's value), and seating 500.

It was renamed after the union with the Church of Scotland as the Burleigh Memorial Church of Scotland after its first minister the Rev. John Burleigh from 1889 – 1922, in 1945.

The church and hall were destroyed by fire during the 1970s – the hall in 1973 and the church in January 1974.

Ailean McLeman (Roberts) writes, "Back in Herbertson Street, opposite our house, on the corner with Glasgow Road, was the Burleigh Memorial Church, another building where I spent a great deal of my time up to about the age of 15.

My Mum was the church organist at that time. And Dad was a church elder, so every Sunday would find Jim (my brother) and I at church and Sunday school and later on, Bible Classes.

The church hall was at the side of the church. And most week nights for me were spent either at Brownies then the guides, country dancing classes, youth fellowship or singing at the women's guild (one of the drawbacks of having a Mum who played piano for most of the organisations using the hall!).

The Burleigh Church eventually, due to dwindling numbers (I think), amalgamated with Stonefield Church and the name disappeared. I think it may now be St. Andrew's Church."

No 1 Co-op

No: 1 Co-op, Blantyre, Hall, Offices, Shops

Co-op halls, offices & shops, Central Branch stretching from halfway up Herbertson Street, to Jackson Street. This is where you would queue to get your "Divi."

The Co-op was the largest row of shops in Blantyre, everyone at some time or other shopped at the co-op.

We had the Tailors, the butchers, the grocers, the hardware, the fancy goods, the millinery and a huge bakery,

which daily sold every known loaf of bread, biscuits, and yummy cakes.

Around the side entrance in Herbertson Street was the Co-op entrance to the Dancehall. This was held every Wednesday, 7-11pm. Friday night was the late night 7-1am, and Saturday 7-11. 30pm.

Also on Hebertson Street were a Saw and Joinery Mill owned by William Roberts where all of Blantyre went to get any woodwork done.

The Manse for the church on the corner was around here. The top entrance of Herbertson Street was a mixture of two storey tenements and private homes.

The other end of the street finished at Auchinraith Road, which was running at a 45-degree angle with Glasgow Road.

Behind the Co-op, was the cobbled yard, where the carts were unloaded of their goods and the heavy horses would do their business.

Thomas Dunsmuir Hartman remembers. "Jackson street was a little bit more fashionable, in that it contained some private 2 storey homes and bungalows all made of brick with baths and toilets inside the homes, all of the other tenement type homes I have been explaining about here and there, had their toilets on the landings of the staircase, or in the entrance of the close.

There was a side entrance into the back of all of the Co-op stores here in Jackson Street. You went through a large close type opening between the buildings into a cobble stoned square, from there it was possible to enter each and every store for the delivery of goods.

The public was not allowed to use this entrance, especially with all of the horses mingling around, I can still hear the clip-clop of hoofs on the cobble stones and the shout of "whooh Nelly", and of course the habitual smell of dung in the air, remember this was a closed in type square where all sounds and smells being accentuated by the surrounding buildings. It was Hustle and bustle of a certain kind. I know about this, for there was I, standing outside the entrance with my pail and shovel, and waiting for you know what."

Jackson Street – Building at the top of the street was probably named Jackson Terrace.

Some memories of when I was growing up in Blantyre. I hope you find them of interest.

Ailean McLeman (Roberts) remembers,

"It was great to see the pictures of Glasgow Road in Blantyre on your website, especially one of the 'Number One' Co-op building situated part way up Herbertson Street and round onto Glasgow Road towards Jackson Street.

I spent most of my younger days in Herbertson Street in the 'Roberts' building which is mentioned elsewhere in your website. My maiden name was Roberts, and my dad was William (Bill) Roberts, who for many years ran the joiner's business (which was originally his father's) from the workshop next to the Co-op building in Herbertson Street. The house we lived in was right next to the joiner's yard, so Dad did not have far to get to work each day.

The garden at the back of our building backed on to the garden of the tenement at the top right-hand corner of Jackson Street. All the kids from Herbertson Street and Jackson Street used to play in these gardens, and we had many a 'back green' birthday party which everyone attended... any excuse for a get together, which included bringing the furniture out of the houses into the garden... no fancy garden tables and chairs in these days!!!

I remember the Co-op building very well, especially the Co-op Hall. When I was very young and growing up in the late 50s into the early 60s (I was born in 1950), my great ambition was to be old enough to go to the dances held in the Hall on Friday nights. I used to lie in my bed and listen to the music and later, the laughter coming from the dancers leaving to go home. By the time, I was old enough to go dancing I am afraid my interests lay further afield in Hamilton! As my Mum (Betty) and Dad were both members of the Blantyre Choral Union, their annual concerts were held in the Hall, so I at least got as far as going in there to listen to the choir and also to help dad prepare for the concerts as he usually built up the stage!!

I do remember the Co-op shops which were next to the Hall. Going down Herbertson Street from our house, there was the shoe shop, and then the Draper's shop on the corner with Glasgow Road, next to that was the butcher, and the grocer.

There was great excitement when the grocer became a 'self-service' where we had to leave our shopping baskets in a wee locker and use the numbered shopping basket to go around and help ourselves.

I remember following the renovation; some of the marble counters from the old grocers ended up in Dad's yard and my pals, and I had an endless stock of 'peevers!!

Next to the self-service was the fish shop, then the fruit and veg shop and finally at the corner of Jackson Street, there was the electrical shop... at least I think that's what was there!!!

Oh! And of course, the Co-op offices were up the same stairs as the Hall, and we got our dividend made up there!!

At the back of the Co-op building up Jackson Street, was a big blank wall against which my pals and I used to play 'tennis' for hours on end, and I remember that near there, one of the men who worked in the butcher's shop (I think) used to have an aviary where he kept budgies!

Ailean McLeman (Roberts), April 2014

My Grandfather was a master tailor with the Co-op, and this is apparently a photo of the folks who worked in the Co-op, almost certainly at the beginning  of the 20th century. Sent in by **Jean Brownrigg.**

Kidd's Building (Sproat's Laun)

Kidd's Building (Sproats Laun), Glasgow Road
Hughie Kidd's fish & chips & The Smiddy Bar

Mecca Bookmakers, The White Elephant, formerly Hughie Kidd's fish & chip shop, The Smiddy Bar, Elm Street, and Stonefield Parish Church.

The Smiddy Bar – Glasgow Road at Merry's Rows (Elm Street) which must have taken its name from the blacksmith shop that once was active in this area.

Opposite the Wellington Bar, also known as Maggie McGuire's.

Your Memories:

William Ross wrote: "The Smiddy, Vince, his mother, Alsatian and Parrot."

Anyone remember the White Elephant? (Where the couple are standing).

Robert McLeod-Wolohan wrote: "Aye I remember the white elephant you could get anything in there and if I remember correctly, it was all stuff that had been used."

William Ross wrote: "The betting shop was McGuigan's before Mecca, they also had the shop at the top of station road."

Kathleen Duffy: Charlie lifted lines behind Teddy McGuiness' pub before betting became legit then he moved into 2 Station Road before selling out to M. O'Hare many years later. Matt did work with him in Station Road but neither of them worked in Kidd's building. William, I thought Slavin had a shop somewhere on the Main Street.

William Ross: Lost my money in that shop so many times and can't remember who to.

Kathleen Duffy: There was Mulholland's, Weir, Slavin and Charlie Forrest who were all Bookmakers at that time but not sure which one was in that particular shop.

Anne Callaghan: Willie Weirs' then Mecca took over.

Kathleen Duffy: At last someone got it thanks Anne. Xx

William Ross: Correct, 1967 ran out of money when Scotland beat England. Monday pay-out for quite a few.

Thea Borland Mcnamee: Remember white elephant well. Jim Collagen (Call) went with the girl whose mum owned it and also helped out in it. Remember Bunty's the hairdressers across the road as well and wee cafe which I think was also taxi office.

Jeanette Allardyce Ward: I remember it but don't know who owned it.

Anne Gilmour Callaghan: Jimmy Campbell owned it and Jim Callaghan worked there for some time.

Marion Young: Ma auntie Helen's pub was across the road, the Castle Vaults.

Christine Allan Brown: The family that owned it lived in Montrose Crescent but can't remember their name.

Catherine Sneddon: I remember that shop my mum worked in the bookies next door to it. Xx

Diane Cunningham: A do remember going into it way MA mum but don't know who owned it. X

Anthony Smith: Don't remember The White Elephant, but do remember my father going into the Smiddy Bar while waiting for The Dookit to open and calling to tell him it had opened. I was far too young to drink.

Rab Mccarrol: Got my puncture repair kits in there when I was wee lol.

Mary Boyle: Was it Hughie Duffy from Logan Street? I'm not sure but will ask my Mother tonight.

Frances McDonald: Remember the white elephant well but not who owned it.

Liz Jack: Remember one of the Lennon's and his wife worked in it.

Angela Carty: I think it was McMillan that owned it. I think because I remember Jesses McMillan mum was always severing in it!!!!!

Etta Morrison: Kidd's chip shop in same building.

Ethel Watson: I remember it was Mary who owned it.

Mary McGuigan: Aww I remember that. X

Jan Walsh: A yes, I remember it well. 😀

Jim Donnelly: McNamee name springs to mind...!!

Marion Young: A got my skating boots from there.

Nancy McFadden: I remember it very well I used to love to look in the window, also the Smiddy pub at the end that's where my Grandpa Frew drank, everyone knew him as Sanny.

David Scott: Did he have a brother Jim?

Nancy McFadden: No, his son was Jim Frew. My uncle Jim died about two to three years ago... I think I went to school with you.

Blantyre's Ain: Sanny Frew was a great guy, he always had a nice word to say. He used to sit on the wall in Auchinraith Road and watch the world go by. I was only about 10 years old but he had time for me.

David Scott: Jim used to come over and watch the fitba with me in the Tact hall and went to a couple of games with us (when we had a spare ticket). Great guy. What's your own name (take McFadden your married name)?

Nancy McFadden: I remember when he went to the over to the hall and I know he was very fond of you. I used to come back to Blantyre every summer when my mum was living.

Nancy McFadden: He always sat on the dyke and would talk to everyone ...

He was a character. He used to chop sleepers for firewood and the smell of chopped wood always makes me think of him.

Margaret Cunning: Was your mother's own name Nancy Frew?

Anne Gilmour Callaghan: Jimmy Campbell owned it. I remember it at the other side of the road.

Merry's Rows, Blantyre

Merry's Rows and the Salvation Army - Elm Street

We then had Elm Street, which formerly was Merry's Rows, pronounced locally as Murray's Raws, which ran back to Auchinraith Road.

This is a shot of the Salvation Army doing their thing at Merry's Raws.

Owned by Merry & Cunninghame, coal masters, they consisted of 46 single and 50 double-apartment houses.

They were built with brick, and were erected in the late 1870s, and described as a very poor type of house with low-ceilings and mostly damp. The rent per week, including rates in 1914, was 2s. 4d. and 2s. 11d. for single and double houses respectively. The water supply was by means of stand-pipes at intervals along the front of the row. The houses had no sculleries or sinks, and all the dirty water was emptied into an open gutter at the front of the rows. There were wash houses to every six tenants, and a flush-closet to every three tenants. Bins were used for refuge, with a daily collection. The rows had no coal-cellars or drying-greens. A man was kept for tidying up the area...

Duncan Slater wrote, "I was born in #79. That is the house with someone at the door, also I can give you the names of some of the people who lived here, in 1937 all the people were moved to new houses on Priory and Calder streets.

#1 Croft Family (Frank)

15 Croft family (Robert)

20 Kalinsky family

22 Woods

24 Duncan

39 Schlothaeur

43 Longmuir

64 McInally

86 Patterson

79 Slater

81 Carabine (with 8 children, one who played football for Scotland, Jimmy)."

Duncan Slater remembers, "On the other corner of Murray's Raws was an Iron Duke. This was an open-air toilet made of cast iron. It was real handy for the men in the later years when the buses started to run, you could stand there and have a pee and still look through the perforated mesh at the top and see if your bus stop. It coming down the road. This was right at the bus stop, it could not have been pleasant for the ladies queuing up for the bus.

Church of the Nazarene

Church of the Nazarene

The Blantyre Holiness Mission, who used to worship in the Caldwell Hall on the corner of Auchinraith Road, began in 1907, and became the Blantyre Pentecostal Church. Who purchased a Nissan Hut in 1910, and erected it in Jackson Street. They united with the Pentecostal Church of the Nazarene in 1915.

When the flats were built in Elm Street in 1952, they asked the Council to lay a path to the rear of the Nissan Hut to gain access.

This later became the main entrance and the layout of the interior of the Church completely reversed to reflect this.

After many years of meeting in the original hall, a new church, on Elm Street, was built and officially opened and dedicated on Sunday 24th October 1982. For nearly 100 years, the witness was maintained in Blantyre, a ministry that concluded on Sunday 24th September, 2006. The church was officially closed on its centenary, 2007.

The church was sold to St. Andrew's Church of Scotland and named, 'Nazarene Hall.'

Your Memories:

David Thomson: Grandpa's auld church Ina.

Ina Sanders: remember it brings back memory and Mr. Mackie was the minister there. That's where I went when I was a wee girl with my mum and gran.

Jessie Mclachlan: David is that wer Liz and our Andrew got married xx.

Liz Campbell: Good memory Jessie.

Christine Brown: They were very happy days I loved Hawthorn Place. Beyond the swing park was the old man's rest lol.

Elm Street and St Andrews Parish Church

Annie Murdoch Anderson Black: I remember going into that park and swinging on the rails when I was a wee girl, then heading down further to Bunty Hairdressers for the haircut, aww I am home sick now ...

Mary Borland: I used 2 go back way to the park then go and sit in the old man's rest and make daisy chains when the sun was out xx memories xx.

Christine Brown: Smashed my leg on the frying pan it was sore lol.

Len Northfield: Loved that swing park, especially the frying pan. Or whatever that big cone thing was called!

Marie Cathcart: I lived at number 11d for years. And it was Oor very own Rosie Law that did the painting on the wall in the park, it's still there to this day. Xx

David Hay: played a lot in that swing park.

Ian Mccaul: The Elm Street warrior's lol.

Thea Borland Mcnamee: I remember Mrs Dent well and next to park was the Train's. Upstairs fae Mrs Dent was the Currie's I ran aboot wi Chris Rock's who a think

was Mrs Dents grandson, and across the landing was the Paterson's.

Billy Paterson split ma heed wi a brick after dropping it from the shute in Swing Park.

Mae Donnelly: And Mrs Dent she lived across the road, Mrs Craigie lived next door to my gran!

Annemarie Aitken: Wee Auntie Agnes. X

Angela Taylor: Nettie Brown my wee gran. X

Mary Boyle: My nana Mrs Mogan or Minnie, the name she preferred was best friends and upstairs neighbour to Agnes Dent. I remember her and Nettie Brown fondly. I was born at 20 Elm Street. Xx

Moira Mulvaney Pacheco: Team Dent was my brother's pal.

Tracey Ann Campbell: Aw my mum's wee auntie Agnes, brings back memories. X

Henerson Janette: ma Grannie Brown that's who am called after.

Hannah Mcaleenan: my gran stayed around the corner in Hawthorn Place, wee Martha.

Danielle Scully: aww ma wee granny Theresa. Xx

Etta Morrison: remember Nettie Brown and her daughters. Think they lived in same close as Muirhead's... We lived in Beech Place.

Thea Borland Mcnamee: Remember the Blythe's well... Betty and Mary. Mrs Blithe used to keep her purse in her bra, a used to go get shopping for her along wi Mrs Callaghan. Wee Teenie Smith 'n Jessie Nisbet an' ma grannies.

Stephen Morrison: My gran stayed in 22 Alex & Jenny Blythe.

Mae Donnelly: I remember Mrs Mogen, Nettle Brown, Kelly and Wilson, my granny lived in number 13C, me and my sister used to stay.

Carolyn Patterson: My Grandparents lived around the corner as well in Hawthorn Place Tam and Catherine Barrie. X

Lynne Dunsmuir: I stayed in 18a next to the park...

Anna Konno – Cavanagh: Theresa O'Neil, she was my Aunty. My Granny Madge lived in No13. I remember Elm St and the park.

Mae Donnelly: We stayed upstairs from Teenie Smith, next door to Mrs McInally, what great days those were!

Thea Borland Mcnamee: Lynn wis she no in Hawthorn Place or wis that Betty Kelly's mam? Stayed last hoose in Elm Street doon stairs.

Lynn Kelly: May Young Breen your aunty Lizzie Kelly was my granny. X

Janette Brown: ma Granny stayed opposite it #11 Elm Street.

Stonefield Parish Church

The foundation stone of the new Church, originally known as the 'Chapel of Ease', was laid in May 1878 by the Rev. Stewart Wright of Blantyre Old Parish Church and Provost John Clark Forrest.

It was the Provost, who donated the land between Elm Street and Church Street where the Church was built.

It was completed in 1880 and cost £5,000 to build (in excess of £560,000 in today's money) and seated 900 people.

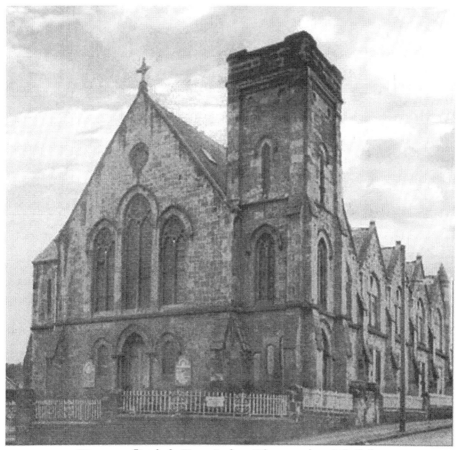

Stonefield Parish Church 1960

The steeple was removed because of subsidence. Note the iron railings which encircled the church.

In 1902, the bell from Blantyre Mill which used to summon David Livingstone to work, was presented to Stonefield Parish Church as a coronation gift.

It continued to be used as the church bell until it was given in 1922 to Low Blantyre Public School. It is now back in the Livingstone Centre.

Sadly, the Church was destroyed by fire on 3rd September 1979 and demolished in 1980.

The fire was apparently caused by a workman's blowtorch being left on when he was working in the roof space.

The new St. Andrew's Church was built on the site.

Thomas Dunsmuir Hartman remembers, "When we Travel west from Murray's Raw's on the Main Street, the next block was taken up by the Stonefield Parish Church and the Church Manse.

They were built in the 1880s and of course the Street running off from the Main Street was called Church Street.

One of the features of the Church was its steeple, and tower, housing a large bell, which when rung could be heard throughout most of Blantyre. Another feature was the large-size masonry stone wall with black iron railings with various gate openings at front and side, the front gates being the most impressive. The church burned down in September 1979.

All of these iron railings and all iron railings without exception in the whole of Blantyre, and anything else with iron in its content was cut down, early 1940s, and used in the war effort. This was very necessary at the time but not a pleasant sight to see after it was done, there was a nakedness throughout the whole village and for many years after the war ended and even up to the present day, most of the iron work has never been replaced.

Most of the Population of Blantyre today has no memory of this event and accepts it as is, but these iron railings throughout Blantyre lent a slight Victorian tinge of privacy to the various buildings and surroundings.

If you are walking through Blantyre and are passing a wall take a look, and you will most likely see small pieces of iron embedded in the masonry.

Church Street was a fairly upscale area to live in. Most if not all the homes were of a large masonry stone just like the church, they were a bungalow type home with all the latest conveniences. A small Street with roughly 6 homes east side and 10 on the west side.

Situated three-quarters of the way down on the west side there was a small wooded area which ran from Church Street through to the next street west called Logan Street, this small wooded area was called St John's wood, why I do not know? In all my years living there, I had maybe heard it called by this name a couple of times at the most, and yet the name has stuck in my memory.

There is a story to be told on this little wooded area which I will cover when we move on to the Logan Street Saga.

Church Street ended into a pasture for cows at its top end, unlike most of the other streets running south which so far have all finished up in Auchinraith Road".

This is part of a conversation between **Thomas Dunsmuir Hartman** in Chicago and **Margaret** in Queensland Australia on TalkingScot.

Your Memories:

Sheena Thomson: I was married in this church in 1969.

Jane Paterson: Our friends were married there also. X

Sandra Goodall: It was a beautiful church such a shame about the fire. I went to Stonefield and St Andrews, and a church is about the people so it's still a beautiful church.

Helen Henderson Mclaughlin: I was married there a few months before the fire and it was beautiful inside and out.

Masonic Buildings

We next come to Church Street and the Masonic Buildings built in three stages. The first shop on this block was a Millinery Store which sold all kinds of cotton, needles, and lace for the local gentry. The next shop was a greengrocer.

The next large door on the block was the entrance to the Masonic Lodge or Masonic hall as we called it, big double door with brass fittings, quite in contrast to the other doors around.

Mary Boyle: I remember this block well. First ground flat was owned by my Aunt Cathy McQueenie. She used to park her ice cream van behind the telephone box.

Obviously, as time passed, the shops changed in both ownership and type of produce sold. Here we have Miller's (not sure if this is Matha the Pole's Shoe Shop before relocating).

Entrance to the Masonic Lodge and Hall, Greenhorn Flesher's, i.e. Butchers, then a Printer & Stationers and James Houston.

More recently we had Dr Hutchison's surgery, Millinery, Greengrocers, Masonic Temple & Hall, Bowie's Florist, fruit & veg, James Aitkenhead Butcher, later Craig's the Butchers, where the cow's sheep and pigs were strung up in the store, with some in the refrigerator, but most of the time they just hung up in the store.

Bob Craig was lucky that he was not far from the local slaughter house in John Street and could get his fresh meat very quickly. Then we had Mathieson's the

Jeweller, Scottish Clydesdale Bank, the Priory Bar and then Logan Street.

For those of you, who are a wee bit lost, here is an aerial photo which puts it into perspective.

Middle left, Stonefield Parish Church, then Church Street, Masonic Buildings, Priory Bar then Logan Street.

The Drill Hall is above Masonic Buildings.

Top of John Street, bottom right with Castle Vaults on the corner of Glasgow Road.

Your Memories:

Jean Gibson: It was Davidson the butcher, Craig's was opposite Ness's school.

Moyra Lindsay: My mum started working in the fruit shop when she turned 14 that was in 1933. Mrs Young owned it then. Davidson's lived in one of the semidetached bungalows opposite your gran in Broompark Rd. Mrs D was a lovely lady.

Mae Donnelly: I remember going in Bowie's before school in the morning!

Robert McLeod-Wolohan: The Priory Bar was my local pub when I was a teenager. That seems so far away now, wish I could go back to the good old days lol.

Len Northfield: The slaughterhouse and butchers, before Peter Craig took it on, was my grandfather's, Jimmy Aitkenhead.

John Mcgaulley: Davidson's the butchers, I worked there in 1964.

The Priory Bar – Glasgow Road at Priory Place

The priory bar was a fairly large bar compared to the other pubs in Blantyre, and it was central so it was very well patronized by the miners, and they did sell a very good McEwan's pint.

The pub had a main bar room with a large nearly round type bar with tables around to sit down on, which was fairly unique in Blantyre, as in most pubs you stood at the bar, as close as the crowd would let you, and drank your pint.

The floor like the butcher's shop was covered in sawdust to catch all the dribbling's and spittle's of beer, there was a lot of smoking going on so the place was always reeking of smoke and fag-ends everywhere with the occasional spittoon scattered around, hence the use of the sawdust, they just sweep up every night and in doing so collected all of this garbage.

They also had a private room which was held in reserve for large family parties or business gents with deals to discuss.

Another smaller room was for the ladies, where all the old local grannies and others could go in and have a wee dram. This room was very private and had a sliding window which opened directly on to the bar, allowing only the bartender to see who was ordering the drink. Everything was hush-hush about this room and about the people who used it.

There was also another Sliding door where you could go and order out a few bottles of beer (The original carrie-oot) and have your tin pail filled up with draft beer. This was sold by the pint and was a little cheaper than buying it at the bar. The miner liked that drop of beer to sup as he was washing himself in the big tin tub in front of the fire.

On a Friday, you would see a lot of kids making for the carry-out with a jug or container in their hands, no one ever questioned a child's age or why they were in the pub. It was always taken for granted that he was there for his dad's beer.

The Priory Bar - Glasgow Road at Priory Place (Logan Street)

Another view of The Priory Bar showing the side entrance to the Lounge Bar in Logan Street.

It was often frequented by Free Masons because of the adjacent Masonic Hall.

The wee white building to the right was a bookie's office. The punters must have thought they were in heaven, Masonic Lodge, pub and bookies in one block.

Davie Tallis, Mary Meechan and Caroline Baird's mum worked behind the bar, and Caroline's dad was on the door. That's where they got together.

Most of the inhabitants of Logan Street would drink here, as did my friend, Jim Cornfield and his dad, not only because of its close proximity, but also because they sold a good pint of Tennent's beer.

Just to give you your bearings, this photo is looking east from Logan Street on the right.

GLASGOW ROAD, BLANTYRE

Where it says, Wines is the Priory Pub and the pointed roof beyond is the Masonic Building. The pointed roof opposite is the Castle Pub at the corner of John Street.

The boy on the right is standing outside the Ironmongers, J.C. Sweet's cut price shop on the corner of the Turner's Building on the right which had a park next to it, where the brass and silver bands would practice, and then there was the new Drill Hall.

Your Memories:

Caroline Baird: My mum worked behind the bar and my dad was on the door, always hear them talking about it, that's where they got together.

Eleanor Duncan Nailon: I remember going to the Priory with my mum on a Saturday afternoon, the good old days. I think I was 11.

Maggie Tallis: My dad Davie Tallis worked there, so did my aunt Mary Meechan, brings back good memories.

John Cornfield: I was in this pub once or twice when I was a boy, my dad frequented it as a young man as it was my granddad's local being of good Logan Street stock.

Bim Mcskimming: It had best pool team ever.

Kathleen McDermott: Good memories of that pub. They had a great sing songs in there.

Liz Daley: Lots of memories of that pub, all good.

Fiona Broadley Semple: Love this pic... we lived in the house above, it was huge ... I used to climb up and sit on the roof... my bedroom had the Wm. Youngers man outside it... memories.

Jean Brown: Fiona I remember your home so well, we had great fun playing in it... it was huge! X

Logan Street Territorial Force Association.

Drill Hall F Coy, 6th Cameronians.

There was a territorial drill hall for the Scottish Cameronians Rifles Regiment in Logan Street where a lot of soldering went on and never more so as on the 3rd September 1939, when war was declared.

You could not move up or down the street because of the amount of bodies, all trying to enrol in the army, they were shipping them out by the truck loads, where to, I never did find out. They were all so keen to go.

Next to the drill hall, was the place called St John's Wood. This was an area of about 3 acres of trees and ran between Church Street and Logan Street.

Drill Hall, F Coy, 6th Cameronians

It was in here that one of the greatest parties ever held in Blantyre was held, and that was VE NIGHT.

Amelia Kane wrote: "I have fond memories of this building. Which was renamed The Elizabeth Scott Centre in my time. Our family lived near the top of Logan Street & there were great youth clubs, play schemes there. It created great community spirit. Happy memories here, thanks for sharing."

Blantyre Post Office

Dating from 1960, this was the main Post Office in Blantyre at the corner of Logan Street and Glasgow Road, in what used to be Turner's Building.

A map surveyed in 1859 shows the post office of the time on Station Road, just within the confines of the Mill

Village where most of the population of Blantyre resided.

The post office was eventually moved to the Clydeview Shopping Centre.

Opened in 1980 as part of Blantyre's redevelopment, the shopping centre is busy, although not very easy on the eye.

The Post Office has now moved to the Old Co-op Building adjacent to Station Road on Glasgow Road.

The Turner Buildings ran from the Post Office along Glasgow Road until it reached Craig Street.

Turner's Building, this was a row of three-story tenements with the bottom house going all the way back to the back side of the building. The 2nd and 3rd floors were reached by a freestanding staircase to the back. All toilets were outside on the Landings.

The building included J. C. Sweet on the corner which was demolished and replaced by the Post Office, then there was a General Store, Dr Stewart's surgery, Scobie's Sweet shop, Co-op Chemist, Ladies Hairdressers, & Dr Gordon's Surgery and then Craig Street.

N.B. Despite what you may have read elsewhere, there has never been a Post Office on Stonefield Road.

Your Memories:

Jane Paterson: I used to go to the back door in the morning and pick up the mail in an old-fashioned leather satchel the cross the road to Little's for the rolls. I was the Office Junior in Blantyre Engineering in Forrest St. Down past the Vic's Club in 1974 then promoted to the Buying Dept. I was trained on the old fashioned plug board (switchboard) ahh lovely memories...

Boski Bell: A can mind going in one door and coming oot the bottom ae Logan St, even when it was mobbed, coz there was always at least 4/5 fast workers on at 1 time. MINTED!!!

Thomas Barrett: When I was a boy till they knocked it down it was known as the new post office.

Alan Burnett: God a blast fae the past.

Maryon Allan: I always called it the old post office coz it wis only there a cpl of years after I was born till they moved it to the pet shop.

Mattie Taggart: We used to get our family allowance out of it on a Monday nothing for the first one and 7 shillings and 6 pence for the second one about 35 pence, so that is what you got. I don't think you could do much with that.

Mary McGuigan: All the queues before 9, my dad used to be there at half 8 why I don't know lol x.

Mary Wood: My sister Helen worked there.

Christina Frame: I remember seeing this being built!

Sadie Dolan: Loved running in one door and out the other lol great memories!!! Used to go for my mams family Allowance.

Margaret Bell: Me tae Sadie. They were the days. Not a care in the world. Post office, then Little's the bakers for the rolls. Xx Brilliant, remember the queue on a Mon morning lol. Xx

Christine Brown: They used to come to the back door for their giros so they would be first in. I worked there as a cleaner, we also had a zephyr zodiac car lol.

Carolyn Patterson: I used to queue up every week with my mum to collect the family allowance... lol great memories.

Nancy McFadden: Loved how cool the tiles were in the summer, and buying stamps to save for my summer holidays.

Annie Murdoch Anderson Black: Remember the telephone boxes in there and my Uncle John's Zephyr Car, thank you so much for sharing all these memories that we have in Blantyre.

Bill Sim: My aunt Lilly worked at the Post Office as a cleaner. My sister Cathie, who worked for Blantyre Engineering, first visited the new Post office when it opened in 1960, to collect her firm's National Insurance stamps.

Harper's Garage

Harper's Garage is at the bottom left of the photo on Craig Street and to the right is the Central Building.

Across Glasgow Road is Hart's Land or (Hert's Lawn) as they say in Blantir.

Photo Source **BritainfromAbove** Sent in by **Andy Lynch**

On the right-hand side of the photo (although not too clear) is Stonefield Primary School, better known as Ness's.

Near the middle is the Wee School with the dining room at the back. (White building)

The road to the right is Victoria Street and where it crosses Calder Street is the Police Station and across Calder Street is Calder Street Junior Secondary School.

To the right of Calder Street J.S. School is the Health Centre opposite McAlpine's in the Park.

Thomas Dunsmuir Hartman remembers, 'Craig Street as we once knew it has been cut in half by the new shopping centre, Main store on the sight being 'Asda supermarket'. It took up the first half of Logan Street, Craig Street and Victoria Street one huge store and parking lot.

Where the Turner's Building ends on the Glasgow Road, there was an open piece of land before you hit the corner of Craig Street. Why this was never built on in my lifetime in Blantyre. I do not know, as it had a very prominent position on the Main Street.

This piece of land ran for about 100 yds. On the left-hand side of Craig Street travelling south and was also a shortcut for us Logan Street kids to cut across for our trip to school and to make our way west through Blantyre.

On the other corner of Craig Street stood Harper's Garage, this was the main garage in Blantyre for Repairs and the fuelling of any cars that came through the village and was the main garage for the hire of Limousines for weddings, funerals, etc.

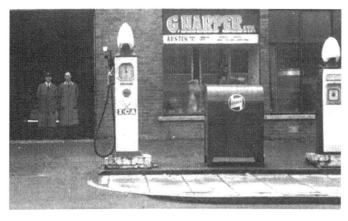

Gilbert Harper was the original owner and builder of the garage in 1934. Next to it was Watts the dentist with Oreste's a wee bit further west.

Brian McLaughlin who owned a local undertaker's business, Felix McLaughlin's, later purchased Harper's garage and ran the business from there. It was known then as The Central Garage.

There were about six private bungalows after the open space, then a sawmill and Joiners yard. Then about another 100 yards of 2 storey Tenement type buildings, with the stairs and

The garage was demolished in 1979. Photo by Jim McGuire

toilets attached to the back side of the building. We are now about half-way up to the left-hand side of Craig Street.

If we go back down to the start of Craig street on the right-hand side going south.

The Harper's Garage and the work's yard took up about 100 yards and where it finished it was on the same line as the Bungalows on the other left-hand side of the road, and here we had the start of about six bungalows on this right-hand side of the street, a bit of uniformity.

But unlike the other side of the street where we had a line of 2 storey tenements. On this side of the road, we had a long line of attached single homes with a confectionery store at each end of this block, both of which did very well with the three schools in near proximity. Calder Street School (senior), Ness's School (junior) and Auchinraith School (junior).

At the end of the Bungalows on this right-hand side of Craig Street was an opening which a lot of the kids used as a shortcut over to Ness's School and for anyone travelling west. This entrance opened up on to a field or waste ground, where all the kids in the neighbourhood met to play, it also led over to the Honeymoon in Victoria street where I was born, so as you can imagine I knew this area fairly well, even after we left this area I went back often to play with my wee pals.

This is part of a conversation between **Thomas Dunsmuir Hartman,** Chicago and **Margaret** in Queensland, Australia on **TalkingScot**.

Your Memories:

Alan Baird: The colonel served his time as a mechanic in there.

Janette Brown: ma Auntie Marion Aitchison worked in there until it closed. She died not long ago.

Elspeth Shirkie: My dad worked there.

Bill Sim: Wee Brick Bradford took the boys in our class at Calder Street J.S. School down to Harper's Garage one day to see the new arrival of the Ford Capri, not the model that we all fell in

love with, but the original model as we see here. So, they had changed from British Leyland to become a Ford Dealership.

The building from Harper's Garage going west on Glasgow Road is the Central Building, also called Hill's Paun building, which included The Ale House – A Public House opposite the Central Bar, which served only Ale, hence its name. It closed in the early 1900s then opened as Hill's Pawnbrokers, latterly Oreste's. Then Dr Gordon's surgery, Haddow's Dentist, Head Master's Bungalow, Ness's School and then Victoria Street.

Ness's School

Glasgow Road and Ness's school, corner of Victoria Street after Annfield Terrace was demolished. Hastie's Farm on the right.

Sent in by **Jack Owens**

The windows are boarded up so this is just before the school was demolished in the mid-sixties. It was later replaced by the "Broo" and then by Casper's night club and is now the Public Library. All things considered, I would have preferred that the school remained, as it had so many memories for thousands of people and a place in history with the likes of Major John Ness. This will never be said about Casper's or the Library.

This waste ground was cleaned up and used as an open Market on Tuesdays, which became very popular.

Major John Ness

Monday 26th October 1875 was the opening of Ness's School, as it was affectionately known, was named after Major John Ness, who was the Headmaster of the Blantyre Works School from June 1st 1856 - 1874, prior to becoming headmaster of Stonefield Parish Primary School, formerly known as Stonefield Parish School, where he remained for 32 years.

The School was demolished in 1978 and became the Labour Exchange, then Casper's Nightclub and is now the Public Library.

It's a little-known fact that Major Ness was primarily responsible for one of only two visits from Africa to Blantyre by David Livingstone. He wrote to him when he was attending lectures in London asking him if he would give an address at a soiree of the members of the Blantyre Literary and Scientific Institute. Livingstone originally declined saying that he had to return to his adopted Country, Africa, as his work was by no means finished. He also stated that he could not speak well in English and had no wish to learn again.

Ness did not give up and approached Livingstone's Mother, who lived at Peacock Cross in Hamilton, for her help. She wrote to her son and so David Livingstone returned to Blantyre and attended the soiree.

Front View of Ness's School 1904

Major John Ness, having spent fifty years of his life as a Head Master, both at the Blantyre Works School and Stonefield Parish School, must have been a character of influence in all matters to do with Blantyre.

Front view of "The Wee School"

The Wee School, as it was affectionately called, was behind the main Ness's School.

Jack Owens: Classroom on the left was where Miss Brown Knocked the "Left-handed Devil" out of me and left me scarred for life.

Rear of Wee School and Dining Hall

L/h Victoria Place known locally as the Honeymoon, (Annfield Place)

The Wee School and Dining Hall

Ness's and the dining hall were used as tech-drawing and metalwork classes by Calder Street School.

This is part of a conversation between **Thomas Dunsmuir Hartman** in Chicago (known as TDH or Drapadew) and **Margaret** in Queensland Australia on TalkingScot.

Hello TDH

Just a quick question to you, have you heard of a school referred to as The Ness's School?

Margaret

Thank you Margaret, I do know Ness's school very well as I was born 30yds from the school in a miners raws with the very unusual name of THE HONEYMOON. I KID YOU NOT. How it got that name I could never find out, still trying. There is a great photo on the front cover of OLD BLANTYRE showing a policeman, the building directly over his shoulder is Ness's School.

Hello Drapadew

The reason I asked was that my Granddad John Morton was the school Janitor there for many years till his death. When my brother visited Glasgow and the Masonic Lodge (which my brother and Dad were members, also my Granddad) he was well remembered as Johnny Morton from Ness's school. I am not sure what year he started there but at his death in 1945 age 71 it is recorded that he was a School Janitor so guess he was still putting in a day's work in 45.

Love the name of your Row, and I too would be interested in knowing why it was named that.

(Note from Bill: It was nicknamed, "The Honeymoon", because Victoria Place or Annfield Place was where newly marrieds' were housed in a single room.)

Your Memories:

Carolyn Patterson: Can anyone remember the markets that used to be held at the front of Hastie's around 1972/1973 or maybe just a little later??? They sold everything lol. X

Stuart Christie: I attended Ness's for a time in the early 1950s and I have vivid recollections of a coal fire burning in the classroom; it must have been winter.

Patrick Mcdonagh: I remember years ago coming back from another adventure over in the leafy and rich streets of Bothwell, after a night of being a nuisance to the locals, one of many schemes to make a penny was to go behind the Silvertrees Hotel, and get the empty Babycham bottles, you could get lot up your juke and top bucks for them, off we would go back to Blantyre we would go to the Cosy Corner, we went to cash them in, we were barred from the Village Bar at an early age, after we cashed in, up to Vince's, we went for a bag of chips and a packet of fags between us, and a bob or two for school in the morning.

One night on this bit of wasteland at Hastie's Farm, we spied a big yellow bulldozer and being foolish boys we started it up. What a fright we got, the noise was deafening, could not turn it off, thankfully it did not move, but you never seen a bunch of boys move so fast in your life, just another day in the life of a Blantyre boy.

Helen Grieve: Looks like it was taken from my mums back garden. We went to that school, well my big brother and me, wee brother was the first P1 at DLMP.

Richard Rankin: Can mind the market at front of Hastie's, especially the toffee apples hanging on the top bar of the sweetie stall.

Tracey McDougall: Brilliant Bill, never knew that one! B4 my time though.

Julie Anne Lindsay: I work above the library, never knew there was a school there.

Mary Wood: What a great photo... This part of Blantyre pops up in my dreams... Strange...

Tom McGuigan: Was the Broo in that building too or Labour exchange to give it the proper name, remember going in with my Da on one of the few occasions he had to sign on.

Jim McDougall: Fond Memories my first school 1947. And of my big sister Margaret dragging me to school.

Frances Clelland: It was a pub before it was Casper's, was talking to my brother about this tonight, neither of us can remember the name of the pub can anyone help driving us nuts!!

Carolyn Patterson: I can remember getting off the school bus to go to the markets that were there for some time.

Ann Millar: I went tae Ness's School then fae there I went tae. D. L. M. P. S. and that wisnae yesterday.

Police Station

Police Station. In 1915, there were seven Police officers living in the Police Station, One Inspector, Two Sergeants and Four Constables. The Inspector paid an annual rent of £ 20, and the Sergeants and Constables paid £15.00 per annum.

The School Janitor across the road at 4 Calder Street paid £18.

Blantyre Police Station today, photo by **James Brown**.

Just to get our bearings, here we have an Aerial View of Victoria Street showing Ness's Primary School, The Wee School, Victoria Place AKA, 'The Honeymoon,' Blantyre Police Station, Calder Street Secondary School and the Health Centre across from McAlpine's in the Park.

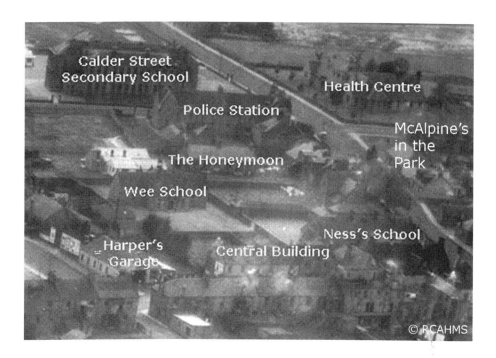

Your Memories:

Laurie Allan Crothers: I remember being at a birthday party in one of the flats upstairs. They were massive inside.

Fran Mcdermott Walters: Our school bus was taken there many a time lol. X

Sadly, at the time of wring, the Blantyre Police Office is scheduled to be closed. To become what? A block of flats? Or worst still, to be demolished?

Public Library

Do you remember this wee Library in Calder Street across from the Miners Welfare?

Built in approx. 1953.

Uncle Cyril wrote: I joined the library on the first day it opened, I then borrowed a book from the Children's Section, read it, and tried to return it on the same-day...

Before the library was built it was an area of humped grassy mounds where we played Cowboys and Indians on the way home from the Dookit's Saturday matinee...

Photo by **Jim Brown**, Feb 9th 2008 just after it closed.

The Library was replaced by a block of Flats.

Your Memories:

Thomas Hamilton-Hailes: I remember the first time I was allowed into the Reference Room: it was like being permitted to enter a cathedral unaccompanied.

Ann Millar: Aye bit a never studied in it, was always gittin told tae shhhhhh, and that wis offie hard fur me to shut ma mooth. Lol

John Mc Dermott: I think I learned more in there than I did at school.

Stuart Christie: Wonderful place, fantastic resource and great librarians; it's where I read The Communist Manifesto, Catch 22 and Stephen Leacock's Arcadian Adventures of the Idle Rich — among many others ...

Ann Higgins Crossar: We used to study for our Highers in the reference room there. Then go to Lightbodies for a chip buttie!

Lynn Cameron: My sister used to work here, she was prob the one who told ye to shhhhh, ha-ha.

Jim Brown: Photo taken Feb 9 2008. Ah remember reading Stuart Christie and Albert Meltzers Floodgates of Anarchy.

Blantyre's Ain: Was that just before demolition Jim?

Jim Brown: Aye it was quite close to the time.

Dorothy Hunter: the steelwork was erected before the war and was not completed till after.

Linda Halpin: Certainly do, loved taking out the LP's when you couldn't afford to buy them... lol

Eleanor Duncan Nailon: Remember we used to go behind library for history lesson.

Margaret McGuigan: I loved this place teenage reading.

Margaret Nimmo Lehmann: Yes, I remember going there in the 60s.

James Gribben: the librarian should have told the wooden floor soosh.

Helen Stewart: Spent many a time choosing books when I was young always got a fine because I was late taking them back. X

Jack Owens: Great place to spend time.

John McCourt: Remember paying the fines for taking back the books late.

Mary Brown: I worked there for a short time when I was a teenager!

Helen Grieve: Remember when it opened. I was round there to get my wee library ticket as soon as it opened.

Angela Timoney: Many a happy hour spent in there.

Margaret Mcculloch: Yes, Maxine I took u there lol

Midlifecrisis: Lorraine N Colin Used to go up n get books for my gran. I'd come bk n she'd say I've read that lol. Xx

Frank Glancy: Used to play football at the side of it lol

Marianna Caserta: I might be wrong coz it was a very long time ago but I think I might have gone to the Latchkey Club after school in there? Can't remember if they moved us there from one of the school buildings or vice versa but it looks familiar.

Shug McNeill: Shhhh

Isabell McGinty Cain: This photo brings back happy memories, when I was a child I thought this was the end of Blantyre, I use to go to the library with my (Maw) my gran every second day, through my Maw I became a lover of reading.

Robert Henderson: Went in there every week.

Elaine Currie: The wee librarian always said shh shhh shhhhhhhh … he he. Xx

Karen Rouse: We used to study in that wee library for our exams Joanna Barrett, Mary-Louise Blue, Emma Welsh and Lorraine Hughes.

Maria L Azul: Lol. Ahhh studying....

Karen Rouse: Think it was the wee front room we studied in. You were allowed to talk in there ha-ha!

Uncle Cyril: I joined the library on the first day it opened, I then borrowed a book from the Children's Section, read it, and tried to return it on the same day...

Before the library was built it was an area of humped grassy mounds where we played Cowboys and Indians on the way home from the Dookit's Saturday matinee...

Blantyre's Ain: Can you remember what year it was built Cyril?

Uncle Cyril: I was in primary, about ten year's old, so I guess it would have been built around 1953...certainly early 50s.

Mary Queen: Remember the dude librarian with long red bushy hair lol ahhh a roll and chips from Lightbodie's was the game sweeties from super sweet.

Eleanor Ferguson Kelly: It had a unique smell...must've been the polished floors. Wonderful!

John See: Of course. There used to be a wee short cut down the side of it and onto the lane behind Asda that we used to take when we are in Primary school across the road.

Mazie Brown: Distant memory seems so long ago

Tracy Stirling: Loved the smell of the old books in there lol.

Theo Priory: Oh, yes and being told to shhh!

Stephen Allan: I do remember the library.

Annie Miller Scoular: I do remember!

Marian Maguire: Yes, a lovely wee library, and far easier to access than the present one if you, have mobility problems.

Chris Good: I think I've still got a book to return to it

Winifred Murphy: My cousin and I loved the library and read our way through children's and adults sections....

Elizabeth Dobson Grieve: Was in there a lot when I was younger.

Catherine Stewart: Why do they always say it will be better loved this building got 4 books at a time, have never been in the new one.

Julie Anne Screen: I loved that wee library, was sad when they knocked it down.

John Hand: I remember it very well. But I didn't know that they had knocked it down as I live 200mil away in Portknockie and I haven't been back for about 10 years.

Jane Davies: Yes, I remember it well in the late 40s/early 50s when I read all the Agatha Christie books there.

Sally Fisher: I remember it well I used to go in there from Calder Street School. X

Moira McMenemy: Brilliant wee place. Sad loss to Blantyre.

Anna Carroll: Lived beside it, before Asda was there

Gerry Gillies: My uncle frank and auntie rose worked there.

Susan Walker Graham: Loved this library.

Edith Bulloch: was there every day when I was young.

Fiona Allen: Yes, I loved this place. X

Keith Mccormack: Asda got s knock back as they wanted to build on to their store councillors said it was a listed building but they did and gave permission for the flats.

Laurie Allan Crothers: Couldn't believe it when they pulled it down. Thought it was a listed building, but then I thought the PO building at the bottom of Logan Street was listed and look what happened to that.

Helen Whyte Dyer: loved that place.

Congregational Church c1880

Neil Gordon gives a very good account of the previous Congregational Church building in his book, 'Blantyre – An Historical Dictionary', before it was demolished in 1954.

Neil wrote: 'Written on a parchment, found behind one of the foundation stones, when the church was eventually demolished in 1954, was a short history of the church which read, Rev H Liddell called the church "Evangelical

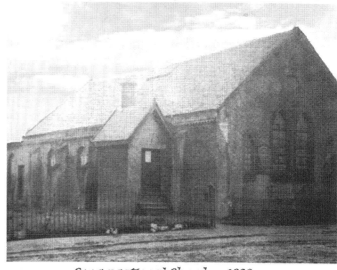

Congregational Church c1880

Union Church," and construction commenced on 10th April 1878. In 1878, the Rev William Wylie was accepted as minister and was inducted on 5th May that year.'

The church was demolished when it was discovered that underground workings had made the building unsafe. In 1920, when the structural faults became apparent, a special fundraising effort was started in order to finance the reinforcement of the church and re-slate the roof, which was in need of repair.

The present church was constructed on the same site at

Craig Street, which was formerly called, 'Slag Road' and was probably owned by John Craig, a local landowner, who, thought Neil, was also a benefactor of the early church considering that his property was used as a

temporary church in 1877. The present Congregational Church was constructed and opened for worship in 1958.

Your Memories:

Nancy McFadden: This is the church that I went to when I was growing up, what a great minister was Mr.

Patterson and Mr. Livingstone the head of the Sunday school, I still have a Sunday school prize from there.

Ian Dino McDougall: I remember Mr. Patterson too. I think he was the school vicar? Happy memories.

Laurie Allan Crothers: I went to this church and the Sunday school when I was young. Long before Mr. Patterson. My sister, Mhairi, got married there in 1979. A lovely wee church.

Blantyre Miners Welfare Society & Social Club.

The Welfare Institute was established in Blantyre in 1928 with the social club being opened in 1958, the Bowling Club in 1964 and most recently, the Resource Centre in 2008.

The original Miners Welfare was partly funded by Andra McInulty and the Auchinraith Silver Band.

Charles McGuigan,

back row fourth from the left. Mr. Scott seated last right hand side.

Your Memories:

Hi,

What a great joy, looking at photos of the Old Blantyre to see my Grandpa – Robert Scott – 104 Victoria Street, Blantyre.

Seated last on the right-hand side.

We came to Australia in 1958, so I never saw him again after that.

My brother John continued the family tradition of caring for his fellow workers, Trade Union Secretary and finally A Federal Member of Parliament for the Australian Labor Party.

He has just published his Memoir – "Glasgow Road to Canberra" He will be delighted that his Grandpa is on your web page.

Thank you for brightening my day all the way to Adelaide, South Australia.

Regards,

Mary (Scott) Sitters.

John Cornfield wrote: All of my family who have lived since the welfare opened all on every side have used this place. My mam and dad had their Wedding Reception in what is now the Resource Centre. We also had my mam and dad's funeral reception here. For me, a big club with a big place in my heart. Long may it prosper.

Margaret Stewart: My wedding reception was held here in 1969.

Carole Marie Deplacido: My wee work place.

Calder Street Junior Secondary School

Calder Street Junior Secondary School, built 1912, later to become Auchinraith Primary School. The Building was demolished end of June/July 2011 and replaced by a modern building, losing all of its previous character. I find it very sad that this fabulous Red Sandstone Building, a landmark in Blantyre, was allowed to be demolished.

On 1st July 2011, I got a phone call from my sister Essie. She was almost in tears. She said, "They're demolishing Calder Street. You'd better get yourself down here quick. I don't believe it." I had no transport that day but ran as fast as I could, with camera in hand, and couldn't believe what I saw! I took these photos, some from standing on the Police wall.

Head Masters Office - No More

Reduced to a Pile of Rubble

So, so Sad

New Auchinraith Primary School

Replaced by a pre-fabricated, characterless, eyesore box...

Your Memories:

Annie Murdoch Anderson Black: I loved Mr. Bradford, he really helped me get my English O'Level and I had a class reunion many years ago and we were all delighted to see him there. I was so sad to hear he had passed away. He gave me a lovely card with beautiful sentiments in it and I still have it.

Elizabeth Dobson Grieve: I went to that school as well and my late father attended as it was Calder Street junior secondary. It's a sad loss.

Robert Crothers: I went to it... Joe Maize was head teacher.

David Brown: I was there between 1964 and 1968.

Mary Sambou: I went there 68 to 72 best years of my life.

Robert McLeod-Wolohan: I went there between 1963 till 1967, it was a brilliant secondary school and Wee Brick was the best teacher there at the time, so sad it's gone now.

Ina Sanders: That's the school I went to.

Mary Davies: My old secondary school.

Paul Hudson McGowan: A great looking old building. It should have been saved and renovated or something but just to tear it down and then replace it with a Pre-fab is just plain wrong. In terms of architecture they have been ripping the heart out of the place for years.

Jimi O'neill: They knocked a school down that would have stood as long as the pyramids and replaced it with a tin can!

Alison Walker-Hill: Scandalous!

Margo Haughen: Heart-breaking.

Kathleen McDermott: I agree. I won't know Blantyre anymore with all the buildings being demolished when I come back home. I remember playing netball there.

Carolyn Patterson: I agree, its sad (when I return to Blantyre to visit family, from New Zealand) and more buildings have disappeared, also years ago I was back and the public park had houses in it, it's just not right!

Annie Murdoch Anderson Black: I was back home recently and it tore my soul out to see this wonderful building my school no longer there. I honestly did cry and walked away thinking about the wonderful memories I had in there. Why did they take this down? Lol x This breaks my heart and bloody soul, why did they demolish this school, my Mum, Aunties and Uncles went there? Bloody disgusting!

Allan Love: I always thought that this school was a listed building watch this space the next building to go will be the police station.

Len Northfield: I've watched Whifflet School, over in Coatbridge, being demolished recently. All the memories and laughter and greetin' that went on in, and about these buildings. It does seem very sad that they're replaced by something without character.

Carol Lush: So many memories. Sad.

Fran Mcdermott Walters: Sad to see nice buildings demolished x

Ishbel McKinlay-Wilkie: How sad is this Bill!!

Finally, to remind you how it was before demolition, with the New Auchinraith Primary School behind,

I would like to share this excellent photo by Blantyre Photographer, **Jim Brown** with you.

Victoria Street

Next to Calder Street, Secondary School was Victoria Street, which ran from Glasgow Road, south to Main Street High Blantyre.

Victoria Street, formerly called the 'Clay Road', was never a main thoroughfare and nothing of any significance was ever built on it.

The street had a funny ending to it when it finished at the Main Street in High Blantyre. It narrowed down to a passageway not even wide enough for a cart to pass through, only wide enough at its widest point to let 2 pedestrians pass, shoulder to shoulder.

Immediately on the left after Calder Street, there was a Council Playground which was very popular by both Calder Street and nearby Auchinraith School pupils.

This was one of my favourite places when I was aged 10 to 12. I would visit this playground almost every day after school at Auchinraith Primary.

From here to the Main Street in High Blantyre, all the rest of Victoria Street is taken up by a Council Scheme known locally as the 'Crescents.'

The scheme has gone through at least 3 types of renovations over the past 70 odd years, but they are still standing and looking good.

The Health Centre has been extended from Calder Street along Victoria Street and past the Health Centre is a Playing Field belonging to the Calderside Academy on Calder Street. This used to be an open field where the farmer from Stonefield Farm allowed his cows to graze.

This is now only used for the outside activities associated with the Academy.

The Witches Hat photo is actually from the David Livingstone Memorial grounds.

The Blantyre Health Institute

On the corner of Calder Street and Victoria Street is the Blantyre Health Institute. Opened on 12th October 1928.

This Institute was used during the war years like a town hall, everything from Gas Masks, Cod-liver oil, Orange Juice, Ration Books, everything that was in short supply and was controlled by the Government was distributed from here to those who were in the category of essential need.

Thomas Dunsmuir Hartman remembers, "I can remember four things in my life associated to the health Institute. The first would be back around 1937 when we as a miner's family were taken up to the health Institute to be deloused. I think the reason behind this was coming from the raw's into a new council house, they wanted to make sure we did not bring any unwanted little beasties with us. When we came out of there we were all covered in a purple paint. Most families in Blantyre went through this, so it was in no way considered degrading, that's just the way it was. I and my three brothers, well we could not care less but my older sister. She was a different story, mortified I believe was the word she used through her tears.

The second item was around about the same time, and it is quite possible that they both went hand in hand. Our family and a lot of other families were all issued new clothes at the health Institute. These clothes and footwear were all donations from the Toc-H. They consisted of a grey flannel jacket, shorts, a white silvery shirt and a pair of Clakity/Clickety Bits.

For the first month in Blantyre, there were all these kids going around all wearing the same type clothes, but they soon got torn and dirty and were often flung aside. Again, my older sister rebelled with the idea of wearing that ankle-length tie up boots, which immediately singled you out as someone who had to be supported through donations. Nothing would make her wear those boots. She was a red-head and had the anger and spirit that seems to go with them.

The third item was the time when the whole town alphabetically had to go to the health Institute for a Smallpox inoculation (or jab's). I can remember the stories that went about on how sore (painful) it was passed around the town by those that had had their inoculation first the A.B.C.D. It was a painful procedure for us kids, but it was blown all out of proportion, so by the time your name came up you were already petrified of what was going to happen to you. There was a lot of squealing and crying before the Doctor or nurse got anywhere near you, all you had to hear was your next, and it was your turn to do your thing.

I can remember I was pretty good at it. This was the inoculation that left you marked for life.

Two or three days after the jab's the whole injection site scabbed over for a couple of weeks and when the scab had formed into a crust, it then dropped off and left you scarred for life. Furthermore, around about this same time in Blantyre we had tuberculosis cases, Scarlet Fever, Diphtheria, Scabies, Chicken Pox, and Mumps', Whooping Cough and Poliomyelitis and various other problems. We did not at this time have the National Health Service so any ailments were taken to your local doctor and as most miners in Blantyre did not have the money to spend on a doctor, it was the norm most of the time, to live and survive with it.

There were not too many families in Blantyre that got away without any deaths in the family through all of these illnesses. Our family and a lot of the families that lived around us all suffered through the years 1926-1945. Those were hard times in Blantyre, more so if the head of the family was out of work up until 1939, as many miners were.

The fourth item Margaret, was to do with my own father, although he had worked the pits from when he was twelve until the beginning of the war 1939, he had managed to get himself from being a miner to being a member of the medical rescue team. He had gone to school to learn First Aid and had passed all his exams through the St Andrew's Ambulance Association, putting him in a much cleaner job and environment and a better hourly salary.

When war was declared, he was immediately called into being a member of the National First Aid Post. Their job was to go to various parts of the country where a rescue team was needed. He spent a whole two weeks in the Clydebank blitz during which time we as a family never knew where he was until he came home. The First Aid Post was in the Blantyre Health Institute during the war, and I used to visit my dad often on my way home from school."

The Health Centre still stands on the same spot, Corner of Calder Street and Victoria Street and in 2002 was enlarged to suit population requirements.

Your Memories:

Elizabeth Weaver: Great to hear stories like this. I remember our mother used to say that when weans wore those donated boots to school, other weans would shout "Pairish bits! Pairish bits!" at them, so I can understand the reluctance of the writer's sister to be seen wearing them. I also remember the cod liver oil and orange juice - I can picture them in their glass bottles, lying at the bottom of the pram (wee brother Brian, inside) as we left the clinic. We were given the cod liver oil every night, followed by a spoonful of Virol, "to take the taste away". It was still vile.

Mary Mcguire: Great stories that should not be forgotten.

Christina Frame: Remember this well!

Irene Steiner: The centre also provided sun ray treatment which I attended once each week. I now live in Auckland New Zealand and my sister Ishbel McKinlay Wilkie contributes to this site.

Hastie's Farm

The Late Mr. John Hastie

Noted Agriculturist and Horse breeder

The passing of Mr. John Hastie at the age of 61 years removed a noted and prominent agriculturalist and certainly one of the largest and most successful breeders of Clydesdale horses of his time. Mr Hastie was a son of the farm, being the eldest son of the late Mr David Hastie of Stonefield Farm, Blantyre, who was also a well-known breeder of Clydesdales.

Trained by such a capable judge, it was only natural that the son should have inherited rare and sound judgment, necessary qualities required for a breeder and dealer. In agricultural circles, he was perhaps one of the most kenspeckle figures in Scotland and his record of service in the interest of the farmer and in horse-breeding is one which could not be excelled by many men.

Hastie's Shire Horse

Thirty-one years ago, the firm of David Hastie & Sons took over Eddlewood Farm, where better facilities and conditions prevailed for housing and rearing stock. The success which attended them in Clydesdales has made the name of Hastie more than a household word amongst Scottish breeders and farmers. He was a life member of the Clydesdale Horse Society and also of the Glasgow Agricultural Society, of which latter society he was a director.

Mr. Hastie was also a member of the Highland and Agricultural Society, and for 30 years he was a member and director of the Lanarkshire Farmers Society. He was also a member and director of the Cambuslang, Blantyre and Rutherglen Society until it terminated two years ago. Up till two years he had been a director of the East Kilbride Society, and also held membership of Biggar, Lanark, West Linton, Larkhall and Strathaven shows, at which he was always an exhibitor as a member of the firm of David Hastie & Sons, of which he was a partner until two years ago, when he retired and took up residence in Largs.

As breeders of Clydesdales he may even have exceeded his father's popularity all over Scotland, as this extended all over Scotland. He did a large business both in buying and selling, and his trade in exporting this class of horse to New Zealand, Australia, Canada and other countries was enormous. As a judge of Clydesdales Mr Hastie was recognised and had the reputation of being one of the ablest and shrewdest on the agricultural board, and his services were in great demand. In this connection, his duties took him to the farthest points of Scotland and at all the principal shows his cheery personality was always welcomed. The soundness of his judgment was never questioned, and as an arbiter he was often called in to adjudicate on many agricultural matters throughout the country.

A Great Curler

As a curler, Mr Hastie had few equals, and as a member of Blantyre Club was one of the most successful skips in the long history of the club. His record on the ice, however, travelled far beyond his local prowess, and on two occasions he had the pleasure and honour of being a member of the team that brought the Royal Trophy to Blantyre. He also skipped the rink that won the Harrowgate Cup at Crossmyloof in 1912, and he was one of the most popular curlers in the old Crossmyloof ice rink. In his internationals, he only lost on one occasion, when the game was played at Moffat. During that period a thaw set in, and only another player and himself were able to throw their stones the full length. He won many prizes in the club in single-handed and points games, but owing to failing health he had to abandon further interest in the "roarin" game two years ago.

As a gentleman, Mr. Hastie had a most lovable personality and enjoyed a wide circle of friends. The esteem in which he was held was manifest by the large attendance of well-known agriculturists from over a wide area who were present at his funeral to High Blantyre Cemetery on Thursday. The cortege was met at the cemetery by a large number of friends from the surrounding neighbourhoods of Hamilton, Eddlewood, Strathaven and Blantyre. Mr. Hastie is survived by his widow and one son and five daughters.

Ref: Hamilton Advertiser. 19/11/1932. Page 8.

Hastie's Farm – a working farm till the 1960s and then a Night Club and Restaurant. The best night out in Blantyre at one time. They came by the bus load. There were more marriages joined and broken here than anywhere else. My Mum worked there when it was a farm, and if she answered the phone she had to say, "Blantyre Five O," and not 5 zero or 5 nothing. It is now Victoria Nursing Home.

Stonefield Farm which was known locally as Hastie's Farm was situated in Victoria Street near to its junction with Glasgow Road. In the 1960s the farm declined to such an extent that it ceased to operate as a working farm and was sold by the Hastie family to Mr. Robert Brown, a local Building Contractor, in 1963. In 1964, Bobby Brown leased out the main farmhouse and an adjoining building to a Taxi firm, whilst he himself opened a room at the right-hand side of the entrance as a small Cafe in which he installed a piano and pianist who provided live music for the customers!

The Taxi firm didn't last very long but the Cafe took off, and I am quite sure that it was then that Bobby Brown got the idea that with further adaptations to the remaining buildings, a Restaurant and Bar could be created within whilst retaining the architecture, heritage and historic old world atmosphere of the original farm!

When the conversion was complete, a food and drinks licence was granted. This together with the fine food, drink, audience participation and live music provided by 'The John Doc Trio' (John Doc, Bryce Sloan and John Healy) plus the unique ambience created within the restored barn, was instrumental in making the farm into a high-class Restaurant and Bar, which was considered by many, to be the best in the West of Scotland.

I must say here that it was during this time that many of our local talents came to the fore when they performed in front of a live audience.

Hastie's Farm Staff Party, Bobby Brown, in Centre.

When in 1979 Bobby Brown decided to retire, and sold the complex onto Sam Plotnikoff, a young business man from Glasgow. Sam carried on the same traditions and high standards of the Bobby Brown era, viz; fine food, drink and live music, etc. I think it would be true to say that he improved Hastie's image, when during a slight recession in trade, he refurbished the small Cafe-cum-lounge and opened it up as Bananas Disco and decided to bring some international stars to the Farm. Some of the celebrities, actors and artists who came to Hastie's at that time, not all to perform, but just to see and be seen was, Matt Munro, Ruby Murray, Frank Ifield, Vince Hill, Marty Wilde, Jiminy Cricket, Alistair McDonald, Russel Hunter, Neville Taylor, Brian Taylor, The Dutch College Swing Band, The Livingstone's, Christian, John Cairney, Aker Bilk, Andy Cameron, Hector Nicol, Jock

Stein. Many of Celtic, Rangers and other Scottish Football team's players were seen from time to time.

In 1985, Sam a business man, decided that due to a slight decline in trade and to give himself some time to attend to his other interests in Snooker Clubs, put the farm up for sale. The 'Farm' was taken over by a Company known as Lanarkshire Holdings.

The Company did not have the same interest or charisma as the two previous owners and trade continued to decline. Conversions were made to the main dining area and other areas within the building which were renamed Zigfields, Barnums, Panama Jacks, Bananas, Happy Jacks respectively, but still the decline continued and the complex closed late 1989.

On Hogmanay night, 1990, just minutes before the bells, a fire was discovered in the roof space of the main building. The Fire Brigade was sent for. On arrival, the entire roof was seen to be involved and damaged to such an extent, that the building was considered unsafe and demolition was recommended. Sometime later, the buildings were demolished, and Blantyre had lost the best Restaurant and Bar, with the best in Entertainment, in the West of Scotland. Call it what you may, Stonefield Farm, will always be known as 'Hastie's Farm' to the clientele who still miss it to this day. "Blantir's no ra same withoot it, sure it's no?"

Acknowledgements:

James Cornfield, Sam Plotnikoff, Frank (Jinxy) Regan, John Rodwell, John Cummiskey, Archie Daly, Margaret Allan, Mary McGinty, Andy Dewar, June Finlay, Cissy Long and many other's.

Lon McIlwraith says, "In 1975, Hastie's burned down. My nana Kathy Brown was in South Africa at the time. She sent a postcard which arrived after the fire, in which she said, "Having a lovely time. See you soon. Keep the home fires burning." Little did she know what had actually happened.

Bobby Brown had the place fully rebuilt and open for business three weeks after the fire. The place was just a busy as ever, but it was never quite the same.

This Hastie's Farm photo shows the place after the rebuild, as can be seen by the newer roof covering most of the length of the building."

By the 1950's Hastie's farm started to go through a change where it was turned into a Restaurant and Banqueting Facilities. Over the years, it became very well-known in Lanarkshire and drew a fairly large crowd most nights.

It had to have been going for nearly 30 years before it was sold and in its place now stands a Retirement Home called Victoria Nursing Home.

Further up the street, there quite a Fruit, Vegetable, and Plant Nursery where a lot of the locals bought their tomatoes and seedlings for their allotments or small holdings."

Your Memories:

Lon McIlwraith - Vancouver (Grandson of Bobby Brown.)

Before it was a pub it was a National petrol station and service garage. The disused pumps and wee glass office were still there years later, you had to drive through them into the back-parking lot.

Hi Bill

I'm not quite sure why I looked up Blantyre today but came across the website showing Hastie's Farm. The write-up talked about the time when it was a night club and yes, I was in that too but as I sat at the bar, I was telling my husband that's where the office was, that's where the pit was, garages down that end and Grannie lived over there.

Yes, I am the eldest granddaughter of Mary and John Cunningham who owned and farmed it for many a long year. My aunt Betty is the only surviving child and should you wish to get some older history of Hastie's I'm sure she would love to help you. I remember running around the yard and being told to keep out of the pit where my uncle was working under a car. He also drove the wedding car, and we often were to be found outside the Burleigh church on a Saturday waiting for the bride coming out. Grannie always had a few pennies in her apron in case none had been dropped inside the car - I only found this out many years later.

My other grandparents owned Gilmour's Draper shop on the Glasgow Road - and there is a photograph in the booklet Hamilton and Old Blantyre.

I was so pleased to see the photograph of Hastie's on the website - there is another one, which hangs in Hamilton Ice Rink, and it has the Hastie boys with their Curling Trophy played for on the local pond. This is no small trophy. I can assure you, and they were founder members of the club. The trophy should now be in Hamilton Museum as this is the first year it won't be played for due to smaller club size but my Aunt wanted it to remain within the area.

Thanks for bringing back some very good memories.

Regards

Joan Anderson (nee Gilmour)

Lon McIlwraith: Bobby Broon kept pigs, chickens and even a donkey doon at the end of the yard. Auld Charlie tended to them and kept a wee greenhouse going too. Bobby Broon fed the pigs with all the leftover food and beer slops from Hastie's' three kitchens and bars. An urban farm long after the original farm had gone.

Thomas Dunsmuir Hartman remembers, "On the left-hand corner of Victoria Street looking south, stood Ness's School. On the other side of the street was the start of a tenement type building (Annfield Terrace), which continued up the Glasgow Road. On the corner of this tenement building was a grocery store. (Gibson's shop grocery & provisions).

Further on up past the tenement building was the entrance to Hastie's Farm.

This was a farm as I knew it in the 1930s it had cows and a dairy with a lot of stable space, which was used by the farmer and local carters for sheltering their horses.

I can remember the large cobble stones through-out the yard and all of the slipping and sliding that went on those frosty mornings when they were first brought out of the stables to be harnessed, they seemed to have a sense telling them that they had to tread much more carefully on a morning like this. Most of the horses were Clydesdales."

John Cornfield says, "I worked here on the door when it was Hastie's Farm then the front end was Bananas and the big room at the back was still Hastie's this was when Sam Plotnicoff had it.

Then James Mortimer bought it and changed the front to Barnum's and the back to Ziegfield's, very state of the art nightclub of its time. Two of the doormen who were the best ever in Blantyre who Worked there when it was Hastie's were Mr Terry White and Mr John Rodwell, I have much respect for both who've sadly passed away."

Colleen Mitchell: I used to go there when I was really young for my dinner! Can still remember the inside, good memories.

Boski Bell: Can mind the last few years of HASTIES, before it was turned into ZIEGFIELDS / ZIGGIES. That we aw went tae every weekend, or 50p a drink night, pmsl.

Len Northfield: My first job was at Hastie's.

Eddie Mcguire: I spent the best years of my life ducking and diving oot a that building, wish it was still here. It had a character I have never came across anywhere else, don't know what it is was. I loved the smell, the oak beams, the brass, the food, the big chunky pint tumblers with a handle, don't forget could go on and on great times.

Stuart Oneil: 50/50. Ziggy's on a Thursday nite, the place was heaving! 50p to get in/50p a drink.

Maureen McGilligan Downie: Do u remember the Tuesday Market in front of Hastie's Farm.

Stevie Brown: I would love to have seen Hastie's back in the day. Bobby Brown was my great uncle, and my dad told me how great the place used to be and would be mobbed most of the time. My mum also has fond memories of the place.

Maureen McGilligan Downie: Stevie, my Mum worked for your Uncle Bobby and he used to let me go in after school and wait for my Mum to finish work. I would get a plate of chips and a juice and one day we had a thunder storm and he drove all the workers home in his Rolls Royce, he was a lovely Man. x

Irene Berry Milligan: I had my wedding reception there in June 73.

Carolann Bate Graham: I have so many memories of Hastie's, my Dad (Gary Bate) worked for Sam and we would go down and help wash glasses at charity nights and I always remember the place always being heaving!

Liz Miller: I speak of it often... it was a great place to go. Was a regular, it's so sad how a great place always vanishes ... great memories... born 'n bread from Blantyre... the good old days...

Fran Mcdermott Walters: Happy memories of that place. X

Gordon McInnes Finbow: That's a blast from the past. My mum and dad used to take me there quite frequently.

Audrey Marshall: I remember the market too and the chicken in a basket - 70s heaven!

Catherine McConnell: remember leaving 12 0'clock Mass at communion to get a good table on a Sunday...lol

Billy Purse: my maw worked in the kitchens, so did I, loved it when the teachers came doon a hid their fish n chips an am sitting eating spare ribs and king prawns... magic it was.

Laurie Allan Crothers: My dad worked for Bobby Broon as a builder. He built the big 'back end' as he called it. Thursdays and Saturdays were the big 'singsong' nights. This is where I made my singing debut in Blantyre at the ripe old age of 11. Sang with the John Doc Trio. Brilliant.

Fran Mcdermott Walters: our mammy worked there as well. Betty McDermott, and so did we all in the end lol.

Karen Feelie: I can remember a wee market on the ground where the home was, I was a wee lassie then and that is where a got my ears pierced.

Helen Dyer: I had my wedding reception at Hastie's Farm... 1973... Took my friends daughter to the market to get her ears pierced and she got up and ran away after the woman did the first ear. I had to chase her through the market to bring her back. She didn't get the other one done... lol it was so funny.

Marie McDermott: Was my first job. Helped out in the kitchen when there was shows on. Worked with Cissy. She was the boss. Then I used to clean with my mum.
Betty McDermott: When it was Ziggy's. The women's toilets were worse than the men's. Lol fact. Xx

Fran Mcdermott Walters: Same here sis, then got promoted to cleaning the tables, then there was Zeigfield's... loved it there.

Elizabeth Dobson Grieve: My Aunt Margaret worked there in the early 1920's before she emigrated to Canada, Margaret Clelland.

Annie Murdoch Anderson Black: I remember all of this and when I used to come back home spent some time in these places dancing the night away, home sick again.

Margaret Lappin: Worked in Ziegfield's and Barnum's, great Sunday sesh always! They were the days April!!!

April Mcmahon: They sure were mag lol!!! Ziegfeld memories lol!!!

Anne Bain: Sunday afternoon's sing-along. Me and my friends loved it.

Alice Murray: Have memories of hanging about outside there waiting for my dad to get a pound off him lol. X

Carolyn Patterson: I used to go in there for lunch with my mum and aunty, then when I was older we went to Bananas Disco lol!!!! Those were the days!!!

Annfield Terrace

After Hastie's Farm, on the corner of Victoria Street and Glasgow Road was the start of a tenement type building called Annfield Terrace, seen here on the right, which continued up the Glasgow Road and the Toll Brae.

Glasgow Road looking East

On the corner of this tenement building was a grocery store, Gibson's shop grocery & provisions which was very popular with the Ness's School pupils across the road, for their sweets. Mr. Gibson used to wear a long white coat.

Pictured here is Hastie's Farm on the right and Ness's Primary School across Victoria Street.

This was the start of the Toll Brae, where Heavy Horses were used to pull carts up the brae for a toll. The Toll office was opposite Ness's School, and the horses were stabled in John Street.

When this tenement was demolished, the vacant land was cleared, and this became an open market on a Tuesday where you could buy almost everything from clothes, fruit and vegetables to even getting your ears pierced.

Your Memories:

Mary Summers: Is that the public toilets the wee building on the left.

Audrey Morrison: The road looked so much better then.

Mary Wood: I remember going into Gibson's... I thought it was a wee sweetie shop... You got your sweeties in a wee paper poke... And, who I assumed was Mr. Gibson wore an either a white apron or coat...

Helen Dyer: Mary, I remember those toilets... sometimes had to run and glad they were there... I took my friends daughter to the market to get her ears pierced and she got up and ran away after the woman did the first ear. I had to chasing her through the market to bring her back. She didn't get the other one done... lol it was so funny.

Karen Feelie: A can remember a wee market on the ground where the home was. A was a wee lassie then and that is where a got my ears pierced.

Richard Rankin: Can mind the market at front of Hastie's especially the toffee apples hanging on the top bar of the sweetie stall.

Carolyn Patterson: I can remember getting off the school bus to go to the markets that were there for some time.

The Stonefield Tavern

The next building of any significance is The Stonefield Tavern Glasgow Road at Priory Street. The pub was formerly known as Fred Rae's, and then Teddy's.
It is thought to be one of the oldest Public Houses in Blantyre.

This photo of 1920 is before the Broadway Picture House was built across the road some 19 years later.

Note the overhead tram power lines, in the middle of the road and the gas lamp to the right.

Look how busy the pavement is on the right. My theory is that the photo was taken on a Sunday morning, and the pedestrians are on their way to Church.

The lady standing by the wooden staircase to the left is most probably the photographer's wife.

Duncan Slater wrote: Later when the white building was removed a large Billboard was there, and we used to climb up the back and throw snowballs at the line up's waiting to go into the Broadway Cinema.

Stonefield Tavern Today... The sign says 1556 and depicts a Horse Show, which was when the Brewery was founded.

Your Memories:

Ray Couston: Yeah, it's a Tennent's advert. It's the date that the Wellpark Brewery was founded.

Carolyn Patterson: see I love these photos, I had my very first drink in Teddy's at the age of.... teen lol.

John Ryan-Park: I lived in a house at 223A Glasgow Road, Blantyre. Just at bottom of the Toll Brae, not far from the Stonefield Tavern.

Danny Canavan: Teddy's pub, many a good day and night in there.

Mary McGuigan: I live in England when my fella came to Blantyre with me, he loves Teddy's. X

Kathleen McDermott Parks: I knew this pub as

Teddy's. Many a great sing song in there on a Saturday.

Glasgow Road 1920 Top Co-op Buildings Built 1891

The large three storey block at the left of this 1920's picture was Blantyre's Co-op. communally owned co-operative shops date back to the end of the Napoleonic Wars when they had sprung up in industrial areas hit by post-war recession. The main advantage of shopping at a co-op was the annual dividend that they paid out, sometimes equivalent to as much as ten weeks' wages.

Blantyre's Co-op was registered in 1883 at a time when the population was expanding rapidly because of the new coal industry.

In the early 1940's the wholesale grocer was accused of using child labour, but it survived the scandal and was integrated into the SCWS Retail Group in 1972, when it lost the Co-op label.

Today a Co-op funeral parlour is still housed on the ground floor of the building. The Co-op No2 Branch consisted of two buildings, the three storeys and the two storeys where the telegraph pole is. Then the Knights of St Columba Building, McNally's chip shop on gable end (now Sun House Chinese Take-away.)

John Cornfield wrote: "Yes, you're 100% right, the shop that's now the Saint Andrew's was the Co-op grocers, a mini supermarket.

The bank was where you could go in at the front of it, I seem to remember was clothing and at the back after you went up 3 or 4 steps was shoes, and through the connecting door from the shoe shop was household goods and at the front was men's clothes I think, I might be wrong and everybody got to pay the dividend lol."

Top Co-op early 70's

© James Mc Guire

Ariel & Art cabs, Blantyre black cabs on Glasgow Road.

Jeanette Allardyce Ward wrote: that's right John, got your stamps in the grocer's ha-ha. There was a payment desk upstairs where the bank is where you payed your hp goods. Co-op was from where the bank is right along to where St. Andrews is. I still call the butchers the co butchers. My mum worked in the clothes, etc. of the co-op when she was young. We stayed in Priory Street so it was our main shopping place.

Top Co-op 2000

Co-op Funeral Service (still there), Clyde Star grocers (now Londis and the Post Office), Barbers Shop (now Agnew's Cafe), Co-op Butchers (now Peters Family Butchers), Mackintosh Carpets and Furniture, (now St. Andrew's Hospice).

Your Memories:

John Cornfield: My mam used to get oor school shoes (animal tracker) remember them with a compass under the insole and animal tracks on the sole we got them on hire purchase oot the co happy days. My mam used to call it the emporium.

Marianne Aitken: We used to get oor school uniforms from there... I remember my mam getting everything for the hoose from there and paying "it up" also have memories of said mum talking boot her dad having a "divi" number and people borrowing it!! John a relative of oors, stayed in the flat above I remember ma mam talking about it.

Mary Crowe: I remember my mother telling us it was known locally as the Wee Irish Building. My great uncle lived in it at the 1911 Census.

Jeanette Allardyce Ward: It was part of the co-op. the bank and the funeral parlour were one, you could go in either door and there were a couple of steps inside which took you into the next part, sold clothes and shoes etc., upstairs sold furniture etc.

Fire at the Knights of St. Columba Building

The three-story tenement is the Knights of St. Columba Building on Glasgow Road with McNally's chip shop on gable end. This building was The Post Office, prior to becoming the Knights of Columba. The year is unknown

 but probably in the late 70s. The driveway to the right was to Wm. McSeveney's Coach Builders and the two pillars still stand today.

Photo sent in by **Anthony Smith** and restored by **George Park**.

The Building was demolished and a single-story building built on the site, which is now the Sun House Chinese Take-away.

Y.M.C.A. Building

Besides the usual uses as the Y.M.C.A., The building was also used as the "Home Guard" training H.Q. during the war.

Behind the building shown, was another building used for training, also there were trenches at the back (where some children used to play at being soldiers.)

Later on, the building at the back became Wm. McSeveney's car repair shop, which is now being used as a car wash.

It was stated officially yesterday that Blantyre Police are highly pleased by the response made for volunteers for service under the A.R.P. regulations.

Up until now, over 1,000 men have appeared at the Police Station and agreed to give their services for immediate duty.

The men have already been allocated to districts and sub-districts under senior officers and are representative of all classes within the community, which includes business men in Glasgow, local doctors and business men, unemployed miners and school teachers.

Gas masks have been stored in the local police office for some time past, but now masks are stored in different halls in Blantyre.

Source: Glasgow Herald, September 29th 1938

Note from Bill: The A.R.P. and the Home Guard were formed as a backup to the army, to defend the towns and villages of the United Kingdom in the unlikely invasion of the Germans, but they were armed initially with only what could be scrounged up and private weapons.

They eventually were properly armed and usually consisted of men in reserved occupations, such as miners and those unable to fight due to a medical condition, or those who were too old to fight.

The building has been recently renovated to accommodate the Spice of Life takeaway and William Hill bookmakers.

The Y.M.C.A. was also used as a Disco called The Roxy in the 70s.

THE ROXY

Doon the Roxy on a Saturday night

Dressed to kill oh what a sight

Struttin oor stuff oan the dance flair

The whole of Blantyre seemed to be there

Two bob tae get in or a tin a beans

Ten bob for sweeties that was yer means

Music kicks aff wae some rock n roll

Smoochin some burd tae a wee bit of soul

Smelly toilets and flaking paint

Fae oor crowd ye got nae complaint

Loads of great memories in that wee hall

Generations of people having a ball

Another memory to be wiped away

Gone forever the Y.M.C.A.

At least there calling it a fancy name

But the Spice of Life just is'nae the same

Jimmy Whelan 2010

Your Memories:

John Cornfield: It was the Y.M. for years then Sandy Nisbett used to take us kids and started a disco in 1972. It became the Roxy, named by us who frequented it Sat nite. During the week, we had games and gymnastics where I met the Cushley's, the Hunters and numerous others. It was the place to be on a Saturday nite if u were 10 or 11 even up to 13 lol.

Mary Borland: I remember going 2 gymnastics on Fri nites n also youth discos oh the memories.

Wilma Hannah-Boyle: Luved the wee discos in there!

Eddie Mcguire: We used to call it the Roxy when we were kids. Sat, think it was, 6 to 8pm disco great days and the tuck shop ginger and sweets.

Duncan Slater: Yes, I played in the trenches, also after the war the Thomson's moved in above the hall. I played with Billy and Thomas.

Paul Hudson McGowan: I remember doing gymnastics there too in the early 1970s in my case. Great fun.

Michelle Brankin: Loved going to this place! It really was a great night every time you went x

Catherine McCunnie: OMG remember it well, our wee disco on a Saturday night brill!

Lesley Hartley: I used to go to Highland dancing in there when I was a kid.

Boski Bell: Crackin pic.

Mary Davies: My Gran, me, and my sisters used to frequent this place for our wee tea and chat, happy memories.

Glasgow Road 1908

This was Glasgow Road, photographed in 1908. The Methodist Church, on the left-hand side in the picture, originated in 1893 when it only had a handful of members.

By 1902, services were being held in Dixon's Hall (built by the coal-master of the same name) and the decision to build the Glasgow Road church was taken the following year.

The new church opened in 1905 and was in use until the First World War. After lying vacant for a time, it was bought by Stonefield Independent Co-op in 1925.

It later became the Bethany Hall and was run by the Christian Brethren, who have been active in Blantyre since the first decade of the century.

Glasgow Road 2008

More recently, the church has been taken over by 'The Word of Life Church', an American based Christian group and even more recently, a Children's Nursery.

The Y.M.C.A. is on the immediate right which was recently converted to accommodate, The Spice of Life Takeaway and William Hill's bookmakers.

Oliver's Building, Glasgow Road 1903

As this is an area, I was unfamiliar with, I asked my friend and fellow Blantyreonian, **William Ross**, because I knew that he was born here. He said, "The Post Office became the Knights of Columba, then there was the YMCA, Felix McLaughlin's funeral parlour, The Bank, which is now the detached Ladbrokes betting shop. Next was a cottage, then the Minty's building where I was born on the ground floor, whih is now 265 Glasgow

Road. Minty's had an internal stair to get to the upper floors and a big Penn Close which led to the cottage that Mick Devlin (a local character) lived in.

Car Terminus, Blantyre

Oliver's shop had a large through close to an exterior stair at the back. Oliver's was a Draper's shop which became Hugh's Photographers and Paton's Ladies and Gents Hairdressers. Next was Dr Church's surgery and then Valerio's Cottage where Tommy Valerio and his family lived. On the corner was a Light Fittings shop which became a workshop for Smith's funeral parlour, then we had Stonefield Road."

The iron railings were of course confiscated for the war effort.

The Tram Terminus at the bottom of Stonefield Road near David Livingstone Church, see the Church Steeple in the background.

Your Memories:

Jeanette Henshaw wrote: Hughes photography took ma bro n sis double wedding in Livingstone church and there was a double wedding in St Joseph's chapel same day and he did their photos too. That was 1979 and we all got our hair done in Mrs Paton's hairdressers. X

William Ross: The first building was called Minty's, if you moved back towards the bank there was a pen close leading to the cottage.

Maggie O'Brien: Dr Harken's surgery was there too then becoming Dr Church surgery.

William Ross: After the surgery, you had the cottage. Wee Mickie's son Tommy and his wife lived in.

Lynn Dougela: My mum was born in that building.

Paul Hudson McGowan: I remember Bill Paton's place which if memory serves me right was next to Hughes the Photographer. Thanks for putting this one up Bill. I have nice memories of Mr. Paton.

Jeanette Henshaw: Hughes photography took ma bro n sis double wedding in Livingstone church n there was a double wedding in St Joseph chapel same day n he did their fotos 2 that was 1979 n we all got our hair done in Mrs Paton's hairdressers x

Annie Murdoch Anderson Black: I remember Hughes Photographers so well, I have still got in the family album, a photograph of my little brother which was taken by this photographer, thank you once again for the memories...

Stonefield Road 1903

Stonefield was the subject of a campaign to elevate it to Burgh status in 1878, although the plan didn't get much support from the ordinary members of the public who seemed to equate the promotion with nothing other than higher taxes. A poll was eventually held, which came out against the issue and had local characters such as Tam Todd gloating that the 'fors' had made 'an awfu' show o' themselves'.

Gas lamps and dirt roads.

St. Joseph's Church and School opposite in Glasgow Road. Built in 1878 and was used weekdays as a school and Sundays and Holy Days as a Chapel, replacing the Hall of Worship in Dixon's Rows which was a block of four house units converted into a church hall. The Church could accommodate 620 sittings.

Stonefield Rd. Blantyre

When the Irish and therefore, Catholic, population grew because of the mining industry, further classroom accommodation was supplied in the form of timber huts to the right of the Church.

James McCallum Billboard and David Gibson Grocers.

Who can tell me this shop's nickname?

Mickey's Cafe, Stonefield Road.

On our wander doon memory lane, we are now in Stonefield Road and it's time to pop into Mickey's Ice Cream Parlour for a Mars 'n ice

with Tommy, Nancy and Velma as our hosts.

The Valerio Building was owned by the Valerio Family, and they restricted the sale of cigarettes, chocolate and of course, ice cream to all the shops they leased or rented out in the building. Scobie's Bakers, Benham Newsagent, Chip shop, McCallum grocers, Painters.

Mickey's closed in May 1988. Today the family have a small Crescent named after them.

Mickey and his son, Tommy outside Cafe de Royal.

I have been asking **Claudia Wood**, niece of Velma, for

some family photos and she has given me kind permission to share this fantastic photo of Mickey's Cafe.

Claudia's link to 'Aunty' Velma is that she is cousins with her gran Celia Lombardi (deceased) and her Great Uncle Carlo Lombardi, who were the family of Vincent Lombardi as in Vince's Chippy. Both Aunt Velma and Uncle Carlo are still in Blantyre, and Carlo still lives above Vince's Chippy in the last of the Lombardi flats the family used to have in that block.

Your Memories:

John Cornfield: I remember this shop well big Tommy, Nancy and Velma great people. This was my stomping ground as a youth. I apologise wholeheartedly for the run-around, we gave them myself, Tam Airlie, big Stan, Steph Murray, Stevie Brownlee, Jim McAdam, Barney Welch, Gavin Stewart, Eddie McMillan, Bobby Gilmour, Davy Rantz, too many to name I'm sorry if I've left your name out.

We tormented the life out of them sorry, but we had some laughs, some memories the aroma of this and Peter's down on Glasgow Road was unique, I still can't put my finger on it.

Linda Mcgowan: I remember sitting in Mickeys on a Sunday night waiting for mass 2 finish then when someone came in fae mass I'd ask them what colour the priest's vestment was.... cause my dad always asked me when I got home... oh the little rebel in me... oh! the shame... lol... just actually dawned on me he wouldn't even have known as he didn't go much to mass. Doh!!! To think I ended up being a Eucharistic minister for five years...

Paul McDermott: Enjoyed many a milkshake in Mickey's Cafe!

Thomas Hamilton-Hailes: Many a pinched cheek from Mickie ... and a cuddle thereafter from Velma or Mickey's wife.

Morag Pickering: Loved in there my brothers and sister also went in absolute great cafe handy for the chapel, not dogger like most of yous great memories.

Moira McMenemy: It was always a treat to go to Mickey's. Loved it.

Thomas Hamilton-Hailes: Me and some mates in the air-raid shelter through the close wi' a candle and a packet of 5 woodbines ... and me being allowed to sit in the back of Bessie Benham's on a sack of spuds reading some comics.

Kathleen Anne Obrien: My Grandparents and my Mum and Dad stayed in the building above. Grandparents got a new house in Cypress Ave., and my Mum Dad and Sister Marie moved to the Crescents, Hardie Street, where my Mum was brought up from age 3. My Husband also started his apprenticeship as a Joiner round the back from Mickey's, happy times!

Fran Mcdermott Walters: The chapel escape lol... we were all in there and I recall being sent over for misalettes so we could say we went and what priest was on lol. X

Marie Kelly: Davie Kelly stayed in 218 Glasgow Road when he was 1 with his Mum Margaret (Magunigal) & Dad Donald Kelly you can see the close in the pic.

Carole Mackie Rickard: I still miss Mickey's. My Papa was born above it in 1918.

Gerry Mcnamee: Mars & ice after 12 00 mass with Velma serving you.

Annie Black: Enjoyed the old juke box in there with their lovely ice cream. Here I go again being home sick...

Marie McMillan: I would go to Mickey's and no go to chapel, my dad came in and pulled me way my ears out aww. X

Liz Allan: Ice cream drink on a Sunday with all our pals who should have been in chapel. All the glass jars of sweets on shelves and lots of chocolate and other things in the glass counter and the phone box inside the door.

Mary Meekat: Loved Mickeys... Coke, Ice cream and chopped Mars... Not forgetting the single fags and book of matches.

Edith Bulloch: Remember Peter Valerio's cafe across from Harper's garage, worked in both.

Elizabeth Baillie Alemanno: Fantastic photo..." look how smart they look."!

Anne-marie Hart: Mickey's was the best cafe I used to go in there all the time & get a snowball & ice cream and spring cola ice drink nom, nom, nom.

Margo Haughen: I remember Velma, Wee Mickey and Tommy so well- my dad bought 200 Kensitas Club from Mickey every Saturday morning!!!

Margaret Brown: Great we cafe memories.

Len Northfield: I remember Peter's cafe at the East end of the town too.

Laurie Allan Crothers: Me too Len, same brilliant ice cream as his brother Mickey's. His wee wife always reminded me of Molly Weir. Small with white hair always up in a bun.

Carolyn Patterson: brilliant childhood memories.

Ellen Swift: Went there every Sunday instead of mass.

Isabel Park: Stayed in building across the road from Mickey's, he used to shout up to my gran, send Isabel down I have a parcel to go to the nuns in the Dandy and I would go and take it to the nuns. X

Tracey McDougall: Think a few folk dogged masses in there Ellen Swift! I remember being in once with. Sharon Burt who was supposed to be in chapel + she asked them when they came out what hymns were, so she could tell Auntie Mary that we went!!! The milkshakes were great.

Gerry Gillies: I remember Thelma.

Sally Fisher: My mum used to take me in there as a child they said because I had jet black hair and dark skin I could pass for Italian any day now I have 2 sons the same dark hair and skin they always get asked if their foreign. Sally Boyd x.

Liz Boxall: Loved the ice cream!! And the phone kiosk as you went in!!!

Carol Crombie: I loved the old booths – full of character.

Sharon Burt: Remember it so clearly Tracey but stop carrying stories. Lol x

Tracey McDougall: Ha-ha don't worry that's the worse! The rest are good. Xxx

Helen Dyer: it's also where we used to buy single cigs. Oops! And Paterson Yep me n my best friend Janey McLauchlan went there every Sunday after mass, she would get a hot orange and I would get a cold orange n two packets of vinegar crisps and they sold this chocolate stick with a cream inside oh it was lovely happy memories. Xx

Moira McMenemy: Loved that cafe. Loads of memories.

Carole Jamieson: My friends mum either owned it or managed it for a while, lots of freebies... Dolly Mixtures on a plate!

Ann Millar: Aye brilliant memories n wee Mickey could hardly see the counter he wis a gr8 wee guy.

Marion Smith: went there sometimes at school lunchtimes. Roll, square sausage & broon sauce & a wee glass bottle of coke. Not forgetting the selection of sweets, yummy!

Margaret Wilson: I used to stay across the road from it happy days.

Jacqui Lafferty Draper: Remember going there as a child. Loved it!

Letitia Mitchell: Great wee café.

Helen Grieve: Spent many an hour in there!

Annie Black: Memories indeed.

Jack Owens: Double nougat was ok as well.

William Ross: The story that was told, was wee Mickey made his money selling pea bray penny a cup.

Blantyre's Ain: Looks like I touched a nerve with Mickey's, I just wonder what the kids will recall so lovingly in 40 to 50 years' time!

John Cornfield: Had many a mars n ice and also ice drinks (remember them Valerio's ice cream 2 scoops topped up wi any Robertson's ginger ye wanted) noo that's a blast fae the past mmmmmmm.

Marianne Aitken: Nancy wi the twitch.... Liam Broon well done!!!! .... couldn't remember her name awwww they were the day's mars 'n ice cream ... remember she always wanted you oot... and wee pied good money tae when ma mammy could afford it!! Always wanted tae knock the glasses they were served in.... xxx

Daniel Anderson: Chapel and a cone!!! Hallelujah.

Catriona Paterson: A jaggy juice (Robertson's 5-star ginger beer) ice drink was the biz... we need another cafe like this, the smell from this shop was fantastic.

Liam Brown: oh Mickey's, where the Valerio family used to sell you your fave ice cream, and ice drink then when you sat in to eat, they would shout like hell, at us to hurry up and get oot. got barred when Velma was serving me and Nancy who had a really bad twitch, looked at me and had a twitch, I said I'm getting served, oot ya cheeky bugger was the reply.

Helen Stewart: Great place loved it.

Linda McEwan Ashton: Ma wee mum used to work In Mickey's.

Fran Mcdermott Walters: Best rolls and sausage, then a mars bar ice cream... never could eat all my dinner after that, wasn't supposed to be there lol x Many a good Sunday in there after mass of course. Lol x

Margaret Gallagher: I went here as a child with my grannie when we went up the street n thought it was the bee's knees.

Morag Campaigne: My Aunty Bella worked in Mickey's cafe and when we were in the cafe having a Bovril and cream crackers and a fly fag, a had to hide so she didnae see me ha-ha.

Angela Vallely: Loved going there for ice cream.

Wilma Murdoch MacPhail: Only place I know that you could get hot orange drinks, tried making it at home but it was never the same... I've lived in Australia for 25 yrs. now but it could be just yesterday. Brings back memories of going to Hastie's for soup and a roll at dinner time at Calder Street but if we didn't have enough money for that we went to the wee shop and got sticky bun and sweets, my mum thought we were getting school dinners lol.

Joyce Traynor: Ha-ha-ha, mind used 2 have nephew hame fr lunch fae skool, he never came 1 day, next day he says he was at Cafe de Royal for lunch, I say where?? He says across fae Old Original Bar, ha-ha, psmsl, xx

Eileen Duffy Eger: Still one of my favourite memories!

Linda Mcgowan: I've seen Velma in Asda a few times... think I'll stop & chat the next time. She honestly hasn't changed a bit. She looks amazing...

Elizabeth Dobson Grieve: Loved going to Mickey's as a kid. The ice drinks were always brilliant!

Linda Mcgowan: I used 2 work there 2... luved it... also frequented it with the Ferns family, Kelly's & Gribbens... I was a Gilluley... all fae Hillview Drive, Coatshill. My dad always brought us tubs or single nougats on a Sat after a few pints in Craig's in the days they shut @ 2.30pm... great memories...x

Carole Miller: Does anyone remember the ice cream bananas they sold as well, terrific.

Maureen Brown: Remember going with my dad at least 40 yrs. or so ago, loved going to Mickey's.

Helen Dyer: we used to go there to warm up in the winter get a cup of tea... ice cream was amazing.

Jeanette Allardyce Ward: They done hot cashew nuts, aw they were brill. Used to go there for our bowl of ice cream, a raspberry, every Sunday. Lol x

Paul Hudson McGowan: Ah, Mickie's cafe, some great memories from childhood. Snowball and Ice or an Iced Drink.

Eleanor Duncan Nailon: Ice cream & ginger beer. Great ice cream drink.

Lorraine Barker: I remember having ice cream drinks from there as a child.

Jane Maxwell: My friends and I would get a hot orange when it was cold and a Mars n ice when it was hot. My grandfather would bring irn bru, cream soda and a carton of ice cream every Saturday night to our house and we would all have shakes delicious.

The best cafe in Blantyre the ice cream was made fresh the choice of sweets was huge and the hot roasted nuts were amazing. Oh, and don't forget the little packets of violets and the little hard liquorice delicious.

Sandy Wilkie: Used to go in with my dad, Peter Wilkie, on a Sat morning, to collect the Milk Money for the White Stuff we delivered during the week – the milk was for 3 purposes, to make the ice cream, to sell pint old fashioned gable top cartons to Wee Mickey, Mrs Valerio, Nancy and Tommy's customers and finally, for the wee 1/2 pint cartons that were dispatched from the vending machine which used to be situated against the wall just outside the shop!

You can tell by your memories, how much Mickey's Café was loved and enjoyed.

Frank Benham outside his shop c.1923/24

I hope you still want old photos of Blantyre. The first one is of William Francis Benham (known as Frank) outside his shop in Blantyre. Frank was my Great Grandmothers` brother. He was born in Edinburgh, married in Glasgow and settled in Blantyre (around 1892).

He was married to Elizabeth Ann Pearson Craig (Lizzie), and they had three daughters- Elizabeth (Bessie), Margaret (Meg) and Jane. They also had a son William, who died in infancy in 1895. He was born at Darvoch Cottage in Blantyre. Frank died in 1925 at Craig Rock, Glasgow Road, Blantyre.

The second photo is of Frank Benham, Lizzie Benham, Bessie Benham, Molly Benham (my Grandmother) and

Charles Benham (my Grandfather). The children to the front are my Mum, Helen Benham, my Uncle, Charlie Benham and my Aunt Betty Benham. I believe this picture was taken in Craig Rock's garden.

Both pictures are c1923/4. Bessie married David Campbell and lived near the station as I remember her garden backed onto the rail track near the platform also it was not far from David Livingstone's House/Museum. Anyway, if any of this is of use to you for your website, please feel free to use it.

Regards

Eleanor Stenhouse

Hi Bill,

I was looking at your website and found the photo of Frank Benham outside his shop. It was on Stonefield Road, no 11.

As far as I know, Benham's owned the shop, then it belonged to 2 sisters (I was talking to my mum again and she recalled the name Bessie Benham, so perhaps the shop was taken over by Bessie and one of her sisters), then a man from Holytown owned it.

It then belonged to my mum Sheila Russell and was a newsagent, grocer etc., she became the owner around 1963/64 and she had until the late 70's when it was taken over by the chap who had the newsagents on Glasgow Road (I cannot remember his name, sorry).

I do know that when my mum had the shop, people still called it Benham's, even though he hadn't been in it in a while!

As you may have guessed I'm an old Blantyre lass, although I'm not there now. My family owned the farm at Wheatlandhead. Anyway, I hope that's filled in a 'blank'.

Regards, Elaine Russell

Your Memories:

Kate Mcinulty: Did that become Norris's then at the pen close? X

Blantyre's Ain: Norris's was across the road where the Co-op is now Kate.

Kate Mcinulty: Ok thanks got a bit confused as you do lol. X

Betty Hepburn: I'm related to the Benham's this my mum's Uncle Frank, his wife was Lizzie, had 3 daughters, Margaret (Meg), Jane (Jean), and Elizabeth (Bessie). X

Betty Hepburn: Hi, I'm wondering if someone might have a good memory here, looking for information on a Person that was called Georgie (last name Unknown) and we think she and perhaps other siblings were raised by one of the Benham's. Georgia came out here to New Zealand to visit another Benham relative, would love to find Georgie's family name (is she a relation to the Benham's?

Betty Hepburn: Sorted my question on our mystery on Georgie? She was raised by a Maiden Aunt, Lizzie McCallum + not by the Benham's (just close friends) she did come to New Zealand and had time with her friend, Jeanne Reade, an American niece of the Benham's.

John Maguire: No Norris's was across the road where the Spar shop was, McCallum's was at the end before in cut into the wallpaper shop. Down from Benham's there used to a launderette, and McVey's had a vacuum shop, there was also Gilbert the baker on the other side, the tanning shop is there now, just remembered it was Mr & Mrs Proudfoot who owned McCallum's, they were a lovely couple.

Elizabeth Baillie Alemanno: Omg. Forgot about Benham's!

Liz Allan: I remember Elaine, her brother and mum and dad well. I loved the house they lived in upstairs. I remember as I watched them a few times, her mum was so lovely. My name was Wotherspoon then.

Stonefield Road c1984

With Clyde Star Video before it moved to Glasgow Road.

Upstairs all boarded up, just about ready to start demolition to make way for the Valerio Court housing scheme, named after the Valerio family.

Another view in 1987 showing the Red Lion Pub and 'D' Hall, which used to be Hugh MacCorgarry's D.I.Y. where you got your pelmets made.

© James Mc Guire

'D' Hall was a sort of Youth Club with a TV, pool Table, etc. Known as, 'The Black Hole', someone painted the outside to look like a jail.

Photos by **James McGuire**

The Red Lion c1980

The Red Lion Bar on Stonefield Road, opposite the Commercial Bar. The pub was owned by Sammy Maxwell. Built on the site of the

old Independent Co-op building. Closed because of planned redevelopment. A very popular Pub in its day.

Your Memories:

Betty Brown: There was a baker, which turned into a fish and chip shop, next door to a bookie's.

Ray Couston: I've lived in Blantyre all my life and I can't figure out where that would've been.

Blantyre's Ain: Bottom of Stonefield Road, Ray Couston.

Betty Brown: Hugh McCorgaries was there before the Red Lion. Was there a Co-op before Hugh McCorgaries?

Blantyre's Ain: Yes, there was a Co-op and Hugh McCorgaries used to make window pelmets to order.

Walter Campbell: There was a little den place for youngsters next door just at the right of the bottom picture. Who remembers that?

Gerry Gillies: The black hole.

Div Purse: The Black Hole, William Campbell.

Alisa Tonner: Me!!!!! Were u there the day I found the old coins round the back?

Iain Lambie: Wee tunnel beside Mickey's cafe??

Walter Campbell: Yes, the Black hole. Thanks, that was it. Now I know, I will sleep like a horse tonight.

Walter Campbell: That's right all the young tyre. Brilliant, all these memories will help our alzimers.

Gordon Dunsmuir: I remember being about 7 or 8 and I clearly remember walking home (Camelon Cres.) from buying sweets from the paper shop and there was some typical old boy sat on the red railing round the shrubs (itchy coos) facing the road. He was absolutely steaming, probably been drinking for a week!! Well, as we walked past him, he took a tumble backwards and just lay there in the shrubs with his legs and feet still on the railings... I'll never forget the noise he made when he hit the deck!!

Denise Gilmour Ross Moir: I remember play in here when it closed down and I remember it being pulled down when I was a wee lassie. X

Robert McLeod-Wolohan: Although I was never in this pub, I remember it well. I passed by it many many times. Lol

Tom McGuigan: I remember calling in once after a Celtic match and it was a bit busy and I shouted to Sammy Pint o lager, he replied "How many hands do you think I have." Lol.

Bill Graham: Hahaha, that was Sammy's humour, for those that did not know him he had only one arm losing the other in an industrial accident at Ravenscraig many years before, great character, what ever happened to him?

William Campbell: My old local pub, sat in the wee back room.

Caroline Rundell: I have fond memories if the Union Jack pub as well, which was further up the street.

Steven Robertson: Mate of mine went to the hair dressers next door with a pic of Ali Campel from ub40 and asked if they could make him look like the pic. Guess the answer.

William Kelly: Sammy, a smashing wee guy knew him well from the bowling club.

Ellen Swift: Drank in it. Xx

Gerry Gillies: Sure, it was Hughie McCorgarie the only place in Lanarkshire you could get a glass door.

Margaret Mary Campbell: Uncle Joe's best pal. Lol x

Jamie Carruthers: Remember it well, when I used to say on Glasgow road.

Laine Fitzgerald: Sam Maxwell wish u still had it, mega parties in it. Lol xx

Ann Millar: Oh! Aye, hid miny a guid swally in there, think it wis across the road fae the Priory.

Stephen Allan: I do not remember the pub but I remember Clyde Star video back in the very early 90s, when I was about 5 or 6, shortly before the shops were demolished.

Jeanette Allardyce Ward: Was my dad's regular. X

Andrina Rankin: Was Jeff's the papershop/homeware?

Stephen Allan: Jeff must have moved across the road after the shops were demolished.

Andrina Rankin: That's right, he did. X

Hazel Krawczyk: It was originally on Glashow Road then for years along from Macintosh carpets, Mickeys and the Pub. He moved over to the old cobblers shop when they built Valerio Court, then next to hairdresser when Scotmid was built in the late 90's.

Margaret McGuigan: I remember it had a space invader table my big cousin Sandra Mcguigan took me there and yes, I was under age.

Catherine Davner: great fun, and auld Wullie was a permanent feature standing at the bar.

Hugh Lennon Tonner: Many a good time had in there!

Kevin Law: Used it before Celtic games.

Jane Barkey: Yes, I have happy memories of the Red Lion I met Archie in that very pub.

Anthony Smith: It's not my Sherpa van. Mine was all blue.

Today, as you can see, Stonefield Road looks very different from this 1903 picture.

The shrubs which were on the left is now the site of The Priory Inn, and J Struthers shop has been demolished. Straight ahead was St. Joseph's Church, which was replaced by a new building a little further west, up Glasgow Road in 1905 and the existing building becoming a full-time St. Joseph's School.

The stretch of shops at the right has been replaced by new brick housing.

Dixons Raws c1919

1st Door on left:

Mrs Helen McDougall Paterson, 27 Park Street,

Dixons Raws,

Blantyre c1919 whose family we have been posting recently thanks to her Granddaughter, Mary Wood.

The raw's consisted of seven Streets Starting with Calder Street, Dixon Street, Hall Street all travelling East Park Street all travelling east to West. The other three streets were Miller Street, Govan Street and Carfin Street, travelling North to South.

Helen McDougall Paterson and two children outside 27 Park Street, Dixon's Raws - 1919

Look at the poor condition of the brickworks. Just remember that these houses had earthen floors with no electricity or gas or water closet.

It was not unusual for 10 or 12 adults and children to occupy the two roomed terraced houses.

These are the last four houses in the

Dixon's Rows, Blantyre

Row which served as a Church to the Catholic Mining Community.

As more and more immigrants from Ireland arrived in Blantyre to work in the Pits, they wanted a place of Worship, because at that time

there was no Catholic Church.

They approached the Pit Owners, Messrs. William Dixon and asked, if not, petitioned, for a place of Worship.

As William Dixon's family were Catholic, and one of his sons was a Priest, they allocated the last four houses at the end of the Row to be used as a Chapel, much to the discontent of the Protestant Community.

This block of four houses was the last to be demolished.

Your Memories:

Jim Macfie: I lived in Dixon's Raw's 45 yrs. ago. Think my Da has a few pics somewhere in his house.

Sharon Mcmillan: My mum Delia Roberts and her brothers and sisters were born at Dixon Raw's. Many a story I've heard about the raws.

Carole Miller: Where would Mill, Govan, and Carfin Street have been? Anybody know?

Blantyre's Ain: They ran north to South parallel with Stonefield Road but on the Victoria Street side of the Raws. You can see them on the 1875 Map in the Miners Resource Centre.

Paul Hudson McGowan: Are there any remnants left of these old houses? I'm probably wrong, something tells me there might be something on Calder Street.

Jack Owens: If I mind right there was gas lights on the wall near the fireplace in the front room.

Blantyre's Ain: I think you are right Jack. Gas was introduced in the late 40's I believe.

Christine Brown: My hubby Tony stayed in 21 Park Street.

Jim Macfie: Yes, we lived next door to Shona Mccabe's gran.

Shona Mccabe: My gran lived in Dixon's Raw's and had pictures of the houses, she used to tell us we were spoiled by the standards of living we had and that it made us soft.

Ann Millar: Memories eh!!! A wisnae born bit ma mammy uze tae tell my brothers and me aboot Dixon's Raw's and Rosendale cause that's where ma mammy came fae.

Christine Brown: Ann I remember the day your family moved into Hawthorn Place what memories from there wonderful. Xxx

Joe Sneddon: And we complain how tough it is today.

Mary Crowe: One of the streets was called Miller Street. My Mother was born in number 8.

Elizabeth Weaver: Aye, the good old days eh? While the pit owners lived like gentry... great photo, but glad some things have changed. I see the woman with the wean in the shawl - in the 50s, you'd still see women carrying their babies that way in High Blantyre (at the Co!).

George Mackenzie: Betty - Ye can'ae beat a wee hauf oot in the shawls...

Ann McArdle: Our address was 9 Dixon Street. I was born in Dixon Rows in 1948.

Martin Cummiskey: My grans Auld house. I've got a pic of that.

Annie Murdoch Anderson Black: My Granny used to tell me all about these houses and the living conditions...

Suzanne Wall-Duffy: Were the cottages still inhabited in 1900s? Are they all demolished now? Sorry to ask so many questions... my husband was born in 1954 in Dixon's Rows....just wondered what it would have looked like then.

Blantyre's Ain: They were demolished in the early 60's Suzanne. I used to walk down Dixon Street in 1960 as a shortcut to school and at that time they were uninhabited.

Betty Brown: My name is Betty McGaulley. We lived there for many yrs, like my dad's family before us. They were hard days, 6 living in one room, including the coal?

The Ejection of the Blantyre Widows

We should never forget that six months after the Mining Disaster at Dixon's No1 and No2 Pits, thirty-four widows, whose husbands had been killed in the disaster, appeared at Hamilton Sheriff Court. They had previously received letters from the colliery owners informing them that they must leave their tied cottages. Having failed to do so, William Dixon Limited had raised summonses against them.

When asked by the Sheriff why they had not vacated their homes, each widow stated that they did not have the means with which to pay a rent. The Sheriff asked, "Are you not getting enough money from the relief fund?" Each widow replied "I have not the means to pay a rent with."

The Sheriff stated that it was out of kindness that the company had allowed them to remain in their houses for so long. One widow claimed that they had a cruel way of showing their kindness and that the firm should have carried out the evictions on the day of the explosion as the public would have taken her by the hand.

The Sheriff stated that he could scarcely agree with her and suggested that both the firm and the public had been extremely kind and generous. He then decreed that the thirty-four widows and their children should be removed from their homes in two weeks' time, on 28th May 1878.

The evictions were carried out and replacement miners were allocated their homes. No-one knows what became of these unfortunate widows and their children. In all probability, they had to seek accommodation in the Poor House. There is hearsay that a local farmer offered some of them huts for accommodation, but there is no proof of this. Some of the widows made marriages of convenience with single miners just to have a roof over their heads and bread on the table for their children. The ejection of the Blantyre widows was a sad and disgraceful end to the tragic story of the Blantyre explosion.

Source: **Lanarkshire.com**

Your Memories:

Angela Gilluley: Unscrupulous landlord these cottages were called Dixon's rows an amazing story of a lady called Mary Barbour from Govan who fought for miners' wives and families to keep them in their homes a must read they were treated appallingly.

Mike Steven: Don't know if our family were there but discussing behaviour from the pit owner as their husbands paid the ultimate sacrifice to get his black gold mined for him.

Margaret Brown Burns: Treated like human fodder.

Kate Braid: So very sad.

Helene Duddridge Mcghee: How awful.

Jim Frame: so sad story.

Charlie Dunsmore: Absolutely shocking!!!

Tommy N Rosalind Lynch: So sad, shocking.

John Allan: Total disgrace.

Laura Gilluley: Scandalous.

Margaret McCreadie: Terrible cruel.

Ann Jeffrey: Man's inhumanity to man!

Union Jack Club

Next along Stonefield Road was the Gasworks which suffered a disastrous explosion on, would you believe, 5th November 1921.

There was also the **Union Jack Club**, next to Lethum's Garage, built in 1973. Whitey Johnstone was President, Jim Dunsmuir, Secretary and Jock Haye and Jim Best, the treasurers. It was a very popular Lounge Bar and even more so when a large games room with several snooker tables and a kitchen were added. However, as a private Club, it had rates and V.A.T. to pay, unlike the Miners Welfare which was a Charitable Society, so it eventually reached its financial limits and closed its doors in the mid-nineties. The empty building was burned down on 5th November, 1995.

Anderson Church

The 19th century saw many tensions within the Church of Scotland. Much of these tensions were concerned with the 'call' of a minister to a charge (church): should it be the landowner or the congregation itself? This came to a head in 1843 when about one-third of the ministers left it and formed the 'Free Church of Scotland'. The minister of Blantyre at the time was the Rev. James Anderson, and he broke away with many of his people and formed a branch of the Free Church in the town. A church was built at once simply called 'Blantyre Free Church'. In 1846, the church was burned down. Their new church was built in 1872 on Stonefield Road. It was built of light grey sandstone in shape of the cross (as seen from photo).

In 1900, it became 'Blantyre United Free Church'. In 1929, it went with the union to reform the Church of Scotland and was renamed 'Anderson Church of Scotland', after its first minister, Rev. James Anderson. A hall was built next to it in 1939.

For a few years, it became linked with Stonefield Parish and in 1978 was formally united with Stonefield Parish Church to become St. Andrews. The question of which building was to be used for worship was answered by fire!

The Anderson church, which had been empty for some time, was burned down on 8th June 1978.

The fire in 1978 was caused by a group of 10 - 12 children playing hide-and-seek in the building which was being used to store paper for a  local company. One of the twelve year olds who was prosecuted for the fire told me that he had nothing to do with it and did not know who had actually started the fire.

The church hall remains today as Smith's Funeral Parlour.

Your Memories:

Terry Hughes: I watched that burn down. Spiral costs and all. Wit a Blaze. Was a kid at the time staying up the S.H.A. There's a photo somewhere of it on fire.

Stuart Oneil: It was derelict when we were young. We used to call it "the haunted."

Gary Mitchell: Nice shot of Blantyre Bowling Club too!

John Paterson: Gary the B/C is at the back that's the tennis court at the front.

Blantyre Bowling Club

Blantyre Bowling Club in Stonefield Road which is still in existence today.

Founded on February 3, 1872 and is the only outdoor bowling green left in Blantyre.

Robertson's Laun

Stonefield Road looking towards Glasgow Road. The wooden hut to the right was built by James Little of Crossbasket for his father who had the habit of preaching liberalism in the Street, so to keep him busy and off the streets, his son built this shop and filled it with Hardware. As, he, being a builder, would be his best customer. The shop was sold for £114 in 1938 to James Paton, a Barber and still remains today.

After a short time as a Florists, it has become a Barbers Shop once again.

The next two storey building was also owned by James Little and known as Little's Building. Built of stone, Little's Building was erected c1905 and housed five tenants.

Robertson's Land (Laun) The three-story building with dormer windows was opposite Dixon's Number 4 Pit at Larkfield on Stonefield Road between Burnbrae Road and Broompark Road.

There were a number of shops in Robertson's Laun but probably the most important to children was Caldwell's Ice Cream Shop and Tommy Loughlin, the Cobbler. I remember Betty McGaulley said that she was born in the back shop of the Cobblers. Today, this is now the Larkfield Shopping Centre.

You can just see the spire of the Anderson Free Church in the distance.

Your Memories:

Arlene Campbell: I remember the tenement that Drew's shop is on, it was still standing in the days I would pass on my way to school... mid 70s.

Drew Semple: great pic Bill, my shop, Candelina Yankee store now stands on the tenement ground, brill mate.

Sheena Thomson: My Aunt Betty Littlejohn (nee Paton) had her hairdressing shop in the hut in the 60's.

Anne-marie Hart: I remember going into the shop for sweeties & ice cream in the 70's.

Annie Murdoch Anderson Black: I remember this in early 70's when I lived in Watson Place, just feeling slightly homesick again. I used to get off the 63-bus coming back from the Troc dancing (Hamilton) at the bus stop across the road from there.

Helen Dyer: Me too! I lived behind this building when the new houses went up. Yeah, makes me a little homesick too.

Larkfield No.4 Pit

Going back down Stonefield Road, on the left, opposite Robertson's Laun, we had Dixon's Larkfield No.4 Pit, which was producing coal from 1878 leaving a Bing known as 'Hill 66', where many a battle was fought and won either by soldiers or cowboys.

The Pit was situated where the Larkfield Hall is now.

Russell's Farm

The rest of Stonefield Road was made up of fields belonging to Russell's Farm or Wheatlandhead Farm, to give it its proper name. As we can be seen in this 1940s photo, it was all farmland from Wheatlandhead to Glasgow Road and until the council houses at the beginning of Fernslea Avenue to the West. You can make out David Livingstone Memorial Church and the Parkville on Glasgow Road.

Your Memories:

Paul Hudson McGowan: Spent many a childhood day playing on the Bing. Although the area was flattened and landscaped some 30 + years ago, it's still the Bing to many people including myself.

The Commercial Bar

The Commercial Bar – Stonefield Road opposite Calder Street. Also, known as Murdoch's or Peppers after Tam Pepper, a former owner and notorious teller of tall tales!

Next was Tommy Loughlin Cobblers, Norris Grocery, Gilbert the bakers, Jimmy Sweeney the butcher and then Craig's Building and the Old Original Bar.

Now known as The Priory Inn. Not to be confused with the former Priory Bar at Logan Street.

A popular bar with a community spirit.

Your Memories:

Etta Morrison: Thanks for info about tam pepper. Often heard the saying 'a bigger liar than tam pepper' but didn't know it originated from here...

Jeanette Bryan: Now I know where the saying came from - heard my mum say it many times.

Jannette McAllister: We used to have a great time in there when we came over for the Celtic games from Ireland. Pat had it then brilliant pub.

Jannette McAllister: Ah long time since I heard the nickname brought a smile to my face.

Anthony Smith: Another pub I used to drink in, but not very often as I wasn't a Rangers supporter.

Stephen Allan: It was a Celtic pub when it was the Commercial.

Anthony Smith: I knew it was one or the other as I never was a football fan. Ditto Fallon's Bar.

Walter Campbell: yes, I remember selling them a keg of beer borrowed from the highland games. Got 40 pound and bought some smoking material. He-he.

Danny Canavan: my dad used to work in that when Vincy Mcguire had it, after they left the Smiddy Bar

Fran Mcdermott Walters: Neil Forrest your mam worked here.

Neil Forrest: Yep for a good few years.

Linda Mcgowan: Where the car park is now, next 2 the priory pub.... (Commercial bar)...

Joe Sneddon: The cobbler was on that side also.

Mary Crowe: Tommy Loughlin was the cobbler, there was Gilbert the bakers next to Jimmy Sweeney the butchers.

Karen McLachlan: For years, I have been saying "you tell more lies than tam pepper" and had no idea who he was. Am pleased now to have solved that.

Carol Jordan: My Great Aunt Lizzie Davidson lived in the block of houses just before the Commercial and I remember the cobblers but not names.

Davie McKinnon: Any pics of the owner when it was Murdoch's, he was my wife's Grandfather.

The Old Original Bar

The Old Original Bar – Glasgow Road at Stonefield Road. Also, known as Craig's. Established 1882. The present building was erected in 1903 by Robert Craig.

Called the Old Original Bar probably because prior to it being built, he owned Clive Place at the same location.

Robert Craig also acquired what we now know as The West End Bar, which I believe was a Wholesale Grocer at the time.

With a frontage like this, this must have been a wonderful site for the locals of Blantyre when this building was erected in 1903. It says come on in and give me a visit. The initials R C had been carved out of red sandstone.

The Old Original Bar, Blantyre - 2005

Here we see The Old Original Bar in relation to the bottom of Stonefield Road all the way up to the Commercial Bar. (White Building)

The "Old Original Bar" Mob
(Craig's Tae, You An Me)

A bunch o' the Boys. JC

A bunch O the boys were whopping it up
outside Craig's Auld Original Baur,
They had all been in and had a good sup,
now they were home for the war!

Whilst standing in the cold rain,
a photo was taken by McGuire,
The ale had given them Dutch courage,
to face she who sits by the fire.

Up spoke a voice from within the bunch,
"I'm hame for the trouble I'm intae"
The rest looked in awe at this brave man,
whose name was Jim McGinty.

Cousin Hugh then spoke, but he was alright,
for a bachelor man was he
Not for him, the fear o`a woman,
he was a gentleman and fancy free.

James McFauld and Todd were another two,
both single the same as Hugh
Not for them the wrath o`a woman,
so they drunk the whole day thru.

McBride, McGaulley and Morris, Coulter,
Cummiskey and Finnegan
Cowardly looked at each other,
then turned and went back in again.

I look at this photo now and again,
taken in days o` lang syne,
The reason I'm not in it?
I was in the loo at the time!

"Now the moral of this tale,
is never be a liar
Don't get a photo taken outside a pub in
Blantyre"
Just be like me and go for a pee and never
tell McGuire...

James Cornfield 2008

Blantyre Tram Terminus

The first tram inaugural run from Motherwell to Blantyre was on 6th October 1903.

You can imagine the excitement on this great day. The local inhabitants could now freely visit Hamilton, Motherwell and Wishaw. The service was completely overwhelmed with over 30,000 individuals lining the Wishaw – Blantyre – Hamilton route expecting to get on the Trams on its first day alone.

First Day of Blantyre Trams 1903

Besides being a very popular means of transport for commuting between the towns, the Tramcars were also highly popular with courting couples as a novel way of being able to spend some time together.

The Tram Terminus was at the bottom of Stonefield Road, near David Livingstone Memorial Church.

Blantyre Trams 1903 - 1930

The Hamilton, Motherwell and Wishaw tramways company line was opened on 22nd July 1903 and provided an excellent means of travel from Blantyre to Hamilton, Larkhall, Motherwell and Wishaw. The Western

Terminus at Blantyre was situated 65 metres west of Stonefield Road at Livingstone Church. The first tram inaugural run from Motherwell to Blantyre was on 6th October 1903.

The company extended the line in 1907 to create a new terminus at Dunallon Loop at the West End, Glasgow Road, where passengers wishing to continue to Glasgow disembarked and travelled into the City on trams belonging to the Glasgow Corporation Tram Company which terminated at Priory Bridge.

The Hamilton, Motherwell and Wishaw Company constructed further lines within Lanarkshire to include within its network of Newmains in 1909 and New Stevenson in 1911, making it possible to travel in a circular route around various districts of Glasgow and return to Blantyre via Newmains.

The Company later changed its name to the Lanarkshire Tramways Company but closed on 10th October, 1930 and the old Shoogly Trams disappeared from the streets of Blantyre.

To give your children the experience of riding on an old shoogly tram, you can visit Summerlee in Coatbridge, and even be able to take them down a mine.

Source: **Neil Gordon's** A TO Z Dictionary of Blantyre.

George Mackenzie wrote: My father was born in 1912 and told me his first job after leaving the school was a Conductor on 2 Trams that went I think from Hamilton to Blantyre -

He said they didn't have numbers but instead had names.

They were called "I can Hop it" and "So can I."

Janette Brown: And 110 years later you need to get 2 buses from Blantyre to get to Motherwell or Wishaw, so much for improvement and a better bus service. The public transport service from Blantyre is a total joke.

Elizabeth Weaver: In some ways, it was probably easier to get around than it is now. Fine if you have a car nowadays; not so simple if you don't. Great photo.

Blantyre Community Centre

Next, along Glasgow Road we had Richardson's Garage, owned by Jock and Chrissie Richardson.

They would repair my bike punctures for free. Anyone remember the two Great Dane's, they had?

Blantyre Community Centre, a popular venue for Weddings. My sister Cathie had her wedding reception here.

Jimmy Coulter was the Caretaker for years, and Una Mason Hynds ran the Cafe with her sister-in-law, Sheena Mason from 1989 – 1991. Una's husband ran the drama group and did the sit in order to try and stop it being closed down. Monday night youth Club.

This is where Billy Connolly played when he visited my Brothers Youth Club.

Your Memories:

Eain Gray: James Cushley, remember the tour?

Isabel Park: Took my 3 boys to play school there. Xx

Una Mason Hynds: A used to run the wee cafe in their way ma sister in law Sheena Mason 1989 tae 1991 n my husband woz in the drama group who did the sit in to try and stop it being closed down.

Paul Anderson: I remember that's where all the holiday clubs were run from during school hols! Good times!

Jeanette Allardyce Ward: A mind ae the big Great Dane that Richardson's had.

Marion Smith: My papa was the caretaker in here for years. Jimmy Coulter.

May Hamilton: My wedding was held there 44 yrs. ago shame it's not there now.

Helen Dyer: Remember going to the dances there, lots of fun memories.

Michelle Devine: I used to go and get my lunch in their when I was at St Joes, it used to be a youth club on Monday night.

Liz Ali Ali: My sis worked in there. X

Shug McNeill: The butchers shop was roundabout where Imo is now, old post office.

Andrew Charles: Pity Richardson's used to make faults with cars while they were in for MOT hoping to get work. Used to do disco in Community Centre for YDT. Half of them were drunk with alcohol they were bought from Botterill's around the corner even though they were all under 16.

Robert Henderson: I worked with Jock Richardson's brother in butchering and his brother George stayed next door to my gran for yrs.

Sarah Sked: We went there for our first communion breakfast. My cousin Nan Duffy had her wedding reception in there she married Pat Cain.

Glasgow Road

Glasgow Road between Blantyre Community Centre and the West End was still farmland up till the 50s.

David Livingstone Church, St. Joseph's Church and St. Joseph's Church and School in the background.

This farmland belonged to the Russell family who farmed Wheatlandhead Farm. The ploughman here is probably Will Simpson.

Thanks to **Elaine Russell** for the photo.

The West End Bar

Next there was The Volunteer Arms in Walker's Building, Glasgow Road, West End. Also, known as The Crossguns, owned by Mr. Roberts whose son John owned The Priory Bar.

MacNeil's Building & Pub.

The West End Bar – West End Place, Glasgow Road. Approximately 50-60 yards from The Volunteer Arms. Also, known as Bennett's, a previous owner and The Farmers Club. Latterly owned by the family of Captain MacNeil, who earlier owned The Caledonian Bar in High Blantyre.

A BLANTYRE family have called last orders – after running The West End Bar for the past 74 years.

The MacNeil family waved good-bye to the pub, in Blantyre's Glasgow Road last month – after serving the people from the town for the past seven decades.

The story of the family's association with The West End Bar began in 1925 when Captain Joseph MacNeil, a retired Merchant Navy captain, left the Isle of Barra with his wife Elizabeth to start a new life in Blantyre.

The couple bought a pub in High Blantyre from the Pearson family and renamed it the Caledonian, but locals knew the establishment as "the Hielandmans" in homage to Captain MacNeil.

They ran the pub for nine years before moving their business to Glasgow Road in 1934. They took over The Farmers Club, which is now known as The West End Bar.

Since then, the pub has been run by several members of the MacNeil family, including Donald, Mary, Ian, Joseph and Nan McGhie, who is now the last surviving member of the original family. Nan, who was the licensee of the pub, celebrated her 80th birthday in August.

The third generation of the MacNeil family – Elizabeth Campbell, Kathryn Clarke, Mary-Jo Furlong and Felix MacNeil – continued to run the pub until October this year, 2008.

On behalf of the whole family, Mary-Jo commented:

"Throughout the years, most of the family have continued to work and live in Blantyre. The pub has, and continues to be, a well-known landmark and is renowned for its support for local groups.

"It was a very difficult decision within the family to leave the licensing trade. So many of our patrons are extended members of our family.

"Generations of the same Blantyre families have journeyed with us through the years.

"But none of us have children and there was nobody to pass the reins to.

"We all have other jobs and Felix, who was the bar manager, is looking for a new career.

"We would like to thank all of our friends at The West End Bar for their continued friendship and loyalty throughout the years.

"We wish every success to the new owners Maura, Mick, Dougie and their staff."

When James Cornfield traded me this photo, he said that at this time the building was a Wholesale Grocers owned by Robert Craig of the Old Original Bar. You can clearly see the sign, 'Wholesale' but whether it referred to Grocers or Wines, I can't be certain. The men gathering are probably waiting for transport to Bardykes Pit to start their shift, said James.

Next is Bardykes Road & Blantyre Boundary.

Your Memories:

Elspeth Shirkie: I was born in the room upstairs 1949.

Kathleen Duffy: I was born in what's now the Lounge (formerly a Room and Kitchen) in 1948.

Sheryl McPhee: I remember the wee paper shop in the now DeVito's, I think and Hughes the photographer or am I getting it wrong.

Elizabeth Gallagher: I was born right upstairs in my granny's back bedroom.

Carole Marie Deplacido: I worked in there.

Ina Sanders: I lived not far from there. I lived in Strathmore Ave

Fran Mcdermott Walters: Lived right across the road on South View, we called it Peters Cocktail Bar lol x

Helen Dyer: Been in there a few times... lol

Nancy McFadden: My dad's, Uncle Jim and Jimmy Meek's pub.

Bardykes House

Wilkie's, Bardykes Farm

Sandy Wilkie wrote, "Bardykes House on Bardykes Road in Blantyre, South Lanarkshire (now known as Bardykes Farm and Bardykes Farm Nursery), was designed in the late 1800's by a Glasgow architect who is now becoming rather famous, though not quite as much of a household name yet, as the City's other world-renowned architect, Charles Reny-MacIntosh. His name was Alexander Thompson but as there were two British architects of that name registered at the same time, our Alexander's name was amended to differentiate them, by reflecting his own very individual and idiosyncratic design style based on his southern European ideals, to become known as the Scottish based, "Alexander Greek Thompson" (9 April 1817 – 22 March 1875)."

The Wilkie family

Wilkie's Farm serving Blantyre and surrounding regions with Milk and Dairy Products since 1900. And was a very popular location for local children because of the Horse and Pony riding and the many Gymkhanas that were frequently held there.

Compulsory Purchase Order

Sandy Wilkie wrote, "In the late 50s, the house fell into considerable disrepair thereafter and was eventually bought by 'Speculator' as my dad described him, a Mr. Loan from Helensburgh, who planned to get a hotel licence then sell it to "The Brewers" for a handsome profit. However, that never came to pass and after further deterioration, he eventually sold it via Joe Daly (father of Alan) and Jimmy Rusk (local council valuer and father of the famous hairdresser family), to Peter and Margaret Wilkie. They were almost homeless at that time, because the 2 nearby farms in High Blantyre known as Birdsfield and Bellsfield, (we milked the cows at the latter and filled it on the former), were being "taken" by the 5th District Council via a "Compulsory Purchase Order," to build Council Houses. Demolition actually started whilst we were still living in the site!

On 5th April 1957, mum and dad plus their 3 weans under 5, Dinky the Alsatian dog and Minky the tortoise-shell cat, moved in on the horse-drawn milk float pulled by Janet (or was it Nell? - Janet was a liver chestnut Irish mare and Nell was a flightier black mare), to Bardykes".

Sent in by **Margo Haughen,** nee Wilkie

Fascinating and great that the owners put down some history to Bardykes.

Sandy Wilkie, who still lives at the house, wrote a short history of the House and Family which was sent in by Margo Haughen nee Wilkie. This can be read in full at: blantyre.biz/short-history-of-bardykes-house/

Your Memories:

Margo Haughen: I was a Wilkie for my sins! We moved into Bardykes in 1957, having lived at Birdsfield Farm before it was compulsory purchased to build Kirkton. I have some research of the building's history my brother Sandy (who still lives there) did fairly recently - if you're interested I could ask my daughter to send a PM copy to you, also a more recent photo for the website?

Blantyre's Ain: Margo, that would be absolutely fantastic. Local History must be recorded for prosperity. Your daughter can email me on bill@blantyre.biz

Elizabeth Weaver: Of course, Blantyre and High Blantyre had farms all through my 50s childhood - despite the pits, Blantyre was still quite rural. Changed days.

Ruth Haughen: My family has lived there since the 50s and still live there now...

Ruth Haughen: Aye Peter was my grandpa... still did milk until about 20 years ago. Dad was still a milkman there until Wiseman's bought it over I think. What do you remember Auntie Deborah Buhagiar?

Deborah Buhagiar: Not much, I think I was drunk or hung over the few times I was there!! We used to visit your mum in her caravan mostly.

John McDermott: Really good to know your family still lives there Ruth. I had many a happy time there as a milk boy.

Elizabeth Weaver: I remember Peter Wilkie too - my brother was the same age as Sandy and one of my uncles worked on the farm way back when they still had milk carts and churns.

Margo Haughen: Who was your uncle, Elizabeth - I may remember him?

Carol Jordan: I was born in 1972 and I used to go over to Willkie's for my gran when I was a kid, sometimes there were geese acting like guard dogs.

Helen Dyer: My friend's gran worked there every morning for years, till she was too old to do it anymore. I think they let her keep going just to give her something to do. Lol such a sweet lady wee Mary Dickson.

Alan Baird: Twa pints tae the yella door ya wee fecker.

Margo Haughen: Alan, that's how my dad spoke to all of us milk boys/girls... pleased to say, he was lovely in private!!

Jock Stein's Cottage 1905

Jock Stein's Cottage, on Bardykes Road. Jock Stein was a local character who had a large mole on his face. Jock would hire out his Cart or move stuff or anything else for that matter. He kept chickens and pigs at the rear and would collect waste food from schools to feed his pigs. The Cottage on the left is Aggie Baine's before the corner was cut off to widen the road. You can just see the roof of the Barnhill Tavern above it.

Blantyre Cottage Hospital

The old cottage hospital stands at no. 63 Bardykes Road, just along from Barnhill. Blantyre had a fever hospital from around 1860, but at the turn of the century local doctors started to appeal for additional resources, and in February 1906 a public meeting was held to discuss methods of raising funds among Blantyre residents.

Local businessmen such as the coal masters also made donations, but these were not entirely philanthropic since their workers often needed the facilities of a hospital.

Opened in 1910, the hospital was the first of its kind in the county to be paid by public subscription. Despite an article appearing in the Gazette in the 1930s about mineral reserves in its grounds, the building is still standing as a private residence!

Local health services are now catered for by the district health centre in Victoria Street.

The Glasgow Herald – Feb 14, 1939

Blantyre Cottage Hospital to Close Down

 Blantyre Cottage Hospital, which has been a useful institution in the Parish for the past 30 years is now to be closed down.

The annual general meeting took place last night when those present included Mr. James Lawson, president; Mr. Frank Stevenson, honorary secretary; and Mr. Robson, honorary treasurer.

The financial position as outlined by Mr. Robson, agent of the Blantyre branch of the Commercial Bank, showed that the Association was in a hopeless condition. It took between £500 and £600 annually to run the hospital, and for some years past the yearly income showed a deficit of from £150 to £200 per year.

To meet these yearly deficiencies, said Mr. Robson, the board had to go into their reserve fund, and now that fund was exhausted.

Although the funds in hand at the moment are not sufficient to clear off the current debts on the hospital, the committee will make a special effort to have these debts discharged. The nursing staff are to be notified that their services will be dispensed within one month.

The hospital at one time regularly accommodated about 10 patients on every day throughout the year.

The oldest house in Blantyre

'Aggie Bain's Hoose', Brownlee Cottage in Bardykes Road in 1933, one of the oldest inhabited houses in Scotland.

It was built in 1536, and has been in the same family until recently, now owned by Margo Haughen nee Wilkie, and now called Bardykes Cottage. (Opposite the Hoolet's Pub) The cottage had a corner removed in order to widen the road.

In 1915 Aggie owned and rented out the two houses next to the Parkville.

The oldest house in Blantyre – 2008

Miss Agnes (Aggie) Bains house, which may also have been called Sauch Cottage, after gable window and front door removed.

Aggie Bain's Cottage or Brownlee Cottage, before the corner was cut off.

John Brownlie Bain at the door c1933

Margo Haughen: This is the first time I've seen this one... thank you so much.

Your Memories:

Audrey Marshall: Is this listed? Is it still used as a normal house Ruth Haughen?

Margo Haughen: Not a listed building because there had been so many changes to the building prior to 'listing', I'm afraid. The council compulsory purchased the corner for road widening!!!!! And then the dormer was added, followed by replacement double glazing.

Ruth Stannage: A jack hammer could open up that window that's not there now anyone got a jack hammer?

Margo Haughen: Shh! We don't speak about that Ruth-you never know when the surveyor/planners are listening!!!

John Cornfield: Ma dad's fave.

Annie Murdoch Anderson Black: Wow thanks for sharing...

Ruth Haughen: My wee house. It's now known as Bardykes Cottage.

Barnhill Tavern – The Hoolet's Nest

View of the Barnhill Tavern c1930; still standing and still quaint, known locally as 'The Hoolet's Nest'.

Barnhill Tavern (The Hoolet's Nest) dates back to 1745 and was a Coaching House on the main London to Hamilton Palace route.

The above photo was an inspiration for Neil Gordon to do this wonderful oil painting in 1974.

It shows the Weaver's Cottage at the top of Peth Brae, with the Barnhill Tavern (1745) on the right, next to Aggie Bain's Cottage (1536), the oldest house in Blantyre. In the distance, the Cottage Hospital can be seen behind the hedgerow.

Jimmy Brownlie lived in the Hoolet's Nest

Jimmy Brownlie was born in Blantyre and was an outstanding personality in Scottish football over many years, as a goalkeeper and manager.

Almost his entire professional playing career, lasting from 1906 to 1923, was spent with Third Lanark, and as well as playing in 16 of the last 17 internationals before the First World War, he also appeared no less than 14 times for the Scottish League team, and in four Victory Internationals once the conflict was over.

In May 1923, Brownlie was appointed player/manager of Dundee Hibernian, who was renamed Dundee United later that year. He continued to play for a further season, but later made one further appearance in an emergency, at the age of 40 in 1926. His first managerial spell with the club found early success, with the Division Two titles in 1925, and again in 1929, but he left the club in April 1931 on the brink of a third promotion.

He returned in 1934 with the club at a low ebb, one away from the bottom of Division Two, and helped to affect a partial revival before he left again in October 1936.

A third and final spell came in season 1938–39, in a dual role with Sam Irving; both men were also appointed as directors of the club at this time. In May 1939, Brownlie announced that he was giving up both roles due to the pressure of his other business interests.

SAW LIVINGSTONE IN 1856

DEATH OF JIMMY BROWNLIE'S father.

Mr James Brownlie, father of Jimmy Brownlie, former manager of Dundee United, died yesterday morning at the residence of his widowed daughter, Mrs Alex. Wardrope, Hunthill Road, High Blantyre. He was 94.

Mr Brownlie was born in the Auld "Hoolet's Nest Inn" in the Barnhill district of Blantyre. He had a vivid recollection of seeing Dr David Livingstone when he paid a visit to his birthplace in Low Blantyre village on December 30, 1856.

Dundee Courier - Friday 17 November 1939

Your Memories:

Christine Brown: My uncle Jimmy married old Mary from the Hoolet's.

Stuart Oneil: As a young boy, I remember playing in the garden and going into the house above the pub. The Macdonald's were friends with my dad and uncle.

Lyn Lappin: I worked there for a few years when Pat had it. Great wee pub. X

Margo MacDonald

Fifty years ago, the proprietor was Nelly Moir, eventually succeeded by Peter MacDonald the piper. More recently, Margo MacDonald of the S.N.P. and M.S.P, and an Independent, who passed in April 2014 was the landlady. (p.s. I used to call in on my way home from work, and Margo would serve me in her bare feet.)

Her daughter Petra is married to one-half of The Proclaimers, Craig Reid.

Your Memories:

Alison Walker-Hill: Petra was at school with me... Zoe a couple of years below I think! X

Jeanette Allardyce Ward: Petra was at school with me too. Hoolet's was my dad's favourite pub many, many yrs. ago lol. X

John Mc Dermott: I delivered her milk in morning.

Paul Hudson McGowan: My dad's pub of choice too for many a year. I remember the MacDonald's well.

And as it is today, now called 'The Hoolet's, with your host Mick Flynn giving you a warm welcome.

That brings us to the end of our Wander Doon Memory Lane, Glasgow Road, Blantyre as it used to be.

I hope you have enjoyed the journey as much as I have.

I have certainly enjoyed being your guide on this Pictorial History of Glasgow Road.

I know that, somewhere, my friend and Mentor; Jim Cornfield has a smile on his face, finally knowing that Glasgow Road, and the places he loved, have been recorded for future reference as they were, before changes were made, which devastated the unique character that Blantyre once enjoyed.

Best regards to you all,

Bill Sim

http://blantyre.biz

p.s. Most of the comments and memories in this book originated in Blantyre's Ain website or its Facebook page.

About the Author

Bill Sim was born in 1948 at Baird's Raws, Blantyre, second youngest of six children. With no shoes and three muddy streets to play in, his early childhood was an adventurous journey daily. The family were rehoused to Fernslea Avenue in 1953 and Bill, 'William,' in those days, was taken there on top of a barrow load of coal.

Fernslea Avenue was like a mansion to the family, whose total furniture amounted to three brand new mattresses, the previous furniture having been burned because of wood worm. There was a magic switch on the wall of this modern house, that only mum or dad could use. When switched, a light would come on and light up the room.

It wasn't long before Bill started to attend Auchinraith Primary School with daily adventures before and after school. He took a shortcut through Dixon's Raws which were due for demolition and then climbed two fences of a football ground which brought him to Victoria Street, just across from the swing park where he headed for every day-after school.

His main education took place at Calder Street Secondary School under the careful eye of 'Wee Brick' Bradford, Matheson the maths' teacher, 'Wee Robbie', the Arts teacher and Miss Cameron the music teacher. As a school prefect and winning both Junior and Senior Sports Championships, Bill enjoyed his time at Calder Street very much.

At the age of Seventeen, Bill left his beloved Blantyre to pursue a career in Sales and Marketing. This involved much traveling and further education in specialist courses.

Bill became a lecturer for British Leyland at their Marketing Centre in Studley, Warwickshire, which involved developing courses in Sales and Management within the motor trade, writing corresponding courses, Sales Training scripts for training films and of course, much traveling.

Bill then became Sales Director for a Training and Consultancy firm specializing in the motor trade and caravan industry and was the main character in a twelve-hour sales training video, made for the Caravan Council, for translation into Scandinavian and European languages.

He then started and developed his own Sales and Management Training and Implementation Company, again in the motor trade, Caravan Industry and Holiday Park Sales. He enjoyed his clientele of large Motor Groups, particularly Ford, and the many Millionaire Holiday Park owners who employed his services, on site and at Conferences and Seminars throughout Europe.

Prior to retiring, Bill came back to Blantyre in 2000 from Bali in Indonesia, where he was Project Director for a Holiday Sales Company.

Back in Blantyre, he started a Blantyre History web site, Blantyre's Ain, in 2003 and continued to add to it throughout the years.

This 'Wander Doon Memory Lane' is five years in the making, being interrupted by four months of serious illness.

Bill has decided to make all the proceeds from the book to go to local charities and good causes.

Made in the USA
Columbia, SC
20 June 2017